BSA

CROWOOD MOTOCLASSICS

BSA

The Complete Story

OWEN WRIGHT

The Crowood Press

First published in 1992 by
The Crowood Press Ltd
Ramsbury, Marlborough
Wiltshire SN8 2HR

Paperback edition 1997

British Library Cataloguing in Publication Data

A catalogue record for this title is available from the British Library.

ISBN 1 86126 064 4

Typeset by Footnote Graphics, Warminster, Wiltshire
Printed and bound in Great Britain by
BPC Wheatons Ltd, Exeter

Contents

Preface

To sit down and write a general account of BSA motorcycles was an intimidating challenge considering the vast array of model types that were produced, let alone the compelling history that lies behind the famous 'Piled Arms' trademark. It needed a measure of self restraint to avoid wandering too far down one of the many avenues that deal with the company's involvement in guns, bicycles, scooters and motorcars.

Undaunted by the task, I fell back on a series of articles that I once penned for the BSA Owners Club magazine, *The Star*. These stories dealt mainly with unusual, elderly or thoroughly bizarre topics, so the time had come to succumb to writing about BSA's more mainstream models. I was also fortunate to have once held an interview with Bert Perrigo, Mr BSA himself. Bert is no longer with us but the occasion left me with a lasting impression. The great man was then well into his seventies but was able to provide a young hack with an endless source of motivation in the pursuit of matters BSA.

The following chapters take a look at BSA's company history, scan all the main model types and follow on with a nostalgic review of BSA's competition victories. The book is not a political thriller analysing the reasons why a company with the immense stature of BSA fell into decay after dominating the motorcycle industry for sixty years. Neither does it plunge into every finite technical detail of every model that BSA produced or attempt to laboriously list every competition success chalked up by BSA's hallowed roll call of star riders. But for those who ride or once rode a BSA, I'm sure they'll find it a useful source of reference and acquire a full grasp of the company's exploits that ventured into every aspect of motorcycling. I also hope the reader will discover some new facts and find this title a firm base from which to explore further into the realms of BSA studies.

Owen Wright
August 1991

Acknowledgements

My sincere thanks are extended to all the many friends and enthusiasts who have supported my research and insatiable appetite for good quality photographs. In particular I would like to thank Steve Foden, that un-flagging Librarian of the BSA Owners' Club for opening up the club's considerable collection of archive material. Thanks also to Graham Howie, Jeff Allen, Trevor Bailey, Alan Johnson, John Parberry and Roger Shuffle-bottom for the loan of some very interesting pictures. May your oil pumps never falter!

My grateful thanks also go to Philip Tooth, Editor of *The Classic MotorCycle* for allowing me to rummage through all the bound volumes of *The Motor Cycle* (The Blue 'Un) and *Motor Cycling* (The Green 'Un). The kindest assistance was also given by *Motor Cycle News*.

The Automobile Association pictures are by courtesy of Michael Passmore (a very nice man); and Ann Fitzgerald of the Post Office PR department also answered a plea for some BSA in GPO service material.

It was an honour to correspond with former BSA star riders namely the late Bill Nicholson, Eddie Dow and Brian Martin, who without hesitation made available their own photo albums.

Determined to show something representing BSA's stateside life I'm grateful to Bill Litant (BSAOC New England USA), Barry Smith and Bill Burdett (BSAOC South California USA) for air-mailing over a worthy contribution and also to my long-suffering wife, Susan, whose unlimited patience and understanding helped me to sort out my rotten spelin and lousy ty p ing.

Finally, without the invaluable assistance of Alistair Cave, former General Works Manager of BSA Motorcycles Ltd, Armoury Road, Birmingham, I doubt that this book would have been possible to produce. Alistair has been a generous source of inspiration and information over the years. At BSA, he loyally worked through all the good and bad times, always maintaining a sense of purpose and dignity even when the final curtain was fast closing down. Ever since the dark days of the early 1970s he has continued to support the cause of the Birmingham Small Arms brotherhood.

MILESTONES

1855   John Dent Goodman elected as Chairman of Birmingham Small Arms Association.
1861   Birmingham Small Arms Company formed 'to manufacture guns by machinery'. J. D. Goodman elected as Chairman.
1863   Small Heath factory commences weapon manufacture as power engines are started.
1873   Birmingham Small Arms and Metal Company Ltd formed to deal with massive order placed by Prussian army.
1880   Mr Otto demonstrates his Dicycle to BSA Directors by riding it up and down boardroom table! First three Otto machines delivered 5th August. Company adopt their 'Piled Arms' trademark.
1897   Company title reverts back to 'Birmingham Small Arms Ltd'.
1905   First powered motor-bicycle produced using a Minerva engine. Eadie Manufacturing Company of Redditch acquired.
1910   First all-BSA 3½hp motor-bicycle unveiled at Olympia, London. Daimler Motor Company of Coventry acquired.
1913   Kenneth Holden, chief tester, wins first race on standard 3½hp model at Brooklands, averaging 60.75mph (97.7kph). BSA enter Isle of Man Tourist Trophy races for first time.
1914   Six out of eight BSA entrants finish TT races. Model H, all chain driven, 557cc, 4¼hp introduced. First sidecars built. Great War marks return to mass production of munitions.
1915   Work commences on four-storey 'New' Building for Lewis Gun manufacture. Expansion to five factories employing 13,000 workers at time of armistice (November 1918).
1919   BSA Cycles Ltd formed. Model E 770cc SV Vee-Twin announced.
1921   Tourist Trophy races end in total disaster. Six specially built machine all fail to finish. Commander Godfrey Herbert DSO appointed Managing Director, BSA Cycles Ltd.
1922   Model G 986cc SV Vee-Twin announced.
1923   Model range expanded with introduction of 350cc Model L and 500cc model S 'Sports'.
1924   First production year for highly popular Model B 'Round Tank'. First OHV Model L produced. Harry Perrey leads competition team up Screw Hill and to summit of Mount Snowden.
1926   First Maudes Trophy win with demonstration of sixty climbs of Bwlch-Y-Groes. A. E. Perrigo joins competition department. Model S 500cc OHV 'Sloper' announced. John Castley and Bertram Cathrick set out on eighteen-month World Tour riding Model G Combinations.
1928   Redditch Eadie works closed, all motorcycle production transferred to Small Heath.
1929   Bert Perrigo wins inaugural British Experts Trial. First BSA three-wheeler powered by air-cooled Vee-Twin produced.
1931   New range of wet-sump lubricated, upright cylinder models announced.
1932   Bert Perrigo wins victory trial on Blue Star. Team award won by BSA team.
1933   Ambitious 500cc Fluid Flywheel motorcycle announced but fails to reach production stage.
1935   To commemorate King George V's Silver Jubilee, Empire Star models announced.
1936   Valentine Page joins design department and presents complete new range of M and B group singles, later joined by 250cc C group models.
1937   Walter Handley wins Brooklands Gold Star on dope-tuned M23 Empire Star. Alloy-engined M24 Gold Star announced at Earls Court.
1938   Second Maudes Trophy victory with endurance test using M21 Combination and M23 Empire Star.
1939   James Leek leads BSA in massive war effort by producing vast arsenal of weapons for Allies, plus 126,000 M20 motorcycles.
1940   Fifty-three BSA employees killed in Blitz. Programme of dispersal factories commenced.
1944   Ariel Motors of Selly Oak acquired.
1945   Production of civilian models resumed. Popular model B31 produced, equipped with telescopic forks.

1946	First 500cc OHV parallel twin model A7 announced. Redditch dispersal factory produces twin-cylinder Sunbeam S7.
1947	Return to Isle of Man TT as ZB Gold Stars enter Clubman races.
1948	First of half a million Bantam two-stroke models leaves Redditch factory.
1949	Herbert Hopwood joins BSA and designs 650cc A10 Golden Flash. Harold Clark wins 350cc Clubmans TT.
1950	Harold Tozer wins first-ever ACU Sidecar Trials Star.
1951	Triumph Engineering Company acquired from Jack Sangster for £2½m. Sangster joins BSA board of Directors.
1952	Third Maudes Trophy win as Brian Martin, Norman Vanhouse and Fred Rist sensationally take three stock A7 Star Twins on 4,500 mile (7,240km) test, winning ISDT team trophy. Gene Thiessen breaks world record on Bonneville salt flats reaching 143.5mph (230.12kph) on methanol-tuned A10.
1953	BSA Motorcycles Ltd and BSA Cycles Ltd formed as separate divisions.
1954	Daytona Beach 200-mile (320km) race won by A7 Star Twins.
1956	Bernard Codd wins Junior and Senior Clubmans TT riding Gold Stars. Sir Bernard Docker ousted by Jack Sangster in AGM chairmanship battle. Edward Turner succeeds James Leek as Automotive Chief Executive.
1957	BSA Cycles sold to Raleigh; BSA and Daimler Cars sold to Jaguar Motors. £2.1m profit announced.
1958	First in long line of unit construction singles as 250cc OHV model C15 is announced.
1961	BSA celebrates centenary. Jack Sangster retires after declaring annual profit of £3m. Succeeded by Eric Turner.
1962	Chris Vincent wins BSA's first and only full International TT with A7 Shooting Star 'kneeler outfit'. New range of unit-constructed twin-cylinder A50 and A65 models announced.
1963	Edward Turner retires as Managing Director, replaced by Harry Sturgeon. Ariel production transferred to Small Heath. National BSA Owners Club formed.
1964	Jeff Smith wins World Moto-Cross Championship. 441cc Victor Scrambler produced.
1967	Death of Harry Sturgeon; Lionel Jofeh installed as Managing Director. Umberslade Hall research establishment founded. Queen's Award to Industry granted.
1968	Second Queen's Award presented to BSA. Three cylinder 750cc Rocket Three produced.
1970	Jeff Smith awarded MBE. Thirteen-model line-up including new 350cc OHC Fury shown at lavish London hotel dinner.
1971	BSA-Triumph Automotive Group devastated by £8m trading loss. Eric Turner and Lionel Jofeh depart. Lord Shawcross installed to lead rescue.
1972	Further £3m loss declared by group.
1973	BSA near bankruptcy. Government-sponsored take-over by Manganese Bronze Holdings. Norton-Villiers-Triumph Company formed. Machines bearing the 'Piled Arms' trademark no longer produced.
1974	Triumph Meriden workers thwart attempts to produce Triumph engines at Small Heath. Factory site sold to Birmingham Corporation.
1977	Small Heath factory demolished.

Introduction

There was a time not so long ago when all our metal finished goods used for domestic purposes were all stamped 'Made in England'. It left the purchaser secure in the knowledge that he or she was buying a quality product, cheap but not shoddy and endowed with a certain measure of artistic elegance. As our manufacturing industries continue to shift and recede, the chances of buying British goods have become less frequent.

As far as British motorcycles are concerned, the great names and factories that once dominated the world have all virtually disappeared. Who would have thought that the once all-powerful BSA company could have also been swept away?

The Birmingham Small Arms Company was a creation of Victorian colonial and imperial expansion, providing a ready supply of rifles to kings and empires in an age of romanticism and revolt. They later hurried to the nation's defence during the great world wide struggles against tyranny in the twentieth century.

But when the guns were no longer needed, the company had to look elsewhere for work and began to build bicycles, and later motorcycles, bringing cheap and easily available freedom for thousands.

When in full swing, BSA's main Small Heath factory had 1,142,000 square feet (1,060,918 square metres) of working space and employed 12,000 people. The tremendous industry that took place within a myriad of buildings struck up a cacophany from the heavy boom of the chain hammers to the whine and whirr of lathes, milling machines and the Ryder swaging machines busily turning out high quality poppet valves for BSA motorcycles in the finest William Jessop and Sons Sheffield steel.

The BSA story is a turbulent mixture of pride, anguish, great achievement and calamity. It could be said to reflect Britain's international, industrial and social history for over a century.

The machines that bore a 'Piled Arms' trademark, a symbol of reverence in its own right, were part of everyday ordinary life. Most fell into that undefined area that lay between machinery hand-built by craftsmen and ubiquitous mass production. Some were built to be the best in the world and carried all before them, some were simply dreadful! But to the many riders who once had the use of a 'good old Beesa', they offered much more than those pots and pans that were 'Made in England'.

1

Early History

A Call to Arms

The Birmingham Small Arms Company evolved in a time of international strife and came about as a direct result of the Crimean War of 1854–56. This was a futile campaign of power politics fought by an army that had changed little since Waterloo, almost forty years previously, and that still used the same tactics and hopelessly inadequate equipment.

The shortcomings of the Crimean campaign, scandalized by newspaper correspondents, caused an outcry. The manufacture of weapons was then more or less a cottage industry hard pressed to keep up with the huge demand and wastage of early mechanized warfare. In 1855, sixteen separate small arms manufacturers in the Birmingham locality were called upon by the government to supply rifles, each gun being patiently and painstakingly crafted by hand.

Faced with an urgent situation of demand far outstripping supply, the British Government set up an ordnance factory in Enfield and commenced the manufacture of rifles by industrialized means. The Birmingham trade had supplied 156,000 muzzle-loading rifles for the British army as against 75,000 pieces purchased by the war department from all other sources including the Enfield Ordnance works. But by the time that the Crimean War had run to its inconclusive end in April 1856, more than 2,000 rifles and carbines were being supplied by the Enfield factory weekly.

The Birmingham Small Arms display at the Great Exhibition of 1862. (BSA Archive)

Threatened with the prospect of being put out of business, the Birmingham gun trade tried at first to portray the superiority of the handmade gun but realizing it was a lost cause because of diminishing orders, a meeting was called in June, 1861. This resulted in a resolution to form 'The Birmingham Small Arms Company' with a prospectus declaring that its aim was: 'To manufacture guns by machinery'.

Gunmaking in Birmingham had already been rife for 150 years. The small arms trade had operated a loose system of group contracting, winning orders and sharing out the work. At the time of Waterloo in 1815, it was estimated that some 7,000 souls were employed in the town producing weapons at a rate of 525,000 pieces each year. Historians can delve further into the murky depths of time to discover that when Henry VIII was on the throne central Warwickshire was a hive of metal workers. 'John Leland's itinerary' – a notable Tudor travelogue – recorded iron working as a chief trade in the district; 'There be many Smithes in the towne that use to make knives and all manner of cutlery tools and many lorimers [harness makers] that make bittes; and a great many Naylors [nailmakers] so that a great part of the towne is maintained by Smithes who have their iron and sea-cole [ordinary coal] out of Staffordshire', wrote Leland.

During the English Civil War, Birmingham was a staunchly puritan stronghold and a major source of weaponry for the Parliamentarian armies. In April 1643, Prince Rupert, whilst leading a Royalist force towards Lichfield, captured and destroyed much of the town.

The earliest known contract for the Crown was secured in 1689 for His most gracious Majesty King William III. After some intense lobbying, a Warwickshire member of Parliament, one Sir Richard Newdegate, impressed upon the King that, 'much genius resides in Warwickshire' and that the Birmingham smiths, 'were able to answer the royal wishes'. A trial order was placed for the supply of 200 snaphance muskets each month all for the princely sum of seventeen shillings a piece, ready money.

Vulcan and Mars

The Birmingham Small Arms Company elected its inaugural board of directors in September 1863, with Mr J. D. Goodman taking the chair. From an initial capital of £50,000 bundled up in £25 shares, the gunsmiths searched for a factory site. Several schemes were offered but the founding members of the board chose a twenty-five acre site in open fields at Small Heath, tempted by a promise that the Great Western Railway were to build a station nearby.

The original building was laid out across a road linking the new premises to the main highway through the town, which was later lined with houses for the workforce. Along this road for the next 100 years, millions of guns (and many thousands of motorcycles) would pass, so it was decided to call it 'Armoury Road'.

As a typically grim and austere Victorian place of work, the completed Small Heath factory was like a fortress of red bricks and arched windows arranged in an open square of three-storey towers inter-connected with smaller blocks with two levels. A central tower containing the main entrance arch led the way straight onto Armoury Road and high above the main door was a clock set into a tablet as if to emphasise the importance of punctuality. Just above the entrance arch, fashioned into the masonry, directors and employees alike could look up to a sinister emblem symbolizing the nature of the place of work. It depicted two medieval smiths at work at an anvil, using both hammer and tongs to forge arrows. Underneath was a motto: *Mulciber had aedes habitat Beccona tuetur* (Mulciber (Vulcan) the God of fire dwells in this house. Bellona the Goddess of war looks after it.).

The final touches to the main factory were still being added in 1866 and even as the floorspace became occupied with American-made machinery the local workforce looked

A fine view of Small Heath circa 1866 taken from across the adjacent railway cutting.
(Loaned by A. G. Cave)

on with suspicion, mortified by this incursion of mechanized production. At first, the workers were not directly employed by the company but acted on a contract basis renting out a section of the factory to carry out work on a particular piece. Payday was held on a Saturday when the contractor carried around a bucket of coins to pay his men.

As Victorian industrial progress gathered pace, working practices within the Small Heath factory were often hampered by superstition, some of it almost bordering upon witchcraft. The spring winders who came in from Willenhall and Darlaston, for instance, would not wind a spring after ten o'clock in the morning because they were convinced that to do so would surely break the wire!

A larger part of Small Heath in those days was taken up by livery stables to house all the necessary horse-drawn traffic and one eccentric drover employed by the company refused to let his animals graze on the rolling pastures outside the factory gates but insisted on feeding his stock within the canteen!

After just five years in business, the company received its first British Government

Old hands line up under the main factory entrance arch circa 1870. (Loaned by A. G. Cave)

contract, worth £98,750 for the conversion of 1,000,000 muzzle-loading rifles to breech-loading, based upon a principle evolved by Jacob Snider, a Dutch wine merchant. The order was so urgent that a night shift commenced operation for the first time to achieve a target output of 3,000 conversions a week. The first consignment of 50,000 pieces was delivered after ten months and, incredibly, the final batch reached the government inspectors just a quarter of an hour before the contract period ran out. At the time, it was considered by the War Office to be a miracle. BSA on their part rewarded three shop foremen with a bonus payment of £100 each. An unusual act perhaps during an age of dreadful factory conditions and practices, but the success of their first government work was repeated time and time again and BSA workers benefited from better welfare and prospects rarely found elsewhere.

The company's early fortunes were said to have followed the international situation and luck was riding high indeed when, in

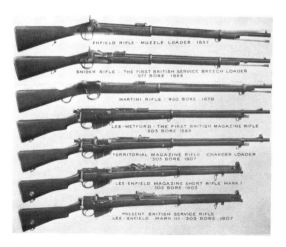

Birmingham Small Arms! Gunmaking was at the forefront of precision engineering during the late 19th century. (BSA Archive)

1873, the Prussian Government placed an order for 40,000,000 cartridge cases. To handle such a vast quantity of ammunition, the Directors put their company into voluntary liquidation and re located its assets into a new company, given the name 'The Birmingham Small Arms and Metal Company'. A factory in Adderley Park was purchased for the specific purpose of meeting the Prussian order. The Adderley Park ammunition business was eventually sold to the Directors of the Nobel Dynamite Trust Ltd (later ICI), in 1896. At that time, the company reverted back to its original Birmingham Small Arms Company title.

But the game of war and the means to supply it were both fickle and uncertain. At the outbreak of the Franco-Prussian War of 1871, BSA were urged into action by a nervous Government to make ready a large order of rifles. After laying down an enormous expenditure for 'tooling up' in anticipation of a contract for 48,000 rifles, France suffered a sudden and total defeat within the year and with the crisis over, all promises of orders evaporated overnight.

The company also had to ride the effects of international arms dealing, diplomatic skulduggery and espionage. For the period between 1878 and 1880, Small Heath went through a traumatic time. With nothing forseeable coming from the Government and a dwindling order book, an auction of obsolete but serviceable rifles cleared out a war department stores depot at Weedon, Northamptonshire. Foreign bidders took away between them, 100,000 firearms, and all the Government made from it was a meagre £15,000. For BSA it was nearly a fatal blow at a moment when a dispute between Russia and Turkey would have generated business, but instead the belligerents snapped up the ex-Weedon stock.

John D. Goodman The Founding Father (1817–1900)

John Dent Goodman was inaugurated as chairman of the Birmingham Small Arms Company in 1863 and immediately delivered their first contract to supply 50,000 Enfield rifles for the Turkish government. He had been the chairman and chief spokesman for the loosely organized Birmingham Small Arms trade since 1855. He was an enterprising, energetic and highly respected businessman with good connections in high government office. He once persuaded Lord Palmerston and his Liberal cabinet to supply desperately needed orders when the Royal Ordnance factory at Enfield should have taken precedence.

Through many periods of slump he kept the company alive by a policy of diversifying into cycle manufacture. By the time of his death, his policies had enabled BSA to become the leading exponent of the cycle business. Weapon production always remained the first priority and he directed his company to act in the national interest, initiating rifle production with or without government orders.

Whatever the field of development, BSA maintained the highest quality standards, employing the most exacting inspection methods then available. The Small Heath factory attained a family firm atmosphere, to work at 'The BSA' was considered prestigious amongst the skilled workers, who forged a strong bond between company and employee for generations as son followed father into the trade. The foresight and vision afforded by Mr Goodman left a legacy that lasted for over a century.

The Sign of the Piled Arms

The harsh winter of 1878 was endured by the people of Small Heath living on the borderline of starvation and abject poverty. The factory had been closed for a year, machines had been dismantled and the main boilers lay cold and silent. The local civic authorities offered some crumbs of relief work and an army of skilled gun-makers found themselves re-employed as gardeners laying out fish-ponds and flowerbeds in nearby Victoria Park.

A delegation of executives went to London to plead for some government work. An order for 6,000 rifles did reach BSA from the War Office but it was too little and too late. Although the factory gates did re-open, the board of directors were operating at no profit and stared desperately at a totally bleak situation. But salvation came from an unexpected source and the story is now deeply engraved into Birmingham folklore.

A mysterious Mr E. C. F. Otto visited the offices at Small Heath one day during 1880, eager to show off his 'Dicycle'. The directors, anxious for any form of contract work decided to entertain Mr Otto's idea. So began a long and distinguished journey into the realms of bicycle manufacture.

The curious device displayed by Mr Otto had two wheels side by side, instead of one in front of the other as later became standard. It must have been a quite compelling problem to gain the necessary knack in achieving balance. Whatever, Mr Otto demonstrated it to all doubters at BSA by riding his machine up and down the boardroom table. This was followed by a trip down a winding staircase of some thirty steps, leaving the directors of a reputable and highly respectable company gasping in his wake. Mr Otto was last seen heading in the general direction of Birmingham at what was described by one elderly director as 'a reckless pace'. Suitably im-

15

Mr Otto demonstrates his Dicycle! (BSA Archive)

pressed by this demonstration, the company decided to take on the manufacture of the Dicycle, building an initial batch of 200 machines.

Aproximately 1,000 Dicycles were made throughout the 1880s. Riders were called Ottoists, and they claimed that learning to attain one's balance only took a matter of minutes, but riding downhill took just a little longer to master!

The saddle was just above the centre of the axle between the two wheels so that the rider could exert his full weight onto the pedals even when facing a stiff breeze, and the drive to the wheels went through spring-loaded belts and pulleys. The Ottoist steered by slackening one of the belts enabling one wheel to turn faster than the other.

After the Otto safety cycle, BSA soon developed their skills and know-how for making and selling their own brand of bicycle. In engineering terms, bicycles and gun manufacture had much in common, since both demanded a high degree of precision and quality. The same rigorous inspection methods employed on military small arms manufacture gave much benefit to the cycle production side of the business.

At the birth of the bicycle enterprise, BSA adopted the immortal 'Piled Arms' emblem to be carried as a trademark on the headstock of every machine. It symbolized the joining together of the old gun traders, and depicted three stacked rifles (a form of army infantry drill) surrounded by a garter.

During the 1880s, BSA introduced their 'Alpha' ordinary bicycle and some 'Beta' and 'Delta' tricycles. They also purchased the rights to manufacture an 'Omnicycle' designed by Mr N. Salaman. This quaint velocipede was a rear-driven tricycle powered by reciprocal motion. Other developments on the tricycle theme soon followed. One was the 'Devon' tricycle, sold by Messrs Maynard, Harrison and Company, which boasted a 'swing frame' which enabled the rider to use his full weight whilst maintaining an upright position.

In 1884, BSA had perfected the 'Safety Bicycle', which was regarded as the forerunner of the present general standard bicycle. In actual fact, it was built purely on the initiative of the factory employees who demonstrated a meritorious degree of craftsmanship by building a few prototypes from crude chalk drawings scrawled out upon the factory floor. The directors turned a blind eye to the caper with the proviso that any material used must come from the scrap bin. In all, about 1,500 BSA Safeties were built, using quite a

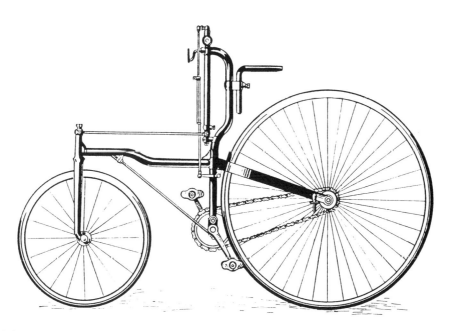

The first BSA safety cycle of 1884, reputed to be made from scrap metal and gun parts.
(BSA Archive)

lot of scrap metal! But cycle manufacture was always of secondary importance to gun-making and company policy was always to act in the interests of the nation.

The War Office decided to re-equip the British Army with the Lee-Metford magazine rifle and awarded a large contract to BSA in 1888. BSA's own army of rifle specialists and technicians had carried out their own assess-ment of the Lee-Metford and reported a number of shortcomings to the War Office, who ignored the warning. It was many years later before the fault was officially 'discovered' and BSA had been producing 1,200 rifles every week!

The intensity of work generated by the Lee-Metford orders forced the directors to abandon cycle making for the next five years and if it had not been for one enterprising gentleman, BSA might never have returned to the world of pedal power. In 1893, George Illston persuaded the company to use its otherwise under-used machinery for the manufacture of cycle hubs instead of shell cases. The astute Mr Illston became the company's first commercial traveller working on a commission of 5 per cent and earned himself the then vast sum of £3,000 a year!

A combination of gun and cycle making enabled the company to ride the slump and boom years that had become endemic to the free enterprise economy. In resuming cycle interests once again in 1893 BSA expanded into the supply of cycle parts for the whole industry. At the Crystal Palace exhibition a full year later, the company was able to put on a considerable display of brackets, cranks, steering heads, seat lugs, chain wheels and pedals.

In 1895, improvements in cycle design and practice gathered pace. A narrower chain line was introduced and the standard crank throw was increased from 6 to 6½in (15cm to 16.5cm). But whatever activities the com-pany was engaged in, its engineers kept to the forefront of developments, constantly re-fining their skills and updating the company's production methods whilst never allowing any relaxation of their standards of workman-ship.

With business on the up, the factory began to modernize with the installation of electric lighting, and the old method of contracting within the premises was ended as all workers became directly paid by the company. Finally, the most brazen revolution of all started as women took their places at the machines for the first time!

2

Growth of an Empire

Novelties and New Models

At the turn of the century, the company began to take an interest in the newfangled internal combustion engine. Just as they were about to commence work on a contract to supply a batch of licenced engines, the South African crisis deepened and brought in urgent government orders for 40,000 Lee-Enfield rifles for the duration of the Boer War.

Whilst the war was raging, BSA kept abreast of bicycle improvements. In 1900, they introduced a free wheel clutch and back-pedalling rim brake, both devices commanding instant success, and thus sealed the popularity of the bicycle thereafter. Pull-up front brakes then followed, along with a complete new range of fittings to suit every type of cycle, be it light-roadster, full-roadster or ladies' open frame style.

With a keen eye on the motorized bicycles that were in evidence all over the Midlands, BSA began to investigate and manufacture some special frames and fittings designed to cope with low-powered engines. In 1905, a spring frame was designed to keep pace with increases in power and speed. An early BSA sales leaflet described their new frames and fittings as 'intended for inclined engines from 2 to 2¾ horsepower.'

In all probability, quite a number of these early BSA built frames were produced to carry a bought-in engine – usually a Belgian built Minerva. (One of these essential pieces of BSA early motor-bicycle history has recently come to the surface and has been acquired for public viewing at the National Motorcycle Museum.)

Before the year was out, another significant development of the pedal cycle business saw BSA amalgamate with the Eadie Manufacturing Company of Redditch. The Eadie two-speed coaster hub, together with BSA's own brand of fittings now offered the largest range of cycle products available and the acquisition gave BSA a good manufacturing base within Albert Eadie's Lodge Road factory where the cycle business could flourish without any interference from gun-making demands.

At the 1909 AGM, Sir Hallewell Rogers, chairman of BSA, announced that in order to meet new trading regulations, the company would widen its policy with regard to the manufacture of a complete cycle, built and inspected to the highest standards. He went on to state that the design section were also to manufacture a complete motor-bicycle, whose frame and engine would be wholly BSA.

In an October issue of *Motor Cycling* and filed under a heading 'Novelties and New Models', a statement read that 'The BSA Company Ltd are producing a single cylinder motor-bicycle as a standard line.' The same article added that an illustration would be available for the Olympia show preview.

The first machine designed and built by BSA made its debut with a proud 'Piled Arms' transfer centred on a green and cream fuel-oil tank. Rated at 3½hp, the BSA looked robust and well proportioned whilst harnessing the best methods and practice found anywhere at the time. It had a bore and stroke of 3.3in × 3.4in (85mm × 88mm) giving a volume of 498cc (a configuration favoured by successive generations of BSA engineers) and the crankshaft developed a quite impressive speed of 1,500rpm! The front fork had two-way springing and as an option, a BSA patent cone clutch could be fitted into the belt driven rear hub, otherwise the basic single speeder carried an auxiliary pedalling chain set weighted to keep the pedals horizontal when not in use.

Immediately after the Olympia show, the 3½hp BSA gathered some very encouraging reports, in which its fine workmanship, oil tightness and good attention to detail were especially mentioned. One test rider climbed Sunrising and Birdlip hills with 'the utmost satisfaction'. Some compared its contemporary practice to that of a Triumph type machine and that, it must be said, was then considered to be high acclaim. 'What astonishes us is that such an excellent example of the touring motorcycle should have been evolved by a concern at the first attempt,' wrote *Motor Cycling*.

The work had been conceived in the Redditch Eadie works with Albert Eadie himself at the head of the team and making his own contribution to the frame and transmission layout. Assisting him was Charles Hyde, another power transmission expert and inventor of many cycle devices that still appear on bicycles to this day. The third member of the design team was Frank Baker, a pioneer TT rider. It was his own hard won experience

---

Albert Eadie The Bicycle Pioneer

Always deeply involved in the early story of the bicycle industry, Albert Eadie was an inventor, engineer and an enterprising businessman. As a leading expert in his day in transmission mechanisms, his patent Eadie coaster hub was a significant contribution to the development of the modern bicycle.

Eadie had been the Works Manager for H. Perry and Co and James Cycles Ltd of Birmingham, before he formed a partnership in 1890 to set up a factory in Hunt End, Redditch, to make sewing machines. They later became involved in bicycles and were registered as makers of the Ecossa cycle, a distant forerunner of the Enfield, New Enfield and Royal Enfield motorcycling story.

In 1896, he broke away and founded his own Eadie Manufacturing Company, moving to new premises in Lodge Road, Redditch, making a wide range of Eadie two-speed coaster hubs, including the famous back-pedalling brake hub and many other cycle fittings. In 1905, the Eadie Manufacturing Company was amalgamated with BSA Ltd, its greatest rival in the supply of cycle fittings. Albert Eadie relinquished his seat on the Enfield board but took up a similar position with BSA, keeping full responsibility for the Redditch factory. He played a prominent part in the design of BSA's first motor-bicycle in 1910 and took out a wide range of patents associated with BSA's multi-spring cush drive, the free-engine hub and a three-speed counter-shaft gear mechanism.

Until he retired in the late 1920s, Albert Eadie retained his involvement in subsequent BSA motor-bicycle designs and up until his death in 1931, he was regarded as an accepted authority on cycle and motor manufacturing.

A 1911 3½hp single speeder sans pedalling gear. (BSA Archive)

of early engines that helped BSA produce a reliable power unit straight from the drawing board. Credit must also be given to BSA's highly specialized team of production engineers who had been trained to produce large volumes of rifles using up to date jigging and gauging methods in order to ensure the highest quality and consistency of every component.

The men at Redditch didn't let matters rest, and improvements and new devices were rapidly introduced. During 1911, a patent two-speed rear hub was offered and later followed up with a three-speed countershaft gearbox. From the 1914 catalogue, a customer could order any permutation of the various transmission mechanisms, each model variation was listed using letters of the alphabet. The model A was the basic single speeder, the model B variant was fitted with the cone clutch, and so on. This system of designation by letters carried on for the next sixty years, right up to the last 750cc A75 Rocket Three!

Eager to prove their new 3½hp machine, seven specially prepared BSAs were entered into the 1913 Isle of Man Tourist Trophy races. There was much to learn however, and only one rider finished in a modest seventeenth placing.

For the 1914 TT races, a team of eight BSA entrants left the starting line, each riding a model D 'Tourist Trophy'. Race tuning amounted to the omission of the pedalling gear and the fitting of an extra large fuel tank. Careful engine preparation was carried out by Mr S. T. Tessier late of BAT motorcycles. Frank Baker, the man behind the original engine scheme was one of the two riders who failed to finish.

The BSA production line began to expand.

A 4¼hp model H with fully enclosed, all-chain drive appeared by late 1913. Its longer 3.8in (98mm) stroke cylinder produced 557cc. The 'Four and a Quarter Horse' BSA remained a firm favourite well into the 1930s, going through a series of redesigns but never losing its reputation as an ever-faithful, all-round performer.

In a relatively short time, BSA had achieved a total commitment to the motorcycle world. Unlike the bulk of the industry which relied heavily on bought-in components, BSAs were built almost totally out of in-house manufactured parts, including the chain, steel ball bearing and even the carburettor!

Determined to make headway into the motorcar business, BSA had completed a series of negotiations that led to the buy-out of the Coventry-based Daimler Motor Company in 1910. Daimler had been one of the oldest names in the British motorcar industry and it gave BSA a firm grasp of the automotive market, supplying not only lorries and buses but also prestige motorcars 'Appointed by Royalty'. Over the years, a number of Daimler-trained engineers were transferred into the Small Heath and Redditch factories bringing their influence and precious expertise into the realms of petrol engines.

Then, just as BSA's motorcycle business was about to further bloom, the heir to the Austro-Hungarian Empire was shot dead on a Sarajevo street corner and Europe marched to war. Once more, BSA moved swiftly to the nation's cause and activities in motorcycle manufacture were of secondary importance.

For King and Country

For many years leading up to the outbreak of the Great War, BSA had been fighting their own commercial struggle against Germany, who had fomented a policy of weakening British industry by giving subsidized bounties and generous concessions to their own munitions firms.

BSA were often placed in a desperate situation when German companies stole contracts by promising seemingly impossible delivery targets. In secret, the rifles were being supplied straight from German government stockpiles, leaving the contracting company to replenish almost at their leisure.

So when Britain went to war it faced a desperate shortage of serviceable rifles, since even BSA's manufacturing base had been seriously eroded. Rather ironically, the British army had almost been on the verge of re-equipping with the German-made Mauser, but in the event, a commitment was made to use the Lee-Enfield Mark III, .303in calibre service rifle, first introduced in 1907. At Small Heath the Lee-Enfield was produced in enormous quantities starting from a meagre 135 to a staggering 10,000 rifles each week by the time of the armistice in November 1918.

The importance of BSA to Britain's war effort was incalculable. The great German offensive in the spring of 1918 was largely halted by a BSA product. It weighed only 26lb (11.7kg), but could fire off 500 rounds per minute with no appreciable recoil. Shots could be fired singly or in continuous bursts, and a new twenty-two or ninety-seven shot magazine canister could be changed in seconds.

The Lewis air-cooled machine-gun differed greatly from other patterns by using the gases released from each bullet explosion to force a stream of coolant air along the length of the gun barrel. Shrouded by an aluminium radiator the gases also acted on a piston which loaded the next bullet. The gun could

Sir Hallewell Rogers Empire Builder (1864–1931)

To accompany the launch of BSA's first motor-bicycle at Olympia in October 1910, the company Chairman, Sir Hallewell Rogers announced, 'Our policy in connection with the motor-bicycle is the same as with our other manufactures, namely to produce only the best and spare no expense in embodying improvements and perfecting the machines, rather than attempt to cheapen the cost with a view to reducing the selling price'. Sir Hallewell was as good as his word, and his policy ensured that the popularity of the BSA motorcycle was built on a firm foundation.

From his inception as Chairman in 1906, he set about a policy of expansion into the motor vehicle world by carrying through an amalgamation with the Eadie Manufacturing and Daimler Motor Companies.

At the age of only 38, Sir Hallewell Rogers was Birmingham's youngest-ever Lord Mayor and he went on to represent Moseley as an MP between 1919 and 1921. As a rich industrialist with interests in banking and gas production, he wielded enormous power in Britain's industrial heartland. During the Great War, he committed BSA totally to rifle, machine-gun and shell production and was on hand to receive a visit to Small Heath by King George V in 1915.

In terms of BSA's motorcycle story it was Sir Hallewell Rogers who created the ideal conditions for Albert Eadie, Charles Hyde and Frank Baker to come up with a design that was by all accounts 'right first time'.

be fired vertically upwards or downwards making it ideal for aircraft armament. Originally designed by Colonel I. N. Lewis, a retired American coastguard officer, the Lewis gun was solely made by BSA and by the end of the war a total of 145,000 guns had been built in a new purpose-built, four storey, west factory at Small Heath.

Under the strong chairmanship of Sir Hallewell Rogers, a man of great political and business stature, the BSA-Daimler company grew mightily and expanded to five factories, employing 13,000 workers, turning out colossal quantities of aero engines, lorries, ambulances and countless weapon types which included thousands of shells, some weighing as much as 685lb (310kg). Vulcan and Mars, the guardians of BSA's house of fire and war, must have been highly pleased with the morass of industry taking place within.

On the home front, a catalogue for the 1915 season consisted of three basic models;

a 4¼hp chain-cum-belt model K, the all-chain driven model H and a 498cc 3½hp model D TT racer. The Redditch factory made their contribution to the war effort by turning out mainly 4¼hp machines destined for the western front, some painted in khaki, others still showing the cream and green that had already become synonymous with BSA.

The war honours may have gone to the 'trusty' Triumph or a Clyno machine-gun carrying combination but one campaign that the BSA story tellers could chalk up concerned the South Africa Motor Cycle Corps numbering 400 men, all ranks mounted on a BSA. Each machine had to carry 140lb (63.5kg) of kit when the SAMC went on a 2,800 mile (4,500km) raid into hostile territory. The Germans may not have been up to much in East Africa but the black mud, soft sand, bug-infested swamps and steamy jungle most certainly were. All 400 machines came back from the campaign intact.

One of the gallant South Africa Motor Cycle Corps in full service kit. (BSA Archive)

After four years of waging a gigantic industrial war, BSA spent some money buying William Jessop and Sons Ltd, an old established Sheffield firm specializing in the manufacture of a wide range of steels, of which so many future BSA motorcycles would see the benefit.

The BSA empire began to re-organize into separate divisions ready for peace-time prosperity. The manufacture of cycles and motor cycles came under the banner of 'BSA Cycles Ltd' and it was Charles Hyde, one of the original design team members who landed the Manager's job.

Trouble Deep, Mountain High

The bright hopes of a victor's peace soon died in the shattered ruins of slump, depression and industrial unrest. The newly purchased Jessop Brightside works was driven almost to a standstill and dividends were paid out to BSA shareholders on only eight occasions over

the next twenty-one years leading up to the Second World War.

BSA Cycles Ltd would provide one of the brighter enterprises in the 'Piled Arms' empire for the following decade. The 1920s saw the introduction of the first in a long line of ever dependable Vee-Twin motorcycles that not only secured a devoted following but earned BSA worldwide fame. In 1924, mass production methods were used for the first time, when the simple and sturdy Round Tank was introduced. BSA motorcycles in one form or another were becoming so popular that the billboard slogan 'One in four is a BSA' was adopted.

There was one unfortunate event that was to be forever ingrained in the memories of BSA men. In 1921, Charles Hyde retired and was succeeded by Commander Godfrey Herbert, DSO, a giant of a man who brought a brave, fresh and adventurous spirit to BSA's motorcycling affairs, driven on by an eagerness to win a coveted slice of competition victories. Joe Bryan was given the reins of the publicity department, operating as a sort of motorcycling impresario, making capital for BSA at every twist and turn. However, 1921 turned out to be so sour that even the silver-tongued J. W. Bryan was at a loss for words.

So far, the Tourist Trophy races had eluded BSA. The directors clung to a dream that the famous wheeled Mercury trophy would one day become the centre-piece on the boardroom table. A secret 500cc overhead, four valve single cylinder machine had been built and had already put in a few impressive laps around Brooklands. After an enormous outlay of time and money, six of these specially built BSA racers were entered for the 1921 TT. The omens were highly encouraging. It was merely a question as to which BSA rider would take the laurels as a team of eight TT-experienced men were assembled and steeled to the task, all smartly turned out in green and cream jackets.

The bikes had duplex frames, cradling an inclined, OHV engine that was bursting with revolutionary ideas. There was a separate, two-port cylinder head and the valve rockers worked on a peculiar vee-groove knife-edge support, unlubricated and operated by square section coil springs. Basically, the bottom end assembly used then standard components except for a purpose-made oscillating oil pump. In all, the BSA 'win at all costs' racers were venomous looking creations that had a large, box-like fuel tank raking upwards to the steering stock. Rumours flew about that these BSAs were the lightest on the weighbridge (not true) and could certainly go like wildfire (very true!).

But on the day of the races, everything started badly and grew progressively worse. The Brooklands trials had not exposed the machines to any twisty sections of mountainous roads. The bikes handled atrociously throughout a practice session already bedevilled by a number of engine seizures. A hasty change of piston material from cast iron to aluminium only aggravated the situation. Valves broke and exhaust manifolds melted as one after another, BSA's lauded TT racers stopped abruptly and were left strewn along the way in utter ruin.

Commander Herbert, barely a month in the Managing Director's seat, vowed that BSA Cycles would never go TT racing again – and they didn't – not for a very long time at any rate.

Fred Hulse was placed in charge of the drawing office and was seconded by Harold Briggs, a young up-and-coming designer. It was a very fruitful partnership which restored some sanity to BSA. In 1923, they introduced a 499cc model S Sports and a medium-weight 349cc model L to expand BSA's range of hard-working sidevalve singles. They then followed up with a 349cc OHV Sports in 1924 and in the same year, the immensely popular model B 250cc Round Tank came along. Two years later, the superb, trend-setting Sloper singles were issued, and BSA now became the market leaders in both manufacturing and design.

Freddie Hulse, a short, dapper little man, was prominent in designing many of the company's motorcycles and three-wheelers. Harold Briggs had been trained at Daimler and his studies of an old Hotchkiss Vee-Twin engine first used in a BSA Light 10 Motorcar just before the Great War formed the basis of many of his excellent engine designs. Briggs would have been destined for further greatness but tragically committed suicide after a doomed love-affair.

Joe Bryan cranked up his publicity drive using a succession of ventures that included mountain climbing and other strenuous tests of ultra-endurance. A troupe of riders were pulled together from a mixture of seasoned trialists and home-grown youngsters to capture a trophy put up by a Mr George Pettyt, an outspoken proprietor of an Exeter-based emporium called the Maudes Motor Mart. The Maudes Trophy, awarded by the impartial Auto Cycle-Union to the best performance in an observed test was always keenly contested for its 'sales pull'.

The 1924 programme of events started, as the ACU watched from the sidelines with every specimen from BSA's seven model line-up being ridden against a stopwatch up and down Screw Hill, a rugged old Caernarfon beacon that contained six very nasty hairpin bends. George Savage, later to become BSA's sales chief, completed the fastest ascent over the three-quarter mile (1.2km), one in twenty gradient on a spanking new

OHV 350 S. Harry Perrey was a mere whisker slower on a massive 986cc model G Vee-Twin combination with one of the younger team members voluntarily requisitioned for sidecar ballast. What a gutsy sight that must have been with the stocky frame of H. S. Perrey never sparing the horses! The next event had nothing like the rigours of Screw Hill about it but was a practical demonstration of BSA's excellent spares and service efficiency.

The ACU were invited to order, from sixteen various dealers, all the parts necessary to build a couple of complete machines, one a long-obsolete 1914 4¼hp model H, the other, its more up to date 1924 counterpart. Three mechanics armed with only a modest outlay of tools completed the giant jigsaw puzzle in just 72 hours. Harry Perrey was called upon to give the old 1914 banger a sound thrashing over 100 miles (161km) of hill climbing around the home counties and furthermore, both bikes started first kick too!

Whilst the spares network was under close scrutiny, Messrs Bryan and Perrey mounted up for what was to be an all-time classic run, the amazing climb to the summit of Mount Snowdon in May 1924. Once again, Harry Perrey captained a team riding a squadron of OHV 350s and a model B Round Tank. Up they all went, along the rocky path beside the old rack-and-pinion Llanberis to Snowdon Summit railway. It was all of sixteen years later that Perrey was to admit in an interview with *MotorCycling* how he was totally grip-

---

Harry S. Perrey Super Showman (1898–1981)

At BSA, Harry Perrey was long remembered as the man who climbed Mount Snowdon in just under twenty-five minutes on one of the firm's brand-new OHV 350s.

Just after the Great War, he landed a job at BSA after reading the small-ads column in a local newspaper, having got through an interview with F. W. Hulse on account of being an ex-army officer claiming to have 'some knowledge of motorcycles'.

As an assistant to Mr Hulse he soon got bored with inter-office politics and managed to get amongst BSA's competition team, working his way up the ladder to lead the section in a sort of 1920s player-coach rôle, winning many medals and trophies for BSA. Some of his more notable victories were a silver medal in the 1922 Colmore Cup Trial and a gold medal in the Scottish Six Days' Trial later that year.

He was involved with the initial testing of the highly successful Round Tank and the first BSA OHV, the model L Sports, combining a quick grasp of engineering matters with all the necessary courage for testing motorcycles to near destruction.

After six daredevil years in the cause of the 'Piled Arms' trademark, Harry moved over to Ariel and carried on in his habitual way, burning life's short candle for the Selly Oak 'Iron Horse'. One escapade had him riding an Ariel 'Flota-cycle' across the English Channel!

Perrey had little time for theory or stuffy drawing offices – he was more at home chalking out his ideas on the factory floor. He nurtured an obsession for weight-saving and probably spent the greater proportion of his time drilling holes or thinning things down. Bert Hopwood, in his published obituary of the British motorcycle industry remembered Perrey for his stock analogy of the street lamp: 'Why is it,' he used to demand, 'that it takes a 10cwt cast-iron lamp post to hold up a feeble incandescent gas mantle weighing only a minute fraction of an ounce?'

In his few years at BSA, Harry Perrey had done a great deal to build up the reputation of the faithful Beesa motorcycle.

Nearly there! Harry Perrey guns his 350cc OHV BSA towards the summit of Mount Snowdon. The photo was actually taken during the following day. Heavy mist and fog prevented a true photographic account of the event. (BSA Archive, loaned by A. G. Cave)

Stop the watch! Harry Perrey pauses for a snack during BSA's Maudes Trophy winning, sixty consecutive climbs of Bwlch-Y-Groes in 1926. The ACU observer, Arthur Bourne (later to become editor of The Motor Cycle), *also grabs a quick bite. (Courtesy* The Classic Motorcycle)*

ped with stark horrifying terror when riding the four and a half mile (7.2km) course up to the 3,560 foot (1,085m) summit with a sheer drop of 2,000 feet (600m) on one side, nil visibility and with gale force winds in full swing! The only mishap was when Perrey nearly slammed into the back of a train that was about to depart from the Summit station!

BSA were mightily disappointed to miss out on the Maudes Trophy, when instead, the ACU handed the silverware to Norton Motors for their 4,000 mile (6,440km) Lands End to John o' Groats epic. But victory came at last in early 1926 when an OHV 350 sports, chosen at random from the production line was shackled to a sidecar and set

about sixty consecutive climbs of the murderous Bwlch-Y-Groes mountain pass that stood over Lake Bala in deepest Wales. With an ACU man in the chair, Harry Perrey completed the task with only minor problems. The Managing Director, Godfrey Herbert was also on hand to witness the event and treated himself to an honorary 61st climb – just to make absolutely sure.

Later that year, two young men set out on another mammoth trial of endurance, a tour around the world! It took 18 months to complete and ran over 25,000 land miles (40,000km) through 23 countries of varying hostility. Each man rode a big model G Vee-

The world tour of 1926–28. John Castley and Bertram Cathrick enjoy the hospitality and privileges of the British Raj in Calcutta. The sidecar inscriptions record their progress so far. (BSA Archive)

Twin Colonial tourer clamped to a heavily laden box car. John P. Castley, representing *The MotorCycle* vividly recalled the saga in his monthly despatches. Accompanying him on the 1926–28 world tour was fellow BSA enthusiast, Bertram Cathrick. Arrested as spies in Serbia, almost fried alive trying to cross the Sinai desert and frozen to the bones trekking over the high Andes, Castley's ripping yarn of around the world in eighty weeks was a grand global salesdrive for BSA cementing a worldwide network of BSA agencies that stretched from Birmingham to

Buenos Aires and beyond. With Castley and Cathrick despatched to foreign fields to fly the BSA pennant, the technical ingenuity of Freddie Hulse and Harry Briggs continued to prepare one particular model, which has long been regarded as a major step forward in the story of the motorcycle – the superlative Sloper. This machine formed the mainstay of large capacity BSAs for another ten years.

The deep recession that loomed in the late 1920s was a bitter reward for the many accomplishments and good designs that marked the roaring twenties at BSA. By July

1928, production of the Sloper singles and all other BSA models became centred on the main Small Heath plant. As a result of these belt-tightening policies, the Redditch factory, where thousands of superb motorcycles had been built, closed its gates.

Blue, Silver and Gold

The mighty BSA-Daimler industrial company creaked and groaned under the trading difficulties of the late 1920s, which had been brought to a head by the National Strike of 1926. Nothing, though, could have compared to the great depression and loss of confidence that followed the stock market crash of 1929.

At the time, the prolific efforts of the Hulse-Briggs partnership had prompted a direct assault on the three-wheeler concept bringing about a cheap and lightweight run-about with a price fixed at only £125 (and later dropped to £98). The TW1 and TW2 Sports three-wheeler BSAs gave sparkling performance and were fitted with independent front suspension, at that time considered to be a very modern feature.

The influence of the old Coventry Hotchkiss motor once built under licence by BSA now came to the fore. Mounted in a transverse position, the air-cooled OHV Vee-Twin engine had 3.3in × 3.5in (85mm × 90mm) cylinders giving a combined swept volume of 1,021.5cc. The drive carried to

Take a telegram! This early 1930s street scene shows half a dozen GPO messenger boys leaving their depot. Machines are 1933 250cc SV B33-1s. (Courtesy The Post Office)

From 1929 BSA began to produce a range of front wheel driven three-wheelers. With growing sophistication, it progressed from a 1021 air-cooled Vee-twin to this handsome example, a 1933 TW33-10 powered by a 1075 four cylinder water-cooled 24bhp engine. (OW)

the front wheels was in front of the crank-cases and a three-speed with reverse drive gearbox spun a pair of shafts through fabric couplings and cruciform Hookes joints. This arrangement fell well short of the constant velocity couplings taken for granted on modern front-wheel driven motorcars. On taking a slippery tight bend, the wheels could revolve in an erratic slow-fast-slow motion giving the occupants some memorable motoring experiences!

The front-wheel-driven three-wheeler went through a seasonal programme of changes. A four cylinder water cooled engine, reminiscent of a Singer design (the Singer car company had moved into ex-BSA-Daimler premises on the Coventry Road

site, adjacent to Small Heath) was available from 1933 before the fourth wheel was added in 1936 to create the handsome BSA Scout built at the Daimler factory in Coventry.

The three-wheeler BSAs joined an extensive range of seventeen different motorcycles and four styles of sidecars that saw in the 1930s. It demanded that a vast range of spares be carried in stock, tying up precious cash and material. But unlike scores of smaller firms that had been squeezed out of business, BSA Cycles Ltd successfully struggled to keep its head above the financial water-line through good house keeping and a selection of small capacity models costed down to the last penny which secured a flow of valuable orders from the GPO and the Police.

A change-over to wet-sump, upright engines with a forward driven magneto and lighting set had commenced for the 250cc and 350cc classes in an attempt to rationalize the product line. By 1931, this was extended to cover the 500cc capacity with a reversion back to the original 1910 engine configuration of 3.3in (85mm) bore × 3.4in (88mm) stroke.

The upright-engined singles offered a more compact wheelbase and eventually displaced their 'Sloper' counterparts. Designed by Herbert Perkins, specially tuned versions proudly carried a six-pointed blue star on the outer timing side cover and captured both the team prize and an outright win in the Victory trial of 1932.

But all efforts at making a standard design with widely interchangeable parts came to nothing when production costs forced a rethink for the smaller capacity machines. To chase what appeared to be a lucrative army contract, an OHV Vee-Twin was built and from that, a new class of high-cam single cylinder sports machines, the first attempt at dry-sump lubrication, came about. They were not successful and a glance through the 1936 catalogue showed that BSA were making sixteen models derived from five basic designs ranging from a 150cc OHV tiddler to the grand old 986cc model G twin.

Joe Bryan deservedly took over the Managing Director's seat at BSA Cycles in 1936 after Commander Herbert had been promoted to the senior board of Directors. Bryan's first

Marjorie Cottle had a very successful career with BSA during the 1930s. She won 'best lady performance' in the Scottish Six Days' Trial for four years running (1932–35), riding a 250cc Blue Star. Here she is explaining the finer points of a BSA Empire Star to show visitors in 1936. (Loaned by A. G. Cave)

Valentine Page The Great Designer (1892–1978)

A Londoner by birth, Valentine Page was apprenticed by a motor car dealer on the south coast, a time he spent tinkering and experimenting with primitive petrol engines.

At the age of sixteen, he had built his own motorized bicycle and had shown enough insight in automobile engineering to win a job within the Drawing Office of J. A. Prestwich, a company specializing in proprietary engine design and supply. By 1920, Page had been appointed chief design and development engineer and spent many a day amid the roar and excitement of the Brooklands race track where he rapidly built up a name for himself by creating a number of record-breaking engines of proven reliability.

His reputation was carried up to the Midlands where a young Jack Sangster gave him a free rein to re-vitalize the production range for Components (JS) Ltd, the factory that made the Ariel motorcycle based in Selly Oak, Birmingham.

With the onset of the great depression of the early 1930s, Page moved to Coventry to take up an appointment with the Triumph Engineering Company. Here he inspired the first commercially viable parallel twin cylinder motorcycle, namely, the Triumph 650cc OHV model 6/1 of 1933, a precursor of the highly successful BSA A7 of later years.

In 1936 he transferred to BSA and before the year was out, his clear, thoughtful and fertile mind had presented the 'Piled Arms' marque with a new range of solid designs, the 'B', 'M' and 'C' group models that were to form the root of BSA productions for the next three decades.

Although Val Page had never been acknowledged as a great stylist, his neat, robust and reliably sound layouts for BSA were modified by successive engineers, usually for the good, but generally never losing their basic 'Page' format.

On the heels of his new 'group' designs some formative work was spent on the BSA A7 twin prototype, which incorporated a proposed telescopic hydraulically damped front fork.

Although he left Small Heath, never to return, in early 1939 for a second spell at Ariel, Jack Sangster sold out to BSA during the Second World War so the BSA connection continued. In the mid-1950s he designed an 'Arielized' version of the popular BSA 650cc twin-cylinder A10 Golden Flash; the Ariel Huntmaster.

But the man who had given BSA a firm product line was not repaid in kind, since a number of Page-inspired Ariel developments fell foul of Small Heath politics. A peppy little belt-driven camshaft 50cc moped that held much promise was cut down by one senior executive because 'it didn't sound like a motorcycle'. Instead the company opted for the flimsy and deficient Ariel Pixie and BSA Beagle. . .

But in the face of managerial adversity came one final success with the imaginative twin cylinder, two-stroke, Ariel Leader. Even though its development was hindered by petty politics within the BSA group, the Ariel Leader won the acclaimed *Motor Cycle News* 'machine of the year' title for two years running.

With the total absorption of the Ariel name into BSA after the closure of the Selly Oak works, Page packed away his drawing instruments for the last time. His final work was an impressive 690cc OHV, four cylinder tourer for Ariel. The engine was arranged with the cylinders in-line almost horizontal and it incorporated shaft final drive with a single friction disc clutch (a design that holds an uncanny resemblance to the modern BMW K series models). It was overlooked by the BSA group just as so many other excellent Page ideas were. Perhaps Valentine Page was just a little too far ahead for the accountancy-minded managers of the day to understand.

act was to entice over to the Small Heath technical department the best designer ever to work within the motorcycles industry. The appointment of Valentine Page was backed with a brief to completely re-draw the main product line. Assisted by Herbert Perkins, Page produced a comprehensive set of designs that were stylish, sensible and right up to date. Only the Vee-Twins were left intact as a full array of dry-sump lubricated models was announced for the 1937 programme, namely a seven model 'B' group consisting of 250cc and 350cc light and medium-weight solo tourers in addition to

the 'M' group heavy-weights built for sidecar haulage or that extra full-bodied sporting appeal. By the end of 1938, another nucleus of 'C' range models were announced. These were cheaper option, coil ignition 250s designed to sell for under £40.

In February 1938, BSA had another crack at the Maudes Trophy. Having issued a list of 1,000 dealers to the ACU, an M23 Empire Star and M21 powered combination headed westwards towards Snowdonia for twenty non-stop climbs of Bwlch-Y-Groes. Then it was back to London for a speed session at Brooklands where the M21 outfit peeled off

After winning a second Maudes Trophy in 1938, BSA repeated the performance during the following year. Harold Tozer driving an M21 outfit and Roy Evans riding an M23 Silver Star are congratulated after completing the final high speed session. The man in the black beret is E. B. Ware, the official ACU observer. (Courtesy The Classic Motorcycle*)*

Albert E. Perrigo 'Mr BSA' (1903–85)

Born within earshot of the Small Heath factory hooter Bert Perrigo was just a boy when in 1915 he witnessed Lewis machine-guns being assembled in the 'New' building whilst the two upper storeys were still being constructed.

With little enthusiasm for his father's bakery business, he began working as a driver, ferrying ex-WD vehicles between dealers. He later took a van driving job with the Bordesley Engineering Company – a small firm who built a motor-bicycle under the name Connought.

After showing a rapid understanding of engines and having a natural ability for riding any type of machine, the Connought people entered him for a 24-hour London to Edinburgh trial where he won the first of many gold medals and trophies in competition trials.

After a brief period with Humphries and Dawes, the makers of the OK Supreme, Perrigo was offered a job with BSA in 1926 as a member of their competition department, and throughout the 1930s, the name A. E. Perrigo became synonymous with BSA's never-ending list of trials victories. Not that the competition world was all glamour – a 1939 issue of *The Motor Cycle* gave an account of BSA's top rider being carried away with a badly gashed jaw and a couple of black eyes to match!

Earlier, in 1928, Bert took part in a publicity stunt. Given a £1 note, he set off with explicit instructions to ride as far away as he could. Taking his trusty '500' that had just given him an overall win in the Cotswolds trial, Bert clocked up 1,670 miles (2,687km) using up eighteen and a half gallons (84 litres) of petrol and just over a pint (half a litre) of oil (petrol then cost nearly one shilling a gallon).

Eventually, Perrigo became BSA Competitions Manager and was responsible for so many of BSA's monumental successes and setting scores of young men on the road to fame. The 1937 Brooklands Gold Star and the 1952 Maudes Trophy victory were just two legendary BSA campaigns planned and managed by Bert Perrigo. As a leading development engineer he enjoyed a close working relationship with many of the great designers who graced the inner design sanctum set beside Armoury Road. Assisting the likes of Val Page, Herbert Perkins, David Munro and Bert Hopwood, the Perrigo touch was applied to everything from Bantams to Gold Stars.

Entirely self-taught, Bert was conversant in every field of motorcycling that absorbed his wide-ranging talents. Whether it was up to the dizzy heights of the boardroom or down in the 'Din house' testing an engine on the dynometer, he always applied a simple, effective and common-sense approach, unlike the scores of highly qualified academics who, in later years, had taken root in the company. As if to confound them all, his final work at BSA was spent liaising with Dr Gordon Blair at Queens University, Belfast working on a computer-orientated project dealing with exhaust systems for advanced two-stroke engines.

He was one of the few people who had the measure of Edward Turner, never shy to commit his point of view in the straightforward way common to Birmingham folk born and bred. (Turner called him 'Bert' when everyone else was referred to in schoolboy fashion by their surname only!)

Whether it was Bert Perrigo the expert rider, salesman, engineer or executive, 'The Gaffer' was both respected and adored during his long career at the BSA and all enthusiasts, who enjoyed his quick wit and good humour, were never refused his advice. They paid him the ultimate compliment of referring to him as 'Mr BSA'.

'Mr BSA' captured in his natural habitat circa 1937. The machine is a B24 Empire Star. (Loaned by A. G. Cave)

100 laps at an average speed of 46mph (74kph). After another hasty trip to the Bwlch for a second helping of twenty, up-hill excursions, the team indulged in a stint of rush hour commuting, criss-crossing London with the gearboxes locked and sealed in top gear. After a total of 1,450 miles (2,333km) had been clocked, the ACU men stripped the engines down and were more than astonished to find no noticeable wear on any of the engine internals. The Maudes Trophy went back once more to Small Heath and to honour their hard-won silverware, a lavish silver-tinted catalogue displaying the 1939 range was presented to all dealers.

Silver was the new colour to adorn every fuel tank, and Silver Star was the name given to the pick of the best and as if the test had not been proof enough of Val Page's engineering excellence, the saga was repeated

again in 1939. All the ensuing publicity generated a full order book as the Automobile Association selected large batches of BSA M20 and M21 combinations for their Road Service Outfits. On a more ominous note, the army were also in the market for large quantities of motorcycles and in the wake of the Munich crisis, BSA began to prepare for another call to arms. But before the blackout came down, there was one more important story left to play out.

On 30th June 1937, a Wednesday, an event long-planned and conceived by Bert Perrigo would eventually bring back victory upon victory for BSA on the racetrack, on the mud-clogged scramble circuit and on the observed sections. . .

Having being persuaded to squeeze back into his old racing leathers, retired racer Walter Handley was entered to race a specially prepared 496cc OHV M23 Empire Star at Brooklands. It was an otherwise quiet, mid-week, three lap, all-comers handicap race but, against a top class entry, Handley set off with a nine second handicap. He ploughed his way to the front as they went into the second lap and eventually hit the finishing line at an average speed of 102.27mph (164.5 kph). The M23 had been set up to run on alcohol with a compression ratio of 13:1 punching out 34bhp. In keeping with the tradition, the organizing lobby pinned a small gold star badge onto Handley's leathers for smashing a 100mph (160kph) average speed barrier.

Back in the drawing office, Val Page pinned up a clean sheet of paper and set to work laying out something worthy to carry the name, Gold Star. Out of it came the M24, an all-alloy version of the medallion winning M23, the pinnacle of Val Page and BSA's pre-war achievements. That history-making day in June, 1937 had not gone entirely to plan however, for in another race, Walter Handley was firmly brought down, throwing man and machine up the track when another rider crossed his path, some reward for a job well done!

But international events were catching up with the world and BSA, instead of embellishing silver and gold onto the panels of super sporty OHV singles, began to daub a liberal coating of best number 3 gas-proof khaki drab onto the humble sidevalve M20s pouring from the production line.

3

Path to Glory, Road to Ruin

The Home Front Line

BSA once more waged a war of mass production against Germany, but this time the factory became embroiled in its tragedy and destruction. The German Luftwaffe had singled out BSA as a key target and issued its bomber crews with specially marked maps pinpointing the areas where Browning machine-gun manufacture, an essential armament for Spitfire fighter aircraft, was taking place. The Small Heath factory was an easy target, the bomber crews easily located the corner of the plant where the Grand Union canal crossed the Great Western Railways metals. On the night of 26th August, 1940, a single high-explosive bomb and a shower of incendiaries landed on the main gun-barrel mill – the only one operating in the country – and 750 vital machine tools were lost. Fortunately, all the workers had been safely evacuated, but rifle production was severely disrupted for three months.

Later that year, on the dark and murky night of Wednesday, 19th November, the main four-storey 1915 building had been lit up by incendiary bombs, and a solitary twin-engined Heinkel bomber scored two direct hits on the southern end of the block. It shattered the building and set off a series of explosions within the main ammunition store. Fifty-three employees lost their lives in the raid, another eighty-nine were seriously injured, and it was six weeks before the last

body was excavated from the twisted and riven remains of the building.

But it was also a night of great heroism for the BSA people, as teams of rescuers worked on throughout the night pulling out survivors while the ground heaved under further attacks of high-explosive bombs. Two of the rescue workers were awarded the George Cross in recognition of their bravery, while another six received the British Empire Medal.

Two nights later, more factory space and many precious machine tools were blown to pieces in a further raid. Facing an increasingly desperate situation, the decision was taken to evacuate the whole factory. When the smoke had cleared from the smouldering rubble, the damage report tallied 1,600 machine tools destroyed. More damage had been inflicted on Britain's munitions supply than during the entire Coventry Blitz.

Defiantly, BSA rose up from the ashes and began to fight back. The hard lessons of the 1940 Blitz had instigated a programme of setting up dispersal factories based mainly in the Birmingham and Black Country areas but some were scattered as far afield as Stoke, Mansfield and the secret 'factory in the caves' at Corsham near Bath. The supply of weapons now began to flow at an ever-increasing rate.

After the war, the company commissioned a book to be written to place on record their astonishing war-time achievements. Donovan

When rapid communications are vital nothing less than B.S.A. reliability will serve our cause.

Thousands of B.S.A. Motor Cycles are now in use by the Army, the Royal Air Force and the Navy, and the number is increasing daily.

Write for the **Motor Cycling Annual** to B.S.A. Cycles Ltd., 47, Armoury Rd., Birmingham, 11

Ward's *The Other Battle* tells how a billion components had been produced, from 67 separate establishments. With 28,000 employees, a grand total of 468,000 Browning machine-guns, 75,000 Hispano and Oerlikon cannons and 1,250,000 Lee-Enfield service rifles were just a small proportion of the company's war-time output. The men and women who, for six years had worked endless shifts, could look back with pride.

If there was one ironic twist in BSA's war story, then it all began back in 1922 when the senior directors held a luncheon in honour of a senior executive who had just resigned in order to pursue a political career. Even though he had worked with Britain's foremost munitions firm, he climbed the political ladder as a great pacifist – his name was Neville A. Chamberlain.

Before the war, changes at the War Office had led to a new direction in policy regarding motorcycles, turning away from overhead valve Vee-Twins to the simplicity of a more easily produced sidevalve single, a 500cc M20 was pitched into a 10,000 mile (16,100km) reliability trial against a Norton 16H of almost identical specification. Both were accepted and BSA received an immediate order for 3,000 machines. Moderate performance, minimal ground clearance but marvellously robust and easy to build, BSA's unlikely recruit to the war effort became a hero during the company's finest hour. In all, over 126,000 M20 type motorcycles were sent to every scene of the war from Birmingham to Burma, accounting for a quarter of Britain's armed forces supply. BSA could rightly claim with all due pride that 'one in four was a BSA'.

The company continued to build up its motorcycle manufacturing empire despite the demands of war and made a number of acquisitions; New Hudson Ltd, Sunbeam Ltd and Ariel Motors Ltd. This latter purchase was lost amid the column inches of a paper rationed edition of *MotorCycling*. The event passed without any comment, since the censors had cut out any mention of the fact that the workers at Selly Oak had downed tools until assurances had been made that the Ariel name was entirely safe in BSA's hands and would carry on in direct competition against their new parent company. In the long term, it enabled the entrepreneurial Jack Sangster to grab a seat on the BSA board and the opportunity to build up a firm power base within the deep corridors of industrial power.

Never Had It So Good

The post-war era from the late 1940s to mid 1950s was the golden era for BSA, when it stood not just as an engineering company, but as an industrial giant that had diversified

Just a few of the 126,000 500cc SV M20s sent to war. The three gentlemen have the seemingly endless task of filling each machine with the correct quantity of oil! (Loaned by A. G. Cave)

into a wide range of product manufacture and material processing. The initials BSA could be found labelled to anything from shot guns and air-rifles, courtesy of BSA Guns Ltd, taxi-cabs from Carbodies Ltd of Coventry, coal-washing plant from Birtley Ltd right down to Monochrome Ltd of Redditch, the pioneers of metal electro-plating.

The war had left a legacy of a huge production capacity with some purpose-built engineering factories calling for work at Shirley and Redditch. To keep the Redditch plant moving, a new elitist, 'gentleman's motor-

James Leek CBE The Great Leader (1892–1977)

Acknowledged to be the best Managing Director that BSA ever had, for without the forthright leadership of Jimmy Leek there would not have been the essential and enormous quantities of Browning machine-guns for fighter aircraft or rifles, pistols, armoured cars ... or even the prodigious hordes of BSA M20 motorcycles!

As a senior BSA executive, Leek once represented the company at the 1935 Leipzig trade fair, an event that left him with a lasting impression, for on the adjacent stand, amid much drum beating and swastika waving stood the feeble figure of Herr Hitler surrounded by his Brownshirt thugs. A demonstration of a bullet-making machine was in full swing and someone made a boastful remark that the bullets were 'for England'.

After being 'entertained' by Hitler's National Socialism, Leek presented a report to his board colleagues advocating an urgent programme of weapon manufacture and so the astonishing and invaluable contribution by BSA to the downfall of the Nazis began.

Born in Morecambe, Lancashire, Jimmy Leek came to BSA in 1912, via the Daimler connection, as a talented production engineer. By the commencement of World War Two he was Managing Director of BSA Guns Ltd where his services were rewarded with a CBE. After the war he became Small Heath's General Manager and Senior Director of both the Cycle and Gun divisions leading the company through its greatest era during the late 1940s and early 1950s. His direct style of leadership instigated a sense of urgency, teamwork and motivation into his sub-directors and managers. He was also an honest taskmaster, known and respected by the workforce for his often surprise visits onto the shop floor or his welcome attendance at the numerous social occasions at 'the BSA'.

In 1945, he helped to set up the Rich Child Cycle Company of New York giving BSA an important outlet into a thriving and highly lucrative USA market.

As a trained engineer, he always selected executives with an engineering background – even his senior sales directors and accountants were former engineers – and all were usually BSA 'born and bred'. He also picked the best engineers of the day, Page, Hopwood, Poppe, and even the styling genius Edward Turner was tempted over to Small Heath during the war, although his allegiance to his former company was too strong (and evidently remained so in later years when he succeeded James Leek as head of BSA Motorcycles).

Jimmy Leek was also a motorcycle enthusiast. There were a number of events held for BSA employees during the 1930s, and the name J. Leek often appeared on the entry list. He was conversant with all motorcycle developments and made many of the key decisions behind so many models bearing the proud 'Piled Arms' badge.

Poor health persuaded him to retire from the board of directors in 1956, when his loss to BSA also marked the high point of the company's fortunes.

cycle' was put into production using the highly esteemed Sunbeam name. At the opposite end of the spectrum, the same factory was given a 125cc two-stroke to build after Small Heath administration had taken up an option that was brought back from the bombed-out ruins of war-ravaged Germany. The parent company unfortunately turned away a chance to build a blimpish looking flat-four, air-cooled motorcar known before the war as the KDF 'people's car' – the Volkswagen!

Motorcycles became increasingly important to the company and anything that had three rifles stamped onto it always held the strongest identity. Centred mainly on Small Heath, lines of civilianized M group sidevalve singles were constantly wheeled from the production track and were soon joined by a new breed of B group OHV singles fitted with telescopic front forks. Then came the first in a long procession of hugely successful A group OHV twins and the re-introduction of the C group 'utility' 250cc singles. All carried a new block winged BSA motif, adopted by the Armoury Road executives to herald a fresh new start. It was a time of high demand at home and abroad in a world frantically re-building and opening out its wide arms for anything 'Made in England'. Putting it simply, any provincial business holding a BSA agency in the 1950s virtually had a licence to print money and realizing that motorcycles were on such a high plane within the company's structure, BSA Cycles Ltd and BSA Motor-cycles Ltd were divided into separate com-panies in the latter part of 1953.

Since the war, Sir Bernard Docker had been installed as the group chairman of the Birmingham Small Arms Company with over-all control of its many activities and subsidiary firms. His family was a rich industrial dynasty and his method of allowing his chief execu-tives to manage their own affairs with little interference contributed to the smooth run-ning of his empire. With Jimmy Leek acting as Small Heath General Manager, Bert Hop-wood, David Munro and Herbert Perkins controlling the design section and Bert Perrigo steering the development and competition sections, BSA were the unquestionable 'leaders of the Industry'. They had a vast sales network, the best quality system and a super-efficient spares and service department.

Everything it seemed, turned to gold, Gold-en Flash, Gold Star and gold medals galore. In the fierce world of competition BSA dominated the Isle of Man clubman TT races until they practically owned the starting grid. In Trials and Scrambles the picture was almost the same because the competition de-partment could easily afford to lavish the best prepared engines and expert support on its chosen team of leading riders. To cap it all there was another Maudes Trophy win, the most spectacular ever and it marked the high watermark in the history of BSA.

The 1952 Maudes 'demonstration' was planned and managed by Bert Perrigo. Three A7 Star Twins were selected at random from a batch of 35 standing in the despatch depart-ment. Each machine was fitted with solo gearing then wired and sealed by an ACU observer. The plan was to embark on a 2,500 mile (4,020km) journey across Europe to contest the International Six Days' Trial at Bad Ausee in Austria, followed by another 2,000 mile (3,220km) tour culminating in a speed test at Oslo airport. The three riders chosen for the expedition were: ex-Ariel and Douglas Trialist, Norman Vanhouse; ex-army trials champion and BSA works team member Fred Rist; and a young chap swiftly making a name for himself in trials under the BSA banner, Brian Martin. For three basic British parallel twins to compete in the ISDT against an imposing entry of more suitably equipped single cylinder machinery, was au-dacious if not downright cheeky! The factory was not allowed to enter a team as such, so the three tendered their entries as members of the Birmingham MCC. Not one team mem-ber dropped a mark and each won a gold medal as well as claiming the team prize. And so to Oslo, where 4,958 strictly observed miles (7,977km) finished with the A7s aver-aging 82mph (131.9kph) from a standing quarter mile (0.4km) sprint. The only mis-haps were a couple of leaking fuel tanks, a handful of burnt-out bulbs and a lost chain-case filler plug! The only item that didn't go

Herbert Hopwood Engineer-Executive (1908–1996)

A working life with motorcycles began amid the drudgery of a filthy iron foundry, and finished fifty years later as Chief Engineering Executive of the BSA-Triumph Automotive group. In between lay a career that touched upon almost every make and model produced in Britain since the war.

Having won a nightschool scholarship in 1926 he was rewarded with a junior draughtsman's job at Ariel where he came under the wing of Valentine Page; he could not have wished for a better tutor. When Page left Ariel, he was seconded to Edward Turner to prepare drawings for his unique Square-four concept.

By 1936, he was Assistant Designer with Ariel Motors (JS) Ltd before accepting a post at the Triumph Engineering Company where Edward Turner had already been installed to manage the design department. Eager to get away from Turner's overpowering personality he moved back to Birmingham to join Norton Motors Ltd and was responsible for their twin cylinder, model 7 Dominator.

Thwarted by Norton's single-minded ambition to win Tourist Trophy races to the detriment of producing a firm base of saleable models, he was invited by James Leek to join BSA as a Forward Product Designer. Within a matter of a few weeks he had been promoted by Leek to Chief Engineer and the time between 1949 and 1955 spent at Small Heath were to be his most 'refreshing years'.

Although adapted from an existing A7 OHV parallel twin design Hopwood's 1949 650cc A10 Golden Flash was one of his most outstanding achievements. It took him only ten days to design it before pushing through a development programme to prepare the production models for the October show.

A greater part of Hopwood's time at BSA was spent developing and modifying existing pattern designs; the 500cc A7 was rebuilt along the lines of the A10 and he also breathed new life into the Gold Stars, making use of better quality die-casting techniques. But Bert Hopwood was also a visionary and presented plans for a radical new racing machine based on a horizontal single cylinder layout codenamed MC1. There was also a promising new 250 intended to replace the aged C11, a step-through 70cc Dandy Scooterette and an electric-start Beezer scooter. Sadly, all these projects fell foul of internal politics, bad preparation or high production costs.

Frustrated by so many in-built difficulties in creating new designs at BSA, Hopwood left to rejoin Norton only to suffer the same restrictions of antiquated production facilities and inept management.

When Edward Turner decided to take retirement in 1963 as head of BSA-Triumph, Hopwood took up the post, partnered by his ever loyal assistant, Doug Hele. They proposed to build a three-cylinder 750 by effectively adding a cylinder to an existing 500cc Triumph. It was only intended to be a stop-gap in order to buy time until they could develop something more elaborate. In the event, it took another six years before the Triumph Trident and BSA Rocket Three entered production.

After the sudden and tragic death of Managing Director Harry Sturgeon in 1966, Hopwood was overlooked to fill the top job and watched helplessly as the final tragic acts of self-destruction brought BSA to its knees.

At the eleventh hour, there was a last-ditch effort to save BSA when a set of 'modular' designs, ranging from a 200cc single to an exciting 1,000cc Vee-Five cylinder superbike, underwent research but it was not to be, since the shareholders backed a Norton-Villiers-Triumph plan to continue making the Triumph Trident and Norton Commando whilst axing BSA from any future plans. Hopwood's (possibly) greatest work remained still-born.

In retirement, Bert Hopwood wrote a damning and compelling indictment of the British motorcycle industry. But it was the BSA A10 Golden Flash that would always remain his crowning glory, a machine that in his own words was 'a very durable bike and it made a lot of money for BSA'.

to plan was when the official photographer, who was following the event appropriately mounted on an A10, developed a nasty bout of appendicitis soon after leaving Paris. . .

'BSA, the most popular motorcycle in the world', said one advertising slogan. 'Lead the way on a BSA', 'Perfect in every part' and 'BSA goes everywhere' were other well used publicity phrases, all of them absolutely true in a decade that moved from austerity days to the 'never had it so good' days and with a seemingly bottomless pit for motorcycle sales, Small Heath still had time for producing over 1,000 bicycles and a similar quantity of industrial engines every week. But against this backdrop of teeming commerce was an undercurrent of discontent.

In 1954, James Leek's health was failing and his attendance at key meetings was becoming less frequent. With knives drawn, others started to rush into the void and three years later, BSA's Chairman, Sir Bernard Docker was unseated from high office by Jack Sangster after an untidy, and highly scandalized Annual General Meeting. Sangster successfully threw off a counter-attack and resumed control of BSA. Previously in 1951, he had sold the Triumph Engineering Company to BSA for £2.5 million in return for a senior Directorship. The press made only a scant mention that the largest producer of motorcycles had bought out its main rival. The Triumph connection had come home to roost as Sangster took little time in appointing his man, Edward Turner, as BSA-Triumph Group automotive chief.

Greetings from Nutley, New Jersey! The man in the hat is 'Theodore Ted' Hodgson who successfully ran BSA USA Eastern operations. The bike is a 1956 350cc OHV B31. (Loaned by Bill Litant)

With a strong smell of asset-stripping in the air, the mighty BSA machine was steadily and systematically dismembered. The Daimler Company went to Jaguar, BSA Cycles were taken on by Raleigh and the industrial engine business was swallowed up whole by Villiers. The sales of these firms realized an unimaginable fortune. In 1956, BSA transmission chain was no longer being made and two years later, Small Heath made its last sidecar. Even the Redditch factory was progressively wound down as Small Heath and the Triumph Meriden factories were organised solely for the purposes of motorcycle manufacture.

Scene Stealers

On 7th June 1961, a centenary issue of BSA Group News was presented to all employees, exactly 100 years after a meeting in a Birmingham hotel called for the formation of the Birmingham Small Arms Company. The 1961 balance sheet had announced a record profit of £3 million. It seemed an appropriate time for Jack Sangster to vacate his Chairmanship and hand it over to one of his supportive accountants, Eric Turner, late of the Blackburn Aircraft Company.

That other Mr Turner had already made his indelible mark on BSA's product range. Whilst the centennial news was being read from cover to cover, plans were already in advance to replace the long-lived and highly acclaimed A7 and A10 twins. The B group pre-unit singles were in the process of being wound down, taking with them the superb Gold Stars, and the old pre-unit C group singles had been long swept aside in favour of a Triumph-influenced, unit-constructed C15. The immortal Bantam had benefited from some cosmetic improvements to its appearance, though there were no engineering changes. The D7 series neatly summed up the current style with its combined headlamp nacelle fork shrouds, rounded triangular tool boxes with composite battery compartment and balanced, gracefully-curved mudguards.

The first to feel the effects of the new order was the proud Ariel Motor Company. Ordered to close down their ancestral Selly Oak base, the makers of the 'Iron Horse' were victims of poor sales and no justification could be given for keeping on another sales team so the Ariel name was hoisted up alongside that of BSA at Small Heath.

Edward Turner retired towards the end of 1963 and another aircraft man took his place. Harry Sturgeon had originated from the De-Havilland Company at Hatfield, after a short period with the Churchill machine company, another BSA subsidiary. He brought into

Our Norah and 'that' Daimler. (Anon.)

The Dockers Naughty Norah and Big Company (1906–1983)

A yacht slipped its moorings one day during the hot June of 1956. On board *Shemara*, a score of Yorkshire miners cheered and applauded as a dazzling blonde danced the hornpipe-jig, dressed in a sailor's uniform.

The dancer was Lady Norah Docker, certainly no ordinary woman. She was an outrageous socialite of 1950s high society, always in the gossip columns, adored and admired by many, but despised by others for her excessive extravagance during a post-war decade of enforced austerity.

Norah Turner came from a lowly background. She was born above a shop in Derby in 1906 but through her considerable determination to succeed, she became a dancer and actress, landing a job in London's *Cafe de Paris*, a renowned hot-spot for the rich and famous. Her charismatic style, vivacious looks and seductive charm made her a magnet for the richest men and two successive marriages left Norah in a very wealthy situation. Her second husband, Clement Callingham, died just a year after they were married leaving her the tidy sum of £250,000.

Never one to accept second best in anything, Norah always insisted on the best things in life. 'While other girls would be satisfied with a fur, I always demanded mink. When other girls would be satisfied with a zircon, I'd insist on a diamond. If I asked for champagne, it had to be pink,' she once remarked. Widowhood did not suit her so she went husband-hunting. It didn't take her very long. . .

At a dance club she saw Sir Bernard Docker KBE, a powerful industrialist and chairman of both the mighty Birmingham Small Arms Company and the Midland Bank. Sir Bernard fell under her spell and they were married in February 1949. So began an era of wild and lavish parties held at the Dockers' estate in Hampshire. One of the most memorable episodes concerned the famous gold plated 'Docker' Daimler. 'When I first drove it I expected eggs and tomatoes to be thrown at it,' she once recalled. 'I must say, right from the start that it was not produced with the intention of reflecting any personal glory to me.'

She had an enormous power over Sir Bernard and she surreptitiously influenced a number of key decisions regarding Sir Bernard's business affairs, some of them directly affecting the prospects of several motorcycle projects. At least one showroom prototype 'got the chop' because the Lady disliked the colour. Of the factory itself, Lady Norah hated its decrepit buildings and once called Small Heath 'A sprawling mass of shabby huts and shacks'. And the directors 'were a crawling, cringing slimey lot. . .' On many a day she could be found grovelling about on the factory floor either playing marbles with the assembly workers or writing out fat cheques for one of the soon-to-be-married factory girls – at least her generosity and love of life never diminished.

Then her rich bubble burst. As a result of allegations about a currency offence, Sir Bernard was forced to resign his chairmanship of the Midland Bank and in a stormy BSA Annual General Meeting in 1956, he was ousted from the high seat of power and the treasured Daimler was confiscated. One of the reasons tabled was an £8,000 bill he had run up for dressing out Norah so that she could attend the Paris motor show in 'suitable attire'.

As if to 'cock a snook' at BSA, Sir Bernard and Lady Norah Docker went out and treated themselves to a Rolls-Royce each and settled down to a happy retirement amongst the very wealthy (but never staying out of the newspapers). In 1958, Lady Norah was caught up in a fracas with Prince Rainier of Monaco over some christening invitation snub. Lady Norah went on a flag-tearing session and invited the Prince to, 'go and jump in the sea'. The Dockers soon found themselves black-listed on the Côte d'Azure.

'Naughty Norah', as the press dubbed her, passed away in 1983 at the ripe old age of 77, when she was down to her last £44,000.

Small Heath a new mood of optimism and motivation. Sturgeon was a brilliant salesman whose driving hand was behind many of the new lavish posters and snappy one-liner advertising catch-phrases that played up to the so-called 'swinging sixties'. 'Get away with BSA' appeared on the 1964 catalogue cover and 'BSA scene stealers' was another.

The American market was by far BSA's largest customer with two main outlets: Theodore 'Ted' Hodgson was President of BSA's Eastern half, with his headquarters at Nutley, New Jersey, while Hap Alzina ruled the Western Coast operations. Ted Hodgson had succeeded Alf Rich Child, the founder of the BSA USA business in 1955, and in his first term at Nutley, he sold 1,446 machines making a profit of $45,000. When he retired in 1968 after thirteen years of trading his sales accounted for 11,225 BSAs with a sales value of over $11 million. In all, he had sold nearly 50,000 machines!

By the mid-1960s, the American influence was beginning to show itself, with an influx of 'flamboyant' colour schemes, high-rise handle-bars and a never-ending quest for more performance to be squeezed out of designs that had really gone beyond their safety bound-

Who's that girl? This 1960s nymphette is hardly dressed for handling a 'hot' BSA A65 Lightning. (Anon.)

ary. But an opportunity to bring about some new designs was missed. BSA badly needed another Freddie Hulse, a Harold Briggs or a Valentine Page; instead the company's objectives were lost amid an influx of accountancy-minded consultants. As time marched on the main-stream range of unit-constructed singles and parallel twins was left sadly wanting.

Some of the cracks that would ultimately bring the company to ruin were starting to show. The parent board had committed a series of blunders by selling off steel-making and machine-tool assets far too cheaply (in one case, the Herbert Machine Tool company acquired a good part of BSA's tool divi-

sion, not for cash but in a payment of shares which became worthless overnight).

After a long and recurrent illness and only three years in office, Harry Sturgeon died of a brain tumour. Sturgeon had been eagerly followed and respected by everyone. His had been the last vibrant regime although it was his own unfortunate remark that BSA were makers of 'consumer durables' that set about a wayward attitude of mind towards motorcycle manufacturing. His replacement should have been Herbert Hopwood, then acting as deputy but instead, Eric Turner went looking for another man with aircraft credentials and chose Lionel Jofeh, a complete outsider.

It was unusual to see Edward Turner sitting on a BSA. Here he is taking the controls of a 650cc A65. Service manager Bill Rawson hitches a lift. (Loaned by A. G. Cave)

Edward Turner Triumph and Travesty (1901–1973)

'A genius', 'brilliant', 'irascible', 'difficult', 'awkward' and 'an egomaniac' were just a few of the terms used to describe this man, who was so much larger than life.

Edward Turner gave the world the vertical twin. There had been previous attempts at building an engine having two pistons rising and falling together on a common crank, but not the way that Turner achieved it. His Triumph Speed Twin of 1937 exploded on the motorcycle world and the repercussions were felt in every quarter, including BSA.

The early life of Edward Turner is shrouded in mystery. He came out of the merchant navy, and once ran his own motorcycle shop in London and even built his own hand-made machine. Convinced that he held the secret special knowledge for successful design he tramped northwards to the Midlands with a book of sketches illustrating a novel idea for a four cylinder engine arranged in a square. At Ariel, Jack Sangster was receptive to the young man's plans and gave him an office in which to turn his ideas into reality.

When Sangster later bought the Triumph Engineering Company, in the mid-1930s he installed Turner to run the design business and his sleek Triumph Twins became a legend. Again, as Sangster began to wield the upper hand at BSA in the late 1950s, Turner's authority was extended to cover the entire BSA-Triumph automotive range. His influence was immediately obvious in the trend for simple rounded shapes, neat headlamps nacelles and exciting colour schemes.

But there was a sting in the tail. Turner's interpretation of basic engineering methods and devices lacked a certain proficiency and calculation. At Triumph, an in-built 'safety valve' ensured that his proposals were vetted, 'beefed up' or in certain instances, completely re-drawn whilst he was away on one of his regular visits to America. They were not so fortunate at Small Heath. The 250cc OHV C15 introduced in 1958 was based on an earlier Turner-designed Triumph Terrier/Tiger Club series. The wretched prototype was described by one development engineer as, 'a poor thing, but we made something out of it'.

Tyrannical, dictatorial and a master of office psychology, Turner considered only his own designs as worthy of being pursued. No one, however, could ever deny that Turner possessed a rare quality for styling and instant eye appeal, and his schemes sold thousands of motorcycles for both BSA and his beloved Triumph.

After retiring in 1961, he carried on in a consultative role and the engineering department found themselves later 'lumbered' with another typically Turner concept, the 350cc OHC twin, Triumph Bandit/BSA Fury. Both were beautifully presented, excellent in style but dreadfully lacking in any technical substance.

For the two successive years 1967 and 1968, BSA's ability to earn dollars was recognized with a Queens Award to Industry. In front of a canteen packed with cheering workers, Eric Turner held the award aloft. Ironically, the occasion masked the true reality of the state of affairs, and it was more of a signal that the end was just around the corner.

Crash Landing

The Manager of a company is like the pilot of an aeroplane, the departmental managers are his instrument panel, telling him if he is flying too high, too low or too fast. The pilot, however, has to decide in which direction to fly and he holds full responsibility for all on board.

When applying this simple analogy of an

aircraft to BSA in 1971, the aeroplane was plummeting out of control, parts of it were already breaking up and if fuel was money then the tanks were running bone dry. The pilot of this BSA jumbo jet was Lionel Jofeh, and at the point of impact he was somewhere in the dark recesses of the fuselage trying desperately to understand the instruction book and even if he had glanced up at his instrument panel, the gauges would have been waving about frantically with all the red lights flashing on and off. The older, more reliable, instruments were for ornamental purposes only, otherwise considered to be disconnected.

As soon as Jofeh had climbed aboard in February 1967, his first and immediate action was to set up a research establishment in an old property, away from the day-to-day affairs of the main factories. The cloistered academic retreat of Umberslade Hall was soon filled with the most eminently qualified technicians, most of them unproductive, 'high salary, company car' boffins. Out of it came very little that any seasoned motorcyclist could recognise as having any relevance. The Umberslade Hall money-no-object think-tank was just another incoherent mess of localized factions pitted against the seething rivalry and downright hostility that was running between Meriden and Small Heath. Not that the two main factories provided a visible dividing line. In the mid-1960s, Harry Sturgeon cleared Meriden of the Triumph Tiger Club and other small capacity products to enable the generously paid Triumph employees to concentrate solely on more profitable big twin cylinder machines. The work was transferred onto the less well-off Armoury Road workforce.

The crash of BSA was so much like many other man-made disasters – a culmination of several events, misunderstandings and bad decisions. Had one, or maybe two of the problems involved been avoided, then the Small Heath-based BSA story might have run for at least another chapter.

Personal self-esteem and egotism had been allowed to rise above the company at senior level. Blind belligerence, demarcation and obstinate militancy ruled the workforce, which for 100 years previously had enjoyed a proud, strike-free family atmosphere. The last ten years of BSA's life had been marked by a steady deterioration of its product line, too many models were long overdue for replacement and when a new design did get to the production stage, it took far too long to have any impact. The A10 Golden Flash of 1949 took a matter of weeks to produce, the Rocket Three of twenty years later took six years!

BSA, if not the whole of the British motorcycle industry since the 1950s, had lost the art of building a small bike. After the dismal failure of the hopeless Beagle in 1965, only the Bantam (which dated back to 1948) was left to shore up the demand from L-plate riders until a monumental decision was taken to wash it away and invite the Japanese to 'waste their time and money on small runabouts'. After all (so the argument ran), the Japanese were doing a great service teaching people to ride so that they could go out and buy a 'real' British-built motorcycle.

One ill-conceived venture after another tore gaping holes out of the company's cash reserves. The 350cc OHC Fury (*see* page 159) was one very expensive fiasco, while the saga of the Ariel 3 was even worse. It could only be described as a motorized shopping basket, but the idea of a 50cc tricycle that qualified in the same taxation group as a moped on account of its narrow rear wheel track, appealed so strongly that BSA fought long and hard in the bidding for the design

By the early 1970s the Small Heath assembly line had a powered track. Here a batch of 1971 singles with Umberslade Hall's oil-in-frame brainchild are being built. (Loaned by A. G. Cave)

rights. It was an amazing device, so they thought, with the front half pivoted so that it could be banked through corners. It was a definite housewives' choice... Only after some considerable outlay in tooling up the factory did they realize that the poor effort was inherently unsafe at certain speeds and only after 20,000 engines had been bought from Holland did they discover its somewhat alarming enthusiasm for seizing up solid. Ariel enthusiasts were mightily sickened and hurt by this careless use of the old Selly Oak name – it was not an Ariel, it was not even a BSA, and the purveyors of 'consumer durables' had been reduced to pedalling trinkets and cheap tat.

The final flourish came late in 1970 when London's Lancaster Hotel was used for a £15,000 bash with over 350 press and trade people. A lavish dinner, dancers and a top comedian warmed up the audience for the top of the bill act, 13 new and revamped BSA/Triumph models lined up under the spot lamps, unveiled to a fanfare of trumpets. Included in the show were the Ariel moped, the BSA Fury and a whole basket of fruit picked from Umberslade Hall, namely some oil carrying frames for the large capacity twins, specially designed for people who stood well over six foot (1.83m) tall. It was like the last supper before impending doom, the eve of a battle against impossible odds, but at least the occasion provided a few stiff drinks to enable them to go down fighting drunk.

The end came after months of fumbling with a myriad of production troubles. Strikes, badly produced parts, engines that did not fit frames and a computer that spewed out orders to build a huge stockpile of unwanted parts, tightened a noose around the com-

50

pany's neck. By the time the first shipments were being despatched, the spring and early summer markets were deserted, leaving shiploads of more unwanted motorcycles to be off-loaded and heavily discounted. The bill showing a £8.5 million loss dealt a shattering blow. Jofeh and BSA parted company in July 1971. Eric Turner clung on grimly until tendering his resignation in November. Lord Shawcross, a senior executive since 1968 was elected to the chair and hastily restructured the company, selling off as many assets as he could find buyers for. The 1972 catalogue was just a mere broadsheet offering the 750cc Rocket Three, Lightning and Thunderbolt 650cc A65 twins and the single cylinder 500cc B50.

Bound together by the desperation of the moment, the Shawcross regime, bolstered by a £10 million finance injection, fought hard and bravely and restored some long lost respectability. Bert Hopwood had answered the call to act as Automotive Chief and initiated a programme for a range of entirely new

Dennis Howell MP inspects a Rocket Three crankshaft as BSA works manager Alistair Cave (right) offers his technical advice. (Loaned by A. G. Cave)

motorcycles built on a modular basis, using common prime moving engine parts. Hopwood's bold, ambitious but realistic plans ranged from a single cylinder '250' to a futuristic 1,000cc Vee-Five cylinder flagship. The basic design 'module' specified a counterbalance shaft with a reciprocating piston type oil pump. After a period of rig testing and development the prospect of building prototypes looked promising until another trading deficit threw BSA onto the rocks.

The last breath of BSA was shrouded in high finance and seedy politics. A deal was struck with the Department of Trade and Industry and Manganese Bronze Holdings, the Glacier bush people who had already collected Norton and a host of other old motorcycle names. The newly formed Norton Villiers Triumph Company was built around the Norton Commando and Triumph Trident, a stable-mate of the 750cc triple cylinder BSA Rocket Three.

As far as the Birmingham Small Arms name was concerned, it was the end. The plan called for Meriden to shut down and transfer Triumph and Norton production into Small Heath but the 1,800 Meriden workers held the opposite view and threw a cordon around their factory to prevent the release of 4,000 machines. A Labour government, brought back to power, legalized the take-over and condemned Small Heath to the bulldozer. In 1977, the vast sprawling mass that once supplied weapons for two world wars and had given employment to generations lay in ruins. The last batch of motorcycles left the assembly line on a Wednesday night in the summer of 1973 – they were not BSAs but a fleet of white-painted Triumph Tridents destined for Saudi Arabia. Someone, in vain, scoured the stores for some winged BSA badges but none could be found. It was a sickening and poignant way to end the story.

4

The Good Old Beesa

Single Cylinder Machinery (1910–36)

The Birmingham Small Arms company adopted a policy that ensured that its finished manufactured goods would always be in great demand even in times of severe trading difficulties. This included all cycles and motorcycles carrying their famous three-rifles trademark. In the main, they were unpretentious machines, not renowned for their sporting prowess – they would more than likely get a little hot and flustered if over-revved – but for price, quality and immediate delivery, a BSA could outgun the rest and keep firing all day long. They became a part of the fabric of everyday life, taking on much of the workload previously done by horses.

In many ways, the first production motor-cycles of 1911 formed the basic mould for the next 60 years. Along every highway and by-way, for the farm labourer, office clerk, village chimney sweep or town charlady, whose sidecarrier would be crammed full of mops and buckets, a good old Beesa outfit was always there to lend a hand. At weekends a BSA combination could take the whole family out on a countryside excursion, courting couples could escape into quiet seclusion or maybe an enterprising young man could pit his sidevalver in a wager and race along a dusty track. A Beesa may not have been something special to brag about in the snug but everyone was just as proud to own one.

Throughout 1911, BSA's Redditch factory sold every motor-bicycle it could make. A 3½hp, 499cc 3.3in × 3.4in (85mm × 88mm) single speeder could be ordered for just £50, while an extra £6 10s would enable a BSA patent 'free engine' cone clutch to be fitted.

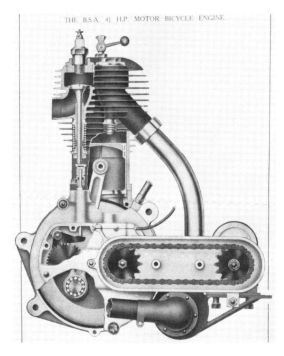

The 'four and a quarter horse' BSA engine measured 3.3in (85mm) bore × 3.8in (98mm) stroke (557cc). The schematic picture shows a 1916 unit in which the offset tappet arrangement can be clearly seen. (BSA Archive)

Selected Single Cylinder Models (Up to 1936)

Model	3½hp model A 'Fixed Engine' (1914)	4¼hp model H (1914)
Engine type	Single Cylinder sidevalve	Single Cylinder sidevalve
Bore × stroke	85mm × 88mm	85mm × 98mm
Capacity	498cc	557cc
Claimed power	3½hp (ACU rating)	4¼hp (ACU rating)
Carburation	BSA Variable Jet	BSA Variable Jet
Gearbox	Single-speed	Three-speed
Ratios	Variable engine pulley ratios from 4.25 to 5.75:1	11.8; 8.7; & 5.5:1
Tyres, front	26in dia × 2¾in	26in dia × 2½in
rear	26in dia × 2¾in	26in dia × 2½in
Brakes, front	Stirrup	Stirrup
rear	Dummy belt rim	Dummy belt rim
Suspension front	Cantilever spring	Cantilever spring
rear	Rigid	Rigid
Fuel capacity	1⅓ gall.	1⅓ gall.
	1 quart oil	1 quart oil
Top speed	45mph	50mph

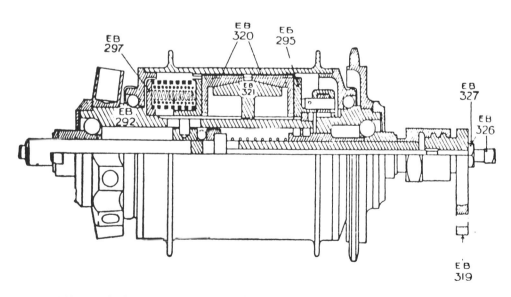

The two-speed 'free engine' cone clutch was combined into the rear wheel hub. (BSA 1914 catalogue)

It had a strong frame fashioned out of weldless steel tubing, pin jointed and brazed into each lug, with front forks to BSA's own double spring cantilever design. The engine followed contemporary practice with separate gear-driven cams, but a number of BSA patents had been registered to cover a free floating gudgeon pin, cush drive and a double chamber carburettor. The drive was taken through a variable vee-belt pulley whereby the rider could take on any incline by first releasing a locknut and then re-setting the pulley between any ratio from 4¼ to 5¾.

BSA's designers were adept at transmission improvements, and a patent two-speed and later three-speed rear hub soon came along. In 1913, a three-speed gearbox controlled by a heel and toe pedal and cushioned by a multi-plate clutch could be fitted on re-

quest. To start the engine, bottom gear was engaged. This automatically freed the clutch. Once the power unit had been fired into life further gear changes were performed on the valve lifter. It was a simple and efficient device that stayed in production until 1922.

To further the needs of sidecar users, a larger 557cc model was introduced by increasing the piston stroke to 3.8in (98mm). It was available with either belt- or chain-driven final drive, the latter version having a handsomely crafted, fully enclosed chain case that would have put some machines, built fifty years later, to shame.

Designated as the model K with chain-cum-belt drive or model H for the all chain-driven version, the 'four and a quarter horse' BSA gave the customer exactly what he wanted – a dependable and versatile trans-

The B.S.A. Three-speed 4¼ h.p. (557 c.c.) Motor Bicycle, with Chain Drive, Model "H"

For solo or combination work the 557cc Model H was a superb all-rounder. Just look at those excellent chain-cases! (BSA Archive 1916)

port, constructed from refined materials, inspected and assembled to precision standards and, at 64 guineas, an affordable price for the mass market.

In 1922, a number of significant improvements to the frame were made. The front forks featured a strong single barrel-shaped spring, centrally placed inside curved tubular webb type forks replacing the earlier cantilever type, and the steering headstock was made from forged steel in preference to the previously used malleable cast-iron material. To signify the changes, the 1923 brochure listed the 557cc machines as the K2 and H2. In all, these wonderfully faithful old sidecar-pullers were made in large numbers. The model K lasted until the end of 1923 and was the last belt-driven BSA, while the more popular model H went through only minor changes until it was superseded by an ultra-modern 'Sloper' design in 1927.

Under the determined leadership of Freddie Hulse and expert engine designer Harold Briggs, a new pair of sidevalvers were added in time for the 1923 seasonal catalogue. The first was a model S Sports, marking a welcome return to the 500cc class after the original model A-derived machines had dwindled from the scene during the war. The second newcomer was a useful 350cc model L rated at 2¾hp and temptingly priced at only 55 guineas.

Both engines still retained a simple upright basis with separate cams and a forward driven magneto, but wide tappet feet and generous cam lobe land areas performed with quiet distinction and lived up to BSA's promise for 'silent timing gear'. There was a new constant mesh, three-speed gearbox too and the rear brake was activated through a parallel motion linkage by the right foot. There were two significant developments during the mid 1920s which assist date identification. For 1926, drum brakes became a

Model	2¾hp model L (1923)	3½hp model S (1923)
Engine type	Single Cylinder sidevalve	Single Cylinder sidevalve
Bore × stroke	72mm × 85.5mm	80mm × 98mm
Capacity	349cc	493cc
Claimed power	2¾hp (ACU Rating)	3½hp (ACU Rating)
Carburation	Amac	Amac or BSA Variable Jet
Gearbox	Three-speed hand-change	Three-speed hand-change
Ratios	14.2; 8.2; & 5.1:1 with 16T engine sprocket	13.3; 7.6; & 4.8:1 with 16T engine sprocket
Tyres, front	26in dia × 2¼in	26in dia × 2½in
rear	26in dia × 2¼in	26in dia × 2½in
Brakes, front	Dummy belt rim	Dummy belt rim
rear	Dummy belt rim	Dummy belt rim
Suspension front	Girder with barrel spring	Girder with barrel spring
rear	Rigid	Rigid
Fuel capacity	1⅓ gall. 2½ pints oil	1⅓ gall. 2½ pints oil
Top speed	48mph	55mph

standard fitting on all models in place of the old dummy belt rim variety and 1927 saw some improvements to the frame layout for both the medium and heavyweight range by way of a lowered seat position.

The Super Sports OHVs

Freddie Hulse's attention had been drawn by a consignment of ex-government British Hotchkiss engines that were left over from the 1914–18 war (the basic engine had been fitted to a BSA light-car built between 1921 and 1924). Its overhead valve gear was particularly neat and it formed the basis for Harry Briggs to draw up a flighty 350cc OHV sports model ready for the 1924 showstand.

At last there was a catalogued model with something to shout about and had there been a works-supported racing programme, who knows what may have come of it. It started out as the plain model L OHV but later, in modified form, it earned the tag 'Super Sports'. It used a 349cc 2.8in × 3.3in (72mm × 85.5mm) upright cylinder, to which a number of special tuning features were added. A detachable cylinder head had polished ports with valve rockers running on ball bearings (early versions employed bronze bushes) and the compound spring valve gear was semi-enclosed; in plain BSA language, that meant the inlet was covered, while the exhaust was open to the weather! All engines came with a certificate to show that they had been bench tested and proven on a test track. Unlike so many BSA motorcycles of the time, the Super Sports had a separate oil tank instead of the normal forward compartment in the fuel tank. Some were turned out in a sedate touring format, but in full race trim it had fishtail exhaust and a cushioned pad fixed to the top of the fuel tank for any-

Mr G. Steck, winner of the Danzig Autumn Motor Cycle Championship in 1928, using a BSA model L Sports of about 1924 vintage. (BSA Archive)

one who wanted to indulge in a spot of high-speed fun laying down low on the tank.

The Super Sports model L earned an obscure nickname, 'the spider'. Could this have been due to the fact that it had a low and spindly profile? Perhaps not, but with the motor whirling at almost 4,000rpm, a 5.4:1 compression ratio and plenty of air in the 27in tyres, it could certainly bat along consistently at 60mph (100kph). After spending another £5 on a 6.5:1 piston and a pair of vicious cams, the giddy realms of 70 to 75mph (115–120kph) were placed within reach and it did its own impression of Birmingham Small Arms fire!

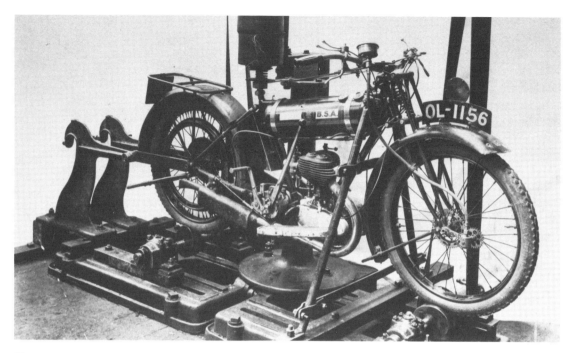

The model B 'Round Tank' underwent lengthy testing before being released for production. Here is one of the initial batch undergoing rig testing at the works. (BSA Archive)

Round Tank, Wedge Tank and a Bike Called X

When BSA launched its lightweight model B in 1924, it was the result of two years of secretive development by Freddie Hulse's team blatantly to corner the market for a simple, run-about four-stroke with few thrills.

Against an aggressively commercial background, BSA were one of four members of a cosy cartel that ruthlessly waged a cost-cutting war that sent the industry reeling. With a rock bottom price of just under £40, the 2.49hp two-speeder was bound to be a winner from the start. It featured a simply constructed sidevalve 249cc, 2.4in × 3.1in (63mm × 80mm) engine having a mechanically oiled roller big-end bearing and a forward pointing magneto drive platform cast integrally with the right-hand engine case. The crank was fixed between ball and plain main bearings and drove an oil pump fitted into the outer cover. There was also an enclosed primary drive case to mask a singular dry-plate clutch driven from a cam-faced shock absorber.

But for all the merits of its moving parts, the one feature that struck any showroom visitor was the cylindrical fuel and oil tank fastened by two metal straps to the frame top tube. Universally nicknamed 'the Round Tank', only BSA's stuffy catalogue description clung stubbornly to its official model designation!

Good for a top speed of 45mph (72kph), the Round Tank was a nippy little thing and

57

Model	2¾hp model B27 'Round Tank' (1927)	3.49hp model L27 OHV (1927)
Engine type	Single Cylinder SV	Single Cylinder OHV
Bore × stroke	63mm × 80mm	72mm × 85.5mm
Capacity	249cc	349cc
Carburation	Amac	Amac (Pilot Jet Type)
Gearbox	Three-speed hand-change	Three-speed hand-change
Ratios	13.6; 9.3; & 6.2:1 with 17T engine sprocket	12.9; 7.4; & 5.4:1
Tyres, front	24in dia × 2⅜in	27in dia × 2¾in
rear	24in dia × 2⅜in	27in dia × 2¾in
Brakes, front	5½in dia Drum	5½in dia Drum
rear	5½in dia Drum	7in dia Drum
Suspension front	Girder	Girder
rear	Rigid	Rigid
Weight	187lb	240lb
Fuel capacity	1½ gall.	1½ gall.
	2¼ pints oil	3½ pints oil
Top speed	45mph	60mph

with a fuel consumption estimated to be near 120mpg (2.356l/100km), no wonder it became exceptionally popular, and enabled BSA to break into the fleet market by winning large orders for a newly inaugurated telegram messenger service. After just one production year, the Redditch factory had cleared 5,000 machines, and four years later, the population of Round Tanks had risen to 35,000.

An ideal choice for the novice, the Round Tank was delightfully snappy to ride with an easy to use, long-handled gearchange lever connected directly to the gearbox and for the folk who lived on the hill, a special set of low ratio gears could be fitted to order. The only slur against its character concerned the omission of a front brake. BSA endured a lengthy courtroom session to prove that the rear dummy rim did in fact have two independent braking controls.

Keeping an open ear to their dealers, the factory came up with a three-speed de-luxe model B finished in a gold-lined, black painted tank carrying only a solitary 'Piled Arms' badge instead of the usual BSA block letters, but then, everyone knew who built the Round Tank.

For 1927, the standard model B took on the three-speed gearbox while both versions had drum brakes fitted fore and aft. The de-luxe lost its cylindrical tank, and instead received a rectangular section, wedge-shaped container, still suspended from the frame tube. This new style was claimed to give a better riding position on account of the lowered saddle height, and for the following year, the Round Tank pattern was discontinued, probably due to a number of competitors who had cloned the idea. Keeping ahead of the field, the 1930 2.49hp model B had a tear-drop shaped saddle tank but for the most part the machine was still very much unchanged from the original dapper Round Tank.

It was a simple fact of life that most people

Model	1.74hp A28 (1928)	B31−1 (1931)
Engine type	Single Cylinder Two-stroke	Single Cylinder SV (Wet-sump type)
Bore × stroke	60mm × 61.5mm	63mm × 80mm
Capacity	174cc	249cc
Claimed power	1.74hp (ACU rating)	6.8hp at 4,400rpm
Carburation	Amac	Amal type 74
Gearbox	Two-speed hand-change	Three-speed hand-change
Ratios	–	14.5; 9.8; & 6.6:1
Tyres, front	24in dia × 2⅜in	25in dia × 3in
rear	24in dia × 2⅜in	25in dia × 3in
Brakes, front	None!	5½in dia × 1in
rear	5½in Drum	5½in dia × 1in
Suspension front	Girder	Girder
rear	Rigid	Rigid
Wheelbase	50in	52in
Weight	180lb	220lb
Fuel capacity	1½ gall. 'petroil'	1½ gall.
Top speed	35mph (optimistic!)	45mph

who rode a motor cycle were not actually motorcycling enthusiasts. This was especially true of the thousands of riders owning smaller capacity machines, who in the general course of an honest day's work were more than happy to get about cheaply without any accompanying drama. BSA's greatest strength was in supplying this insatiable appetite for what the press termed a 'nifty two-fifty', and this was especially so in the heady days of the Round Tank, and continued right up to the days of the simple and efficient C15 of the 1960s.

Competitive price and top quality were the two main attributes that sold more BSA-built motorcycles than any other make. For three seasons, the quarter-litre class consisted of a scaled down version of the wet-sump lubricated upright cylinder singles. On one hand, it gave a degree of rationalization with the rest of the range and with a complete lack of external pipes it offered the would-be pur-chaser a far better and more reliable proposition. However, the depression cut prices to the bare bones and the higher manufacturing costs of oil-in-sump construction could no longer be tolerated. So in 1933, the makers returned to a gravity-fed oiling system with sight feed glass. And the price? £33 15s bought the B33-1 ready equipped with a Lucas maglita and a chrome-plated fuel tank. Now if a 1930s commuter really wanted to beat that, he could have shelled out another £3 for the B33-2 OHV job. But a higher price tag of £46 5s would have probably put the highly refined B33-3 Blue Star only within reach of certain dedicated sportsmen.

In order to stimulate a severely depressed motorcycle industry, the Rt. Hon. Philip Snowdon, Chancellor of the Exchequer, in his 1931 budget shifted the tax level from vehicle weight to engine capacity and set a 15 shilling rate for machines of less than 150cc. This had the desired effect of sending

Nancy and Betty Debenham were a popular pair of 1920s flappers who featured in many of BSA's publicity stunts. Here they are leaving the factory main gate on a 1929 model B, now fitted with a saddle tank. (Loaned by A. G. Cave)

data book claimed a top speed of 47–53mph (75–85kph), yet the little Beesa sold very well indeed and lasted for three years, appearing in the 1936 catalogue as the Light XO. By then, the basic 2.49hp engine had been cleaned up to include an enclosure for the magneto drive. BSA's half-pint singles held fast to 2.4in × 2.7in (63mm × 70mm) engine dimensions, first introduced with the Round Tank, and continued to do so for another generation – enter Mr Valentine Page.

The Sloper, a Thoroughly Modern Motorcycle

With no disrespect to their previous efforts, BSA had acted out of character when they launched their wet sump, forward raked engine design onto the world in August 1926. It was a strident step forward in motorcycle thinking and won instant popularity. Long seen as a milestone in development, the initial 4.93hp OHV S27 really helped the

scores of manufacturers back to their drawing-boards to conjure up something in the ultra-light class.

BSA simply sleeved down an OHV model B to 2in (52mm) and apart from a fuel tank painted in apple green, that was about it! Listed in 1934 as the model X34-0 it was sold at an incredible knock-down price of just £27 17s 6d. It was hardly likely to earn any glory for sparkling performance. A 1934 BSA

Model	S27 OHV 'Sloper' (1927)
Engine type	Single Cylinder OHV (Wet sump type)
Bore × stroke	80mm × 98mm
Capacity	493cc
Carburation	Amac TT
Gearbox	Three-speed hand-change
Ratios	10.9; 6.3; & 4.6:1
Tyres, front	27in dia × 2¾in
rear	27in dia × 2¾in
Brakes, front	7in dia
rear	7in dia
Suspension front	Girder
rear	Rigid
Weight	300lb
Fuel capacity	2¼ gall.
Top speed	65mph

Ahoy there, shipmates! Able Seaman Jack Tar working amidships, bails out the bilge from his 1928 OHV 500cc Sloper. The picture captures a meeting of the Dolphinium MCC at Gosport during the early 1930s. All officers and ratings are sailing BSAs. (BSA Archive)

motorized two-wheeler jump over the broomstick from motor-bicycle to motor-cycle and just like the Round Tank, the affec-tionately named 'Sloper' was seldom referred to by its model number.

Attributed to Freddie Hulse, partnered by Harold Briggs, the Sloper's specification was bang up to date. Both engineers knew their territory well when they developed this famous classic. The saddle tank and the gracefulness of its superbly proportioned engine gave it a style unmatched by anything else at the time. The 3.1in × 3.8in (80mm × 98mm) engine had a detachable 90 degree valve cylinder head, each valve being oper-ated by an alloy steel pushrod concealed in-side a telescopic tube. It ran extremely quietly too, since the timing gear used flat, mushroom-shaped tappets giving ample mat-ing faces with their corresponding cam. The forward compartment of the crankcase held six pints (3.3 litres) of oil, and a submerged skew driven oil pump supplied a feed directly to a double row big-end bearing which ran between a pair of steel flywheels. The crank-shaft lay across a set of ball and roller bear-ings. Oil could be regulated from the saddle by a valve and tell-tale glass located near the crankcase mouth. The oil level could also be checked by a level indicator sited at the front of the oil compartment.

A duplex tubular cradle frame was built up from steel lugs brazed and pinned to each section of tube. Running on 27in diameter wheels, the frame top tube dropped downwards to give a low twenty-four inch riding position. A single dry-plate clutch had a light action and the 7in (177mm) drum brakes were both operated by a separate toe pedal, the left foot controlling the front wheel brake.

BSA could quite rightly claim to be 'the Leaders of the Industry'. The Sloper set a standard that the rest struggled to follow. On an open throttle, the Sloper was not especially fast and the inclined engine tended to throw a greater proportion of its weight towards the front wheel leaving the rear end to skip and lurch on even moderate cornering, but as it was an ideal sidecar machine, this crab-like behaviour was of little consequence.

For an extra £5, a high compression piston and a pair of race cams could be fitted on request. Some customers complained that their 'special tuned' version was indistinguishable from the standard models, so in an off-hand way, an employee working in BSA's production department decided to mark every tuned Sloper by stencilling a red star onto the timing case. This innocent act would later bring about a greater glory to an otherwise hum-drum reputation associated with BSA.

Throughout a long and productive ten year run, six basic model variations on the Sloper theme were built, ranging from a thrifty 349cc to a lusty 595cc, and including side-valve versions and certain de-luxe models with two-port cylinder heads. Sloper production estimates have been placed as high as 80,000.

A number of seasonal changes and improvements (usually to the good) were applied, the most notable of which was the introduction of a forged steel backbone frame member in 1930, otherwise the basic design

Model	I 29 Two-port OHV Sloper (1929)
Engine type	Single Cylinder OHV (Wet sump type)
Bore × stroke	72mm × 85.5mm
Capacity	349cc
Carburation	Amac TT
Gearbox	Three-speed hand-change
Ratios	5.7; 7.8; & 13.5:1
Tyres, front	26in dia × 3in
rear	27in dia × 3in
Brakes, front	5½in dia
rear	7in dia
Suspension front	Girder
rear	Rigid
Weight	295lb
Fuel capacity	2¼ gall.
Top speed	55mph

Model	M33-11 (1933)
Engine type	Single Cylinder OHV (Wet-sump type)
Bore × stroke	85mm × 105mm
Capacity	595cc
Comp ratio	5.5:1
Claimed power	26bhp at 4,800rpm
Carburation	Amal Downdraught
Gearbox	Four-speed hand-change
Ratios	14.3; 9.9; 6.4; & 4.8:1
Tyres, front	26in dia × 3¼in
rear	26in dia × 3¼in
Brakes, front	7 × 1⅜in
rear	7 × 1⅜in
Suspension front	Girder
rear	Rigid
Weight	325lb
Fuel capacity	2¾ gall.
Top speed	75mph

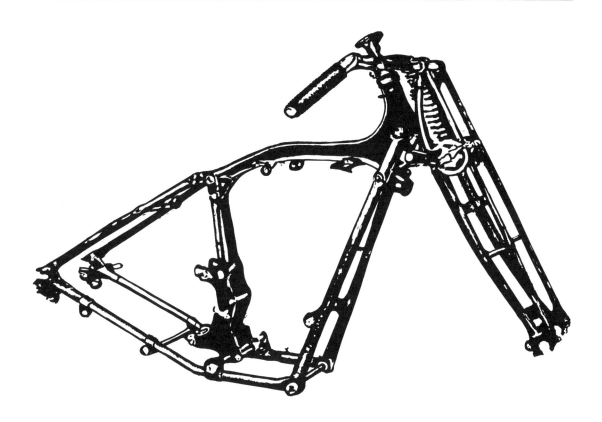

BSA's backbone of forged steel was one solution to the common scourge of frame breakages courtesy of Small Heath's twenty ton drop hammer. The I section top frame member first appeared on the Sloper models in 1930 and became general issue until the late 1930s. (BSA catalogue)

never really changed; and even today, the legendary Sloper has its own highly enthusiastic followers forever spellbound by its sheer elegance and charm.

The Light 500s

As an alternative to the highly successful Sloper series, BSA offered a bike that was lighter, faster and handled the corners more securely. Basically, they were an extension to the hot-footed 350cc model L Super

Sports with a gravity-fed oil pump and forwardly driven magneto.

Produced for the 1929 and 1930 seasons the 'light' 500cc had a detachable two-port head with a 90 degree valve arrangement. The rockers ran on roller bearings and used many of the excellent silent running features found in the Sloper design. Intended mainly for solo work, an extra £6 bought a tuning kit consisting of a high-compression piston and a pair of racing cams. The standard 1929 Light OHV cost £49 10s. For 1930, a side-valve light 500 was listed for those who still

63

The catalogue listed this 1930 'light' 500 as the S30-19. It was intended for fast solo work and employed a gravity-fed mechanical oil pump with sight glass and regulator. The twin-port engine formed the basis for Jack Parker's dirt-track racers. (P. Sole)

Model	**X34-0 (1934)**	**4.93hp Two-port S29 'Light' (1929)**
Engine type	Single Cylinder OHV	Single Cylinder OHV
Bore × stroke	52mm × 70mm	80mm × 98mm
Capacity	149cc	493cc
Comp ratio	7.2:1	–
Claimed power	6bhp at 5,000rpm	–
Carburation	Amal type 93	Amal
Gearbox	Three-speed hand-change	Three-speed hand-change
Ratios	19.8; 12.4; & 7.1:1	11.4; 6.6; & 4.8:1
Tyres, front	19in dia × 3in	26in dia × 3in
rear	19in dia × 3in	26in dia × 3¼in
Brakes, front	5½in dia × 1in	5½in dia
rear	5½in × 1in	5½in dia
Suspension front	Girder	Girder
rear	Rigid	Rigid
Wheelbase	52in	54in
Weight	220lb	–
Fuel capacity	1½ gall.	2 gall.
		3¼ pints oil
Top speed	48mph	70mph

worried about the vulnerability of an OHV layout and in common with the Sloper, the frame was beefed up with a forged-steel I section backbone and a full complement of sidecar lugs. It was classed as a '350 Commercial' with tradesmen firmly in mind.

Blue Star and Empire Star

'I say, that's one of the new 1932 BSAs.'
'Yes, it's the 4.99hp OHV. A good looker too. The new tank design is very smart.'
'And the tank-mounted instrument panel, jolly neat that.'
'Four-speed gearbox, you'll notice.'
'Yes, and coupled brakes – that's another good point.'

So went an unlikely conversation piece between a group of motorcyclists conjured up by BSA's publicity people. The machine in question was bound to pull a crowd wherever it may have stood, for the W32-7 Blue Star was the top notch model from Armoury Road and was part of an extensive range of upright, wet-sump powered models that had first appeared for the 1930 season. Herbert Perkins and David Munro were the chief architects of these elegant BSAs that were built in both sidevalve and overhead valve form and in either 250, 350 or 500cc sizes. To redress the Sloper's balance problems, they pulled the cylinder back to a vertical position and placed the magneto and timing gear above the forward facing oil sump. Sports models could be supplied ready tuned from a bag of bits which comprised double coil valve springs, special cams and a high-crown piston.

In 1932, the sports singles started officially to use the Star motif proudly displayed on the

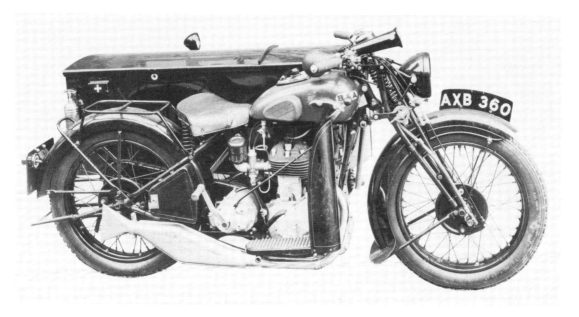

All the ingredients of a hard working BSA are shown in this 1933 W33-6 499cc SV hitched to a heavy box-car. The GPO always specified a full complement of fittings, leg shields, footboards, bulbhorn and 'protectomotor' air cleaner. (Courtesy The Post Office)

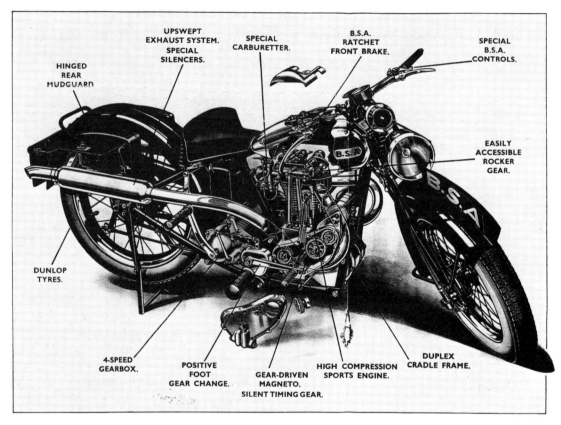

A sectional view of a typical sports BSA. The machine is actually a 249cc B33-3 Blue Star Junior of 1933. (Courtesy The Classic Motorcycle)

timing cover. On later Blue Stars an enamelled star badge in the appropriate colour was inscribed by a number that boasted its top speed rating, '75' for a 350cc, '85' for the 500cc.

After the mountain hopping publicity stunts of the late 1920s, BSA's competition aspirations turned towards reliability trials and Bert Perrigo, 'Mr BSA', captured a cabinet full of silverware. Perrigo was certainly pleased with the Blue Star – he was on a royalty of sixpence for every one that was sold!

In 1933, the 350cc class received a revised cylinder head and new bore and stroke dimensions of 2.7in × 3.4in (71mm × 88mm). The Blue Star range was also extended to include a 250cc model, namely the B33-3, sometimes referred to as the Blue Star Junior. This was fitted with a twist-grip throttle and a fashionable upswept exhaust pipe – that essential item that no self-respecting 1930s tearaway could do without. How the ladies were supposed to prevent ruining another expensive pair of stockings was entirely their problem!

On the opposite end of the sporting singles spectrum, the 1933 catalogue described a

Model	B33-3 Blue Star Junior (1933)
Engine type	Single Cylinder OHV (Wet-sump type)
Bore × stroke	63mm × 80mm
Capacity	249cc
Comp ratio	6.9:1
Claimed power	11.8bhp at 5,400rpm
Carburation	Amal type 74
Gearbox	Four-speed foot-change
Ratios	18.6; 12.9; 8.2; & 6.2:1
Tyres, front	26in dia × 3in
rear	26in dia × 3in
Brakes, front	5½in dia × 1in
rear	5½in dia × 1in
Suspension front	Girder
rear	Rigid
Wheelbase	54in
Weight	332lb
Fuel capacity	2 gall.
Top speed	60mph

Model	W34-9 Blue Star (1934)
Engine type	Single Cylinder OHV (Wet-sump type)
Bore × stroke	85mm × 88mm
Capacity	499cc
Comp ratio	6.9:1
Claimed power	28bhp at 5,200rpm
Carburation	Amal type 89
Gearbox	Four-speed foot-change
Ratios	14.3; 9.9; 6.4; & 4.8:1
Tyres, front	26in dia × 3¼in
rear	26in dia × 3¼in
Brakes, front	7in dia × 1⅜in
rear	7in dia × 1⅜in
Suspension front	Girder
rear	Rigid
Wheelbase	54in
Weight	358lb
Fuel capacity	2½ gall.
Top speed	80mph

machine that went beyond the Blue Star. Based on Bert Perrigo's ISDT-winning machine, the W33-9 Special was made available to the public for the princely sum of £63. *Motor Cycling*'s resident scribe, one Mr Cyclops, roadtested Bert Perrigo's actual machine when it was still coated in the dust and grime brought back from his winning trip to Merano, Italy. In his account for *Motor Cycling* the said journalist had to keep a keen eye on the speedometer, bewildered by its amazing show of speed. (With Bert Perrigo at the helm, it was timed at a mean 92mph (148kph).) Cyclops was enthralled – not only was it very fast, but it was also very strong and responsive through its four-speed gearbox. It handled 'like a dream', and he singled out the brakes as 'tremendously powerful, yet sweet in action'. It really was *the* 'special' of all the machines that Mr Cyclops had ridden, the one he most wanted to steal for keeps.

Always a thoroughly decent and patriotic British company, BSA joined in the flag waving to celebrate King George V's Silver Jubilee in 1935 and announced a pair of 'Empire Stars' for the following season. In pride of place, and reproduced in glorious colour in the 1936 catalogue, was the 'Masterpiece of the industry' – the model Q8 with a 496cc 3.2in × 3.7in (82mm × 94mm) capacity and in full sports trim. A 348cc 2.7in × 3.1in (71mm × 80mm) model R8 with otherwise identical features was the lower capacity option.

Both versions were really further developed Blue Stars with redesigned twin-ported cylinder heads to give more efficient combustion and anti-knock performance. The barrels were cast in nickel-chrome, air-hardened iron which proved to be the answer to the newly introduced leaded fuels which had been playing havoc with cylinder bore life. The engine sump compartments were

Model M10

Listed for only one year, the 1936 M10 was a lusty slogger with a 595cc 3.3in × 4.1in (85mm × 105mm) SV engine. It carried on the tradition set by the old 'four and a quarter horse', model H of 1914. In turn it was replaced by the Val Page designed M21 later that year. (BSA Archive)

Model	Q8 Empire Star (1936)
Engine type	Single Cylinder OHV (Wet-sump type)
Bore × stroke	82mm × 94mm
Capacity	496cc
Comp ratio	5.9.1
Claimed power	–
Carburation	Amal type 76
Gearbox	Four-speed foot-change
Ratios	14.3; 9.9; 6.3; & 4.8:1
Tyres, front	27in dia × 3in
rear	26in dia × 3¼in
Brakes, front	7in dia × 1⅜in
rear	7in dia × 1⅜in
Suspension front	Girder
rear	Rigid
Wheelbase	54in
Weight	382lb
Fuel capacity	3½ gall.
Top speed	85mph

widened to take on an extra half pint (quarter litre) of oil and together with the gearbox casings were buff-polished and coated in an oil stain-resistant lacquer. Then there was the Empire Star green finish for the fuel tank and wheel rim centres, a shade very similar to the old LNER apple green. For the first time, an eight-pointed star badge appeared on the tank, bearing the 'Empire Star' legend.

The Q8 Empire Star performed as well as it looked. It could accelerate from 10mph (16kph) in top gear with no snatch, and cruise effortlessly at 65mph (105kph) without changing a note. The clutch was a new single spring type shielded within its own casing inside the oil-bath primary chain-case. It was light to operate and the footchange gearbox could be flicked through the changes at the gentle press of a toe. 'The Empire Star

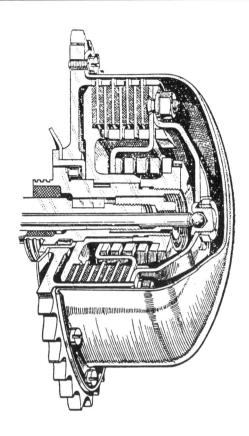

*The single spring 'Empire Star' type clutch
ran 'dry'. The outer pressed-steel dome
prevented the ingress of oil. The type was also
adopted for the 1939–45 WD M20.
(BSA Archive)*

BSA definitely scintillates', reported one roadtest carried out in March 1936.

Included in an extensive 18 model programme were some 'New Blue Stars', a 500cc Q21 and a 350cc R20; these represented slightly lower specified, and hence cheaper, alternatives to BSA's new crack Empire Stars. But for 1937 it was all change again – the Empire Star name would continue but on something totally different which had been brought about by the fertile mind of Valentine Page.

High Cam and De-luxe

For 1935 and 1936, BSA produced a selection of de-luxe singles. Technical details described a progressively new design with the very latest dry-sump lubrication system and a 'high cam' layout. All models came fully equipped with a lighting set and four-speed foot operated gearboxes, with no hidden extras, hence the de-luxe tag was applied to the official model designation. Even so, these high-cam models had not been conceived from a clean sheet of paper, but were merely a spin-off from the J type OHV Vee-Twin engine.

Mid-way through the 1930s, BSA's competition department were looking for a replacement for the wet-sump, Blue Star type, and it did not take too much imagination for someone in the development shop to blank off one of the Vee-Twin's cylinders and see what came out on the dynometer. Long strokes with deep combustion chambers were very much the order of the day so far as 1930s fuel and oils would allow, and in order to reduce pushrod whip to a minimum, a large idler gear sat between the crank pinion and the cam gear placing the camshaft high up in the crankcase. Using the front cylinder of the J type twin, a gear driven magneto sat closely tucked in behind a vertically mounted barrel. In all, five gears made up the timing side gear train which was concealed inside an L shaped outer cover. Both pushrods were operated from a single camshaft and ran in a cylindrical tube. The whole unit looked like a very fashionable 'cammy' engine – even the rocker box cap looked like a cleverly disguised bevel driven cambox, reminiscent of an Excelsior Manxman or Norton International. Only BSA's habit of leaving the exhaust valve open to the weather betrayed it.

The lubrication system was the forerunner of that found on all post-1945 singles with a dual stage gear pump collecting oil from a tank and then sending it back again after it had finished oiling all the main working surfaces and had drained down into the base of the crankcase. As well as better cooling and weight saving, a separate oil tank came in useful for filling in that embarrassing triangular gap between saddle, rear mudguard and rear frame tube.

The 1935 14 model catalogue included a pair of OHV de-luxe debutants. Third in the list of models superbly illustrated with green tinted fuel tanks was a 249cc, 2.4in × 3.1in (63mm × 80mm) version listed as the B35-3. There was also a 348cc issue of the de-luxe style labelled as the R35-4 – 'R' stood for 2.7in (71mm) bore and 3.4in (88mm) stroke; there were other R models in BSA's range but these were the earlier upright, wet-sump 'Blue Star' types which, engine-wise, had very little in common. Frame and cycle parts were shared with the rest of the range except that the R35-4 petrol tank had a small cut-away to clear the rocker box, and there was little doubt that this little quirk was a last minute panic measure when the first models were being assembled!

Attractively priced at £49 for the R35-4 and just an extra £2 for the 350cc option, a good order book should have been secured, but few people were duped by those 'cammy' pretentions. But BSA put down 1935 as a quiet year and the de-luxe singles continued through 1936 as the B3 and R4 with few significant changes. There was also a new recruit to the fold in the shape of a competition R19. Against the standard 350cc model, the R19 had 21in front rim with knobbly Dunlop sports tyres back and front, plus a swishy upswept exhaust pipe. It was supplied with a full set of tuning spares and sold for £58. The R19 was considered as a potential trophy winner, but Bert Perrigo did once comment that after exhaustive tests and trials, the high-cam singles never came up to expectations, and despatch records only indicate that less than 100 R19 Competition machines were ever built.

The 1936 catalogue claimed that 'sporting performance, low running costs are but a few of the characteristics which make these BSA models popular'. The scarcity of a 1935–36 de-luxe single suggests otherwise.

Horsepower – the SV and OHV Vee-Twins (1920–40)

From the earliest times, any motorized bicycle having more than one cylinder was more than likely a Vee-Twin. Ever since the days of Gottlieb Daimler and his *zweizylinder-motor* of 1889, two cylinders joined on to a common crankpin in a single longitudinal plane has been one of the most enduring methods of providing plenty of sidecar pulling power.

BSA were well on the way to completing their own version when the First World War severely interrupted their plans and it was not until 1920 that a 50 degree Vee-Twin model E (during its inaugural period it was called the model A) came about. It was rated at 6/7hp with a bore and stroke of 2.9in × 3.3in (76mm × 85mm) (770cc). Great emphasis was placed upon attention to detail and ultra-reliability as the engine was given long skirted pistons and hefty H section conrods. A mechanical pump backed up with a hand operated plunger, interchangeable valves, roller big-ends and robust alumnium chaincases earned the three-speed countershaft 770cc twin a reputation for long service and it remained in production until 1931.

BSA were very proud of their 'multi' and

Selected Vee-Twins

Model	E de-luxe (1926)	G14 (1936)
Engine type	Twin Cylinder 50 degree Vee-Twin Sidevalve	Twin Cylinder 50 degree Vee-Twin Sidevalve
Bore × stroke	76mm × 85mm	80mm × 98mm
Capacity	770cc	986cc
Comp ratio	4.5: 1	4.5:1
Claimed power	6/7hp (ACU rating)	25bhp at 3,800rpm
Carburation	Amac or Mills	Amal type 76
Gearbox	Three-speed	Four-speed
Ratios	10.0; 5.8; & 4.2:1	13.7; 9.5; 6.0; & 4.6:1
Tyres, front	26in dia × 3in	18in dia × 4in
rear	26in dia × 3in	18in dia × 4in
Brakes, front	Dummy belt rim	7in dia × 1⅜in
rear	Internal expanding	7in dia × 1⅜in
Suspension front	Girder	Girder
rear	Rigid	Rigid
Wheelbase	65in	63in
Weight	320lb	420lb
Fuel capacity	2½ gall. 3 pints oil	3¾ gall.
Top speed	55mph	65mph

they were at great pains to demonstrate that the benefit of three years' development had made it very strong and very well engineered. The fuel tank was supported upon the top frame member by three lugs and they managed to achieve a sufficiently low riding position by curving down the rear section of the tube at the saddle nose.

Valve materials had greatly improved through the necessities of wartime development, and the model E was fitted with a pair of high temperature nickel alloy steel components. The timing gear used the external cam method and the contact area between cam and tappet was more than sufficient to ensure long life under the most severe conditions.

The first rash of changes came about in 1923, although they were only brought about for production reasons. The outer magneto drive cover took on a convex shape to provide a little more clearance for the drive chain, and the exhaust, mounted in front of the cases had a detachable entry pipe instead of the previous cast-in pinch bolt arrangement which was prone to breakage.

The crankcases were restyled into a more oval shape pattern during 1923. Earlier casings had been virtually circular when set against a long oblong magneto drive – 'frying pan' was an apt description often used about them by old hands.

The fuel tank gained a rounded forward nose with an increase in the size of the filler caps and the gearchange gate was altered from an upright position to a forward angle of about 45 degrees. Trivial though these changes may have been, it just goes to show

Horsepower in plenty! This 1922 6hp 770cc model E easily coped with a heavily laden tradesman's carrier. (Anon.)

how reluctant they were at BSA to change a competent machine.

The 1923 programme also included a Light 6 twin. This was a cheaper version of the 770cc twin with slim valanced mudguards and a pressed steel rear chain cover. At £85 it was intended for solo or sidecar use at a time when the trend in Vee-Twin powered motorcycles leaned towards heavy sidecar haulage. The Light 6 kept up with high fashion, putting on a modern rear fishtail styled silencer from 1928 and then adding a rounded saddle tank for the following year. It outlived the larger model E de-luxe by a couple of years, making its final appearance in 1931 when the price had been slashed right down to just £631.

The slightly more expensive model E de-

luxe hardly ever altered at all and stubbornly held on to its flat tank until the end. It usually came supplied complete with a fully enclosed rear chain casing and a full set of tool bags fastened to the rear mudguard.

Only two years after the introduction of the model E another Vee-Twin was built for use as a large taxi-cab – all part of a growing free-for-all business in setting up cheap public transport. So, for the 1922 season, BSA called upon the heavy brigade and listed a model F consisting of two big 'lungs' full of slogging power, and measuring 3.1in (80mm) in diameter with a piston throw of 3.8in (98mm) to give it plenty of thump. 'Pulling power' was what they called it, long before anyone used technical words like 'torque'.

Once again someone at Small Heath had a

change of heart about the model name and it was retitled the model G in time for the 1925 catalogue. It continued in production until the outbreak of the Second World War, winning a staunch following and a world wide reputation for sheer 'pulling power' and a never-ending appetite for hard work.

Whereas the 770cc model E was intended to be flexible and economic, and took up less garaging space than a light car, the big-hearted, eight shirehorse-power twin delivered the mail, dropped off the morning milk churns and carted in a few hundred-weight of coal . . . and all before breakfast!

The ultimate test for this colossal Birmingham Dray came in 1926 when BSA built a pair of extra-heavy duty colonial model G outfits for a two-year circumnavigation of the world. John Castley, a reporter with *The MotorCycle*, and BSA salesman Bertram Cathrick set out on a grand global sales drive for BSA. In all they visited twenty-five countries, and cities as far and wide apart as Constantinople, Cairo and Calcutta, Bombay, Batavia and Buenos Aires. Considering the terrible condition of the roads and the difficulties in travelling between one domain and the next it was an astonishing achievement. Both outfits returned to Small Heath still intact with few mechanical problems to mention after 23,000 punishing land miles (37,000km). It resulted in a model G World Tour twin being catalogued for the next six seasons.

So the unflagging model G plodded on through the years. Drum brakes appeared in 1926, a lowered seat position the following

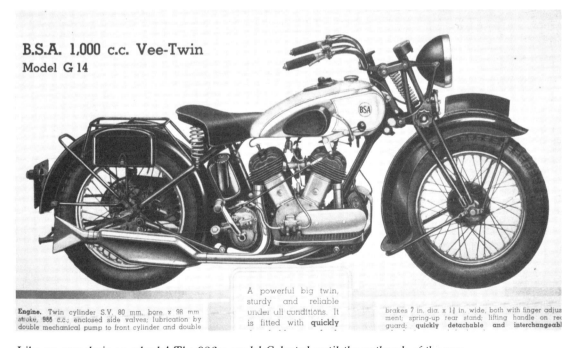

B.S.A. 1,000 c.c. Vee-Twin
Model G 14

Engine. Twin cylinder S.V. 80 mm. bore x 98 mm stroke, 986 c.c.; enclosed side valves; lubrication by double mechanical pump to front cylinder and double

A powerful big twin, sturdy and reliable under all conditions. It is fitted with **quickly**

brakes 7 in. dia. x 1⅛ in. wide, both with finger adjus ment; spring-up rear stand; lifting handle on rec guard; **quickly detachable and interchangeabl**

Like an armchair on wheels! The 986cc model G lasted until the outbreak of the war. This 1939 specimen was finished in silver and chrome. The ignition advance-retard had twist grip control on the left hand handlebar. Footboards were just one of the many rider comforts. (BSA Archive)

Preparing for war. BSA had many buyers for their big capacity model G just before the Second World War. This khaki painted version was probably one of a consignment destined for the Dutch Army. Just look at that front tyre! (BSA Archive)

year along with improved cooling fins for the cylinder head, which extended onto the exhaust outlet. Tappet covers arrived in 1930 along with a three gallon (13.6 litre) saddle tank complete with an integral oil supply. A separate oil container appeared in 1936 when the frame was extensively stiffened with a forged steel I-section backbone. When the final batch left the assembly line in 1940 it still had quickly detachable wheels and a dual supply pilgrim oil pump fixed onto the outer timing cover, giving a direct pressure feed to the big-end bearing, which had hardly changed after two decades of hard labour. Production finally fizzled out during 1940 and after the war the vertical twin had taken a firm hold leaving no room in BSA's plans for a big lusty Vee-Twin.

During the early 1930s, the War Office decided to re-equip the army with a new motorcycle. Whitehall opinion favoured a large capacity overhead valve, multi cylinder machine for policing the far-flung regions of the British Empire. BSA promptly tendered for the contract and came up with an OHV design built around a 500cc, 50 degree, 2.4in × 3.1in (63mm × 80mm) 'high-camshaft' layout.

The quality and ruggedness of BSA's prototype withstood a 10,000 mile (16,100km) test and a significant order was secured in 1932 despite a deep economic depression. It was BSA's first attempt to use a dry-sump oiling system with a positive big-end feed and a separate oil tank.

By 1934, the 4.98hp medium class twin was offered on the civilian market and was catalogued as the J34-11. The engine had a high-camshaft layout with paired cam lobes operating parallel pushrods enclosed inside a nickel-plated tube that hugged the cylinder. It gave a false impression of a sporty bevel gear driven, 'cammy' engine.

In its production form, a sports specification was listed, although BSA were quick to point out that their Vee-Twin 'possesses that characteristic peculiar to medium twins – flexibility so wide that whilst the speed man will be delighted by its maximum performance, the medium weight sidecar enthusiast will find it equally satisfactory. The new twin is amazingly docile and extremely economical.' One roadtest written some years later did agree that the J type Beesa did run smoothly but 'was rather complicated, no faster than a single of the same capacity and wasn't well suited for sidecar work'. The J34-11 was first seen at the 1933 Olympia Show flouting a claimed output of 22bhp from an engine speed of 5,000rpm, enough to propel the 350lb (158kg) twin along at up to 80mph (130kph).

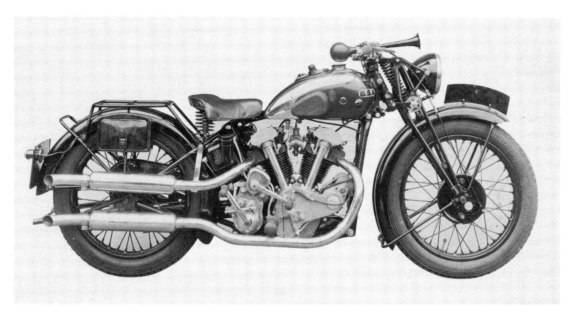

Originally specified for the RAF, the 500cc model J twin eventually appeared in the civvy catalogue in 1934. Note the auxiliary foot-change device often found on the sports Blue Star singles. (BSA Archive)

Making allowances for a weighty forged steel backbone frame, it was actually lighter than many contemporary 500cc singles. The forks and 19in wheel assemblies were borrowed from the heavier sidevalve single-cylinder BSAs.

One of the strangest features found on the OHV twins concerned the gearbox. The army machines had handchange gear selection, indeed, the four-speed gearbox was originally adapted from the wet-sump lubricated single cylinder models normally equipped with a handlever. To convert to positive footstop, a double ratchet and pawl mechanism was added, hidden within a triangular box located on top of the gearcase, a feature which also appeared on certain Blue Star and 'Special' sports singles of the mid-1930s.

Following a time-honoured BSA edict, the inlet valve was covered with a pressed steel cap, while the exhaust valve was left exposed to cool down in the open air and lubricated by that elusive substance long used by engineers – oil mist. By 1935, the model J twin had slid down the catalogue one space to become the J35-12. Sales of these 500cc twins were never very high on the civilian market and it only managed a third year in production when designated for 1936 as the J12. Constabulary authorities were regular purchasers and anyone found committing a road traffic offence in the mid-1930s would probably have been enjoyably chased by a copper mounted on a J12 BSA!

A larger capacity Vee-Twin appeared in the 1936 catalogue and was also listed for three years. The model Y13 was extended in both bore and stroke at 2.7in × 3.7in (71mm × 94.5mm) carving out a volume of 748cc, and offering the kind of qualities that

Model	J12 (1936)	Y13 (1936)
Engine type	Twin Cylinder 50 degree Vee-Twin OHV	Twin Cylinder 50 degree Vee-Twin OHV
Bore × stroke	63mm × 80mm	71mm × 94.5mm
Capacity	498cc	748cc
Comp ratio	7.25:1	5.5:1
Rated power	22bhp at 5,000rpm	–
Carburation	Amal 4/130	Amal 76/001
Gearbox	Four-speed foot-change	Four-speed foot-change
Ratios	14.3; 9.9; 6.3; & 4.8:1 (solo)	14.3; 9.9; 6.3; & 4.8:1 (solo)
Tyres, front	19in dia × 3¼in	18in dia × 4in
rear	19in dia × 3¼in	18in dia × 4in
Brakes, front	7in dia × 1⅜in	7in dia × 1⅜in
rear	7in dia × 1⅜in	7in dia × 1⅜in
Suspension front	Girder	Girder
rear	Rigid	Rigid
Weight	352lb	410lb
Wheelbase	55in	62in
Fuel capacity	3 gall.	3¾ gall.
Top speed	75mph	80mph

sidecar people preferred. Many engine components were shared with the 500cc J. The big-end bearing however, was not. The smaller J had side-by-side conrods connected onto the crankpin, whereas the big model Y had articulated knife-and-fork rods that gave more generous roller contact areas. To the inexperienced eye it was difficult to tell the J and Y twins apart. The bigger machine had less clearance between the rocker boxes and the underside of the fuel tank, and the cycle parts were basically the same as the 986cc sidevalve twin model G, including interchangeable 18in wheels.

Never to be remembered for its trunk-road, mile-eating prowess, the OHV Vee-Twin BSA was still a capable all rounder which could take plenty of punishment, lasted well and had good road and about-town manners.

5

Slogging Power

The M Group Singles (1937–63)

The Val Page-designed M group exemplified everything that was good about BSA. With his straightforward, robust design and solid construction, coupled with a high-quality finish and an extensive spares back-up, the dry-sump lubricated M group models were winners from the very start when they were introduced as part of a completely new production range for 1937.

Made up of five models numbered in a sequence from M19 to M23 they ranged from a 350cc OHV de-luxe tourer, M19, to a top-of-the-range 500cc OHV M23 Empire Star. In between came a couple of side-valvers, the 500cc M20 and the 600cc M21, both classified as 'Tourers suitable for side-car or solo use'. The M22 spot was occupied by a 500cc OHV Sports which was 'ideal for the rider who wants a medium-powered machine with ample reserve of power', according to BSA's 1937 Motorcycling Annual.

M Group		
Model	**M19 (1937–38)**	**M22 (1937–39)**
Engine type	Single Cylinder OHV	Single Cylinder OHV
Bore × stroke	68.8mm × 94mm	82mm × 94mm
Capacity	349cc	496cc
Comp ratio	7.25:1	6.8:1
Claimed power	–	–
Carburation	Amal type 76	Amal type 76
Gearbox	Four-speed	Four-speed
Overall ratios	17.0; 11.8; 7.5; & 5.7:1	14.3; 9.9; 6.3; & 4.8:1
Tyres, front	19in dia × 3¼in	19in dia × 3¼in
rear	19in dia × 3¼in	19in dia × 3¼in
Brakes, front	7in dia × 1⅜in	7in dia × 1⅜in
rear	7in dia × 1⅜in	7in dia × 1⅜in
Suspension front	Girder	Girder
rear	Rigid	Rigid
Wheelbase	54in	54in
Weight	–	375lb
Fuel capacity	3 gall.	3 gall.
	3.5 gall. (1939)	3.5 gall. (1939)
Top speed	–	77mph

Model	M20 (1937–55)	M21 (1937–63)
Engine type	Single Cylinder SV	Single Cylinder SV
Bore × stroke	82mm × 94mm	85mm × 105mm (1937)
		82mm × 112mm (1938 on)
Capacity	496cc	595cc (1937)
		591cc (1938 on)
Comp ratio	5.0:1	5.0:1
Claimed power	13bhp at 4,200rpm	15bhp at 4,000rpm
Carburation	Amal 76/015 (1937–40)	Amal 76/015 (1937–40)
	276 (1940–54)	276 (1940–54)
	376 monobloc (1955–63)	376 monobloc (1955–63)
Gearbox	Four-speed	Four-speed
Overall ratios	15.8; 10.9; 6.9; & 5.3:1	14.2; 9.8; 6.3; & 4.8:1
Tyres, front	19in dia × 3¼in	19in dia × 3¼in
rear	19in dia × 3¼in	19in dia × 3½in
Brakes, front	7in dia × 1⅜in	7in dia × 1⅜in
	7in dia × 1⅛in (teles)	7in dia × 1⅛in (teles)
		8in dia × 1⅜in (1956)
rear	7in dia × 1⅜in	7in dia × 1⅜in
Suspension front	Girder, telescopic 1948–55	Girder, telescopic 1948–63
rear	Rigid, plunger option 1951–55	Rigid, plunger option 1951–63
Wheelbase	54in	54in
Weight	369lb	370lb
Fuel capacity	3 gall.	3 gall.
Top speed	64mph	68mph

Model	M23 Empire Star & Silver Star (1937–40)	M24 Gold Star (1938–39)
Engine type	Single Cylinder OHV	Single Cylinder OHV
Bore × stroke	82mm × 94mm	82mm × 94mm
Capacity	496cc	496cc
Comp ratio	7.5:1	7.75:1 or 12:1 option
Claimed power	–	28bhp at 5,250rpm
Carburation	Amal type 89	Amal 10TT
Gearbox	Four-speed	Four-speed
Ratios	14.3; 9.9; 6.3; & 4.8:1	14.3; 9.9; 6.3; & 4.8:1 std ratio
		11.8; 8.2; 5.2; & 4.8:1 close ratio
Tyres, front	20in dia × 3in	20in dia × 3in
rear	19in dia × 3¼in	19in dia × 3½in
Brakes, front	7in dia × 1⅜in	7in dia × 1⅜in
rear	7in dia × 1⅜in	7in dia × 1⅜in
Suspension front	Girder	Girder
rear	Rigid	Rigid
Wheelbase	54in	54in
Weight	375lb	346lb
Fuel capacity	3 gall. (3.5 gall. 1939)	3 gall.
Top speed	85mph	92mph

All five models generally shared common cycle parts and one mightily strong crankcase assembly with ball and roller bearings taking up drive side support, and a ball bearing on the gear side. A dual stage oil pump sat inside a basement bulge cast into the right-hand case. As a consequence, that 'bulge' would confound all attempts by 'garden shed specialists' to put one of BSA's M type bottom ends into any other make of frame!

The engine was unmistakably Val Page at the peak of his profession – the graceful upward flick of the outer timing cover pointing towards the back of the cylinder and the elegant cast alloy pushrod tower fitted to the OHV machines were typical of his work.

The main strength of the M type BSA, especially the sidevalve M20 and M21 models, was its 'slogging power', that inexhaustible ability to doggedly work on all day under the severest conditions, and withstand any abuse that the most cack-handed rider-mechanic could ever throw at it. A mere 13bhp at 4,200rpm did not appear to add up to very much but once a pair of hefty flywheels had been wound up the M20 would pull anything clamped to its indefatigable structure. In BSA's own words, 'the massive brazed-up construction of the duplex cradle frame' was certainly built to last, with three heavy gauge tubes forming the main backbone. A smaller diameter bolted-up subframe formed two lower engine bearing tubes, the offside having an awkward-looking kink to avoid that oil-pump bulge.

The pick of the bag was the M23 Empire Star, a 3.2in × 3.7in (82mm × 94mm) bore and stroke (496cc) Sportster with all-enclosed valve gear and an air-hardened cylinder. 'Brilliant acceleration, extreme flexibility and magnificent roadholding' were the bywords. The factory's team of special-

Very nice men! The Automobile Association were another uniformed organization that put M type BSAs into service. These jet-age Road Service outfits are equipped with glass-fibre reinforced fairings and box sidecars. The scene is at the top end of Armoury Road leading up to BSA's main office entrance. (Courtesy The Automobile Association)

ists recognized its potential and the type was destined for a couple of Maudes Trophy attempts and some badge-winning exploits around Brooklands' bumpy concrete bowl.

The Gold Star legend began to unfold when, for 1938, another model joined the line-up, none other than the superb M24 Gold Star, an alloy-engined version of the M23 that marked the high point of Val Page's work at BSA. For £92 19s a sportsman could have bought a track-ready, dope-tuned M24, guaranteed to give some real 100mph (160kph) performance.

B.S.A. 500 c.c. O.H.V. Silver Star
Model M 23

The New 500 O.H.V. Silver Star—a magnificent mount for the sporting rider. It is

ngine. Single cylinder single port O.H.V. 82 mm. ore x 94 mm. stroke. 496 c.c.; specially tuned; Air-

steering damper; 3½ gallon tank; new knee gr Dunlop Universal tyres, 3.00—20 front, 3.50—19 r

When it came to sporting success, the M23 not only won the Maudes Trophy for BSA in 1938 but also went on to form the basis of the pre-war Gold Star when a specially tuned M23 Empire Star lapped Brooklands at over 100mph (161kph). This 1939 catalogue entry shows how the 500cc Silver Star looked before the war. (BSA Archive)

Such was the versatility of the M group, as demonstrated by a classic Maudes Trophy win in 1938, that the M20 and M21 sidevalve tourers began to win large contracts painted either in the pre-war khaki worn by the Automobile Association or in various olive-green drab liveries specified by the land armies of Holland, Sweden and Eire. His Royal Majesty's armed forces were also putting BSA's latest sidevalver through an induction training programme after the Munich crisis.

In 1938, BSA made some unpublicized technical alterations. The M21 came in for a bore and stroke change to become a long stroke alternative to the 3.2in (82mm) bore M20, which enabled the same lined cylinder barrel and conrod to be used for both machines. The pistons however, were dissimi-

lar, the M21 component having the gudgeon pin nearer to the piston crown.

For 1939, a new nine-bolt cylinder with angled cooling fins was fitted, along with a new six spring clutch. The timing gears were also revised, being supported between the inner case and a flat steel outrigger plate which enabled the outer cover to be taken off without disturbing the geartrain.

Before the black-out began, there were one or two additional variants. For the gentleman who held strong traditional values the M20 de-luxe was available with an instrument panel mounted in the fuel tank, complete with an oil pressure check button on hand to lend some reassurance about the reliability of that new-fangled oiling system. The de-luxe M20 also had one of those big parallelogram

As an unlikely recruit for the war effort, the 500cc sidevalve M20 was hampered by its low ground clearance but Small Heath could turn them out at the rate of one machine every four minutes. WD M20s were not built to a standard pattern and various equipment and features subject to availability were specified. (BSA Archive)

'can' silencers tipped with a fishtail end-piece. For the more vigorous rider, the M22 and M23 OHVs could be ordered with two-port cylinder heads and upswept pipes, the latter now earning the title Silver Star. There was one casualty, the 350cc M19, whose lack of a useful power to weight ratio meant that it failed to make the grade.

For the duration of the war, the humble M20 went into action and for nearly five years it was the only motorcycle bearing the three rifles insignia. Built in batches of anything from seventeen to seven thousand at a time, the WDM20 reverted back to the single

spring 'Empire Star' type clutch. Some contracts called for a special tank-mounted, Vokes type air filter to prevent abrasive dust and sand particles getting into the engine. When the final 'all clear' was sounded the M20 was rolling off the assembly track at the rate of one every four minutes, and soon a coat of black gloss would replace Army issue gas-proof khaki.

Hard pressed to keep up with the post-war boom, the M21 returned to help soak up some of the extensive stocks of wartime components. The M20/M21 sidevalve singles were the last to receive telescopic forks, and

In 1954, an M21 outfit was every working man's dream, an alloy cylinder head was fitted from 1951 and telescopic forks appeared in 1948 on all the M range. Few would have been concerned about a thirsty fuel consumption of 30mpg (9.423l/100km). (OW)

not until 1948 did the old girder legs finally get assigned to the scrap bin. Any further improvements were merely to keep up with changes brought on by outside supply.

Although the OHV M group models had been killed off by the demands of war production, BSA introduced something of a hybrid in 1948, by taking a 500cc 3.3in (85mm) bore by 3.4in (88mm) stroke B33 engine (in itself derived from the hefty M type bottom half) and mated it into the M frame. The resulting M33 was an admirable general-purpose mount, perfectly suited for sidecar hauling but still a pleasantly useful form of trans-

port in solo form and quite capable of notching up a top speed of 80mph (130kph) with the right choice of engine sprocket.

A new gearbox with an enclosed declutching mechanism appeared in 1950 (the previous unit could trace its origins back into the mid-1930s from the days of the wet-sump Blue Stars). Alloy cylinder heads came in for the next season, a welcome improvement to combat some of the serious overheating troubles that a humble slogger would suffer if left to run on a late spark for lengthy periods. Some degree of mechanical sophistication in the shape of plunger-sprung rear wheels was

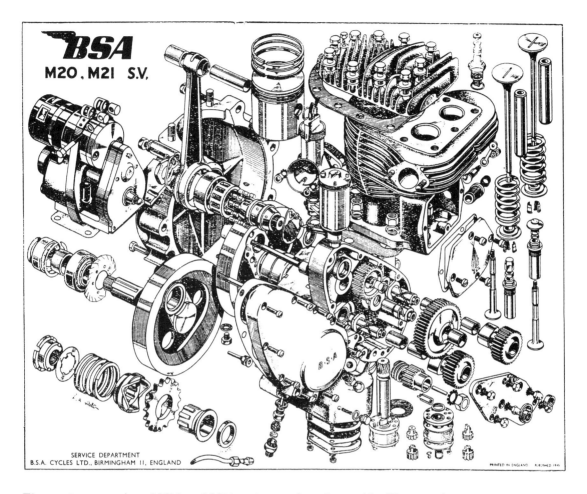

The greater proportion of M20 and M21 parts were interchangeable. The conrods, barrel and cylinder head were common. Both machines had an 82mm bore, yet the pistons were dissimilar. (BSA Archive)

another technological leap forward which was introduced to the M type frame in 1951.

By the end of 1955, the 500cc M20 had been discontinued. The last batches went out with Amal monoblock carburettors and maroon fuel tanks after years of wearing either silver matt or the customary black. All that remained was the M21, still holding on to its diminishing tribe of die-hard sidecar enthusiasts, and orders from the AA to perform tractor duties for their famous daffodil-yellow Road Service outfits. These were to be the ultimate development of the M type side-valver, equipped with a crank-mounted alternator to power a two-way radio system and superbly efficient 8in front brakes.

At the beginning of the 1960s, British Railways had built their last steam locomotive, and it was therefore appropriate that BSA should say farewell to their nearest equiv-

Model	M33 (1947–57)
Engine type	Single Cylinder OHV
Bore × stroke	85mm × 88mm
Capacity	499cc
Comp ratio	6.8:1
Claimed power	17bhp at 5,500rpm
Carburation	Amal type 289 (1947–54)
	Amal type 376 monobloc
	(1955–57)
Gearbox	Four-speed
Ratios	16.7; 11.5; 7.4; & 5.6:1
Tyres, front	18in dia × 3¼in
rear	19in dia × 3½in
Brakes, front	7in dia × 1⅜in
	7in dia × 1⅛in (teles)
rear	7in dia × 1⅜in
Suspension front	Girder, telescopic from 1948
rear	Rigid, plunger option from 1951
Wheelbase	54in
Weight	387lb
Fuel capacity	3 gall.
Top speed	80mph

alent, the final sidevalve engined BSA, which left the works in 1963.

The Working Class – The C Group Singles (1937–58)

If Mr Jones had been an archetypal factory worker (with a slight interest in motorbikes), in the 1950s he might have stopped by at a corner shop every Thursday night to collect his weekly copy of 'the Blue 'Un', sometimes referred to by its more official title of *The Motor Cycle*. Thumbing through the pages, Mr Jones found plenty of news about race-bred and other highly glamorous super-sporty overhead cam racers, or high performance twins, the best that money could buy. These were the things that Mr Jones, and many thousands sharing his predicament

could only hope to dream about, for Mr Jones and his ilk were never likely to own anything more than a pious BSA C11.

The 250cc C Group Beesas were usually brushed aside by enthusiasts who rode nothing less than a '500' as 'utilities'. In more modern times the unfortunate term 'grey porridge' has been heartlessly stuck to what was really a sincerely honest little worker that carried out a thankless task under the most austere circumstances. The C range pre-unit singles introduced before the war represented the best value for money there had ever been and Mr Jones would have ridden his three-speed, eleven horsepower C11 day in, day out without so much as a hint of fuss. Not only were they clean starters every time, thanks to BSA's first use of coil ignition, the double row big end would hold out for ages and obligingly keep plodding along despite those very rare occasions when Mr Jones eventually had a free afternoon to do what could be loosely described as a routine service. But then anyone would have been put off by having to undo all those sixteen fiddly screws that held its pressed steel chain case together.

When the sidevalve C10 was announced in early 1938 and followed up with the OHV C11 during the next year, they illustrated a text-book example of the economics of design, brilliantly executed by designer Valentine Page. The valves were operated from a single camshaft that took its drive straight from the crankshaft pinion and knocked against a pair of bellcrank tappet levers. As for the OHV model, the valve pushrods crossed over each other, working within the confined space of a cast-in pushrod tunnel. The crank pinion also drove a two-stage gear pump hung vertically inside a 'bulge' rather similar to the larger M Group singles, and it also turned a skew-driven distributor that sprouted out of the

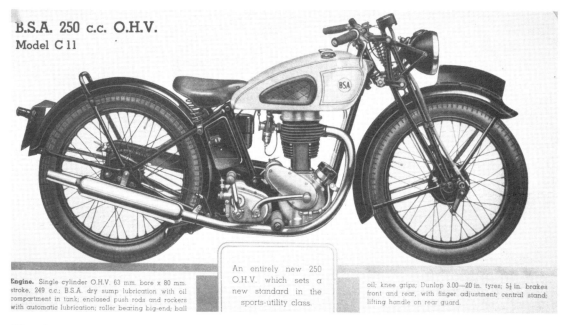

B.S.A. 250 c.c. O.H.V.
Model C 11

Engine. Single cylinder O.H.V. 63 mm. bore x 80 mm. stroke, 249 c.c.; B.S.A. dry sump lubrication with oil compartment in tank; enclosed push rods and rockers with automatic lubrication; roller bearing big-end; ball

An entirely new 250 O.H.V. which sets a new standard in the sports-utility class.

oil; knee grips; Dunlop 3.00—20 in. tyres; 5¼ in. brakes front and rear, with finger adjustment; central stand; lifting handle on rear guard.

Was there ever better value for money? The 1939 250cc OHV C11 had dry sump lubrication, and easy start coil ignition gave it a clean handlebar layout . . . and all for less than £40. (BSA Archive)

forward flank of the engine cases like a mushroom.

On a lowly compression ratio of 5:1 the 2.4in × 3.1in (63mm × 80mm) bore and stroke, 8hp C10 pottered along contently at 45mph (75kph), small beer perhaps but then it returned almost 95mpg (2.9l/100km) and wouldn't complain about the low octane fuel that the non-enthusiast rider occasionally poured into the tank. The three-speed gearbox had fairly wide ratios and hard riding made the valves bounce, indicating to the man in the saddle that it was time to change up to the next cog.

The OHV C11 obviously had a little more snap and could manage a good 60mph (100kph) if anyone felt like racing the bus home. Both models had that big bike feel with a mellow exhaust note to match.

When the jigs and fixtures were recovered for further use after the Blitz, the C10 and C11 simply carried on as if there hadn't been any war at all. Sharing a rigid frame and girder forks they easily betrayed their pre-war origins and some examples still retained an oil compartment and speedometer set into the fuel tank. For a couple of years a de-luxe C11 was available, turned out in azure blue and carrying a full instrument panel display on the tank top, a purely 1930s fashion.

Before 1946 was out, telescopic forks were fitted and 1951 brought along an optional plunger-sprung rear wheel. The softer ride was all for the better when four-speed gearboxes began to appear as something of a sweetener to offset a short-term restriction of chromium plating on the fuel tank.

In 1954, all models underwent a drastic

C Group

Model	C10 (1938–53)	C11 (1939–54)
Engine type	Single Cylinder SV	Single Cylinder OHV
Bore × stroke	63mm × 80mm	63mm × 80mm
Capacity	249cc	249cc
Comp ratio	5.0:1	6.5:1
Claimed power	8bhp at 5,000rpm	11bhp at 5,400rpm
Carburation	Amal 74 (pre-war)	Amal 74 (pre-war)
	Amal 274	Amal 274
Gearbox	Three-speed	Three-speed
Ratios	14.5; 9.8; & 6.6:1	14.5; 9.8; & 6.6:1
Tyres, front	19in dia × 3in	20in dia × 3in
	20in dia × 2¾in (C10L)	19in dia × 3in (1953–54)
rear	19in dia × 3in	20in dia × 3in
		20in dia × 3in (1953–54)
Brakes, front	5.5in dia × 1in	5.5in dia × 1in
rear	5.5in dia × 1in	5.5in dia × 1in
Suspension front	Girder, telescopic 1946–53	Girder, telescopic 1946–54
rear	Rigid, plunger 1951–53	Rigid, plunger 1951–54
Wheelbase	51in	51in
Weight	270lb	270lb
Fuel capacity	2 gall. pre-war	2 gall. pre-war
	2½ gall. 1945–54	2½ gall. 1945–54
Top speed	56mph	60mph

Model	C10L (1953–57)	C11G (1954–55)
Engine type	Single Cylinder SV	Single Cylinder OHV
Bore × stroke	63mm × 80mm	63mm × 80mm
Capacity	249cc	249cc
Comp ratio	5.0:1	6.5:1
Claimed power	8bhp at 5,000rpm	11bhp at 5,400rpm
Carburation	Amal 375	Amal 375
Gearbox	Three-speed or four-speed	Three-speed or four-speed
Ratios	14.5; 9.8; & 6.6:1	14.1; 9.3; & 6.3:1
	Three-speed	Three-speed
	18.3; 12.5; 8.6; & 7.1:1	17.2; 11.7; 8.1; & 6.6:1
	Four-speed	Four-speed
Tyres, front	19in dia × 2¾in	19in dia × 3in
rear	19in dia × 2¾in	19in dia × 3in
Brakes, front	5½in dia × 1in	5½in dia × 1in
		7in dia × 1⅛in (1955)
rear	5½in dia × ⅝in	5½in dia × 1in
Suspension front	Telescopic	Telescopic
rear	Plunger	Plunger
Wheelbase	51in	53½in
Weight	256lb	301lb
Fuel capacity	2¾ gall.	2¾ gall.
Top speed	56mph	60mph

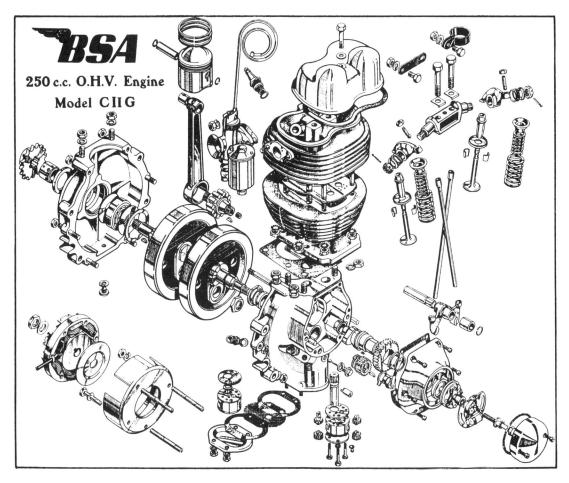

BSA

250 c.c. O.H.V. Engine

Model C11G

The 250cc C11G engine was never noted for its performance and few attempted to increase its power output beyond 11bhp but it reliably supplied a long and high mileage service for thousands of commuters. (BSA Service Sheet)

redesign when the engine was rearranged to incorporate a rectified AC-powered electrical system. A six coil alternator sat at the end of the crankshaft on the output side to provide ample current to feed both the ignition coil and lights. The C11 became C11G, the letter G indicating 'generator'. The bottom offside face of the crankcase took on a sort of rounded nose shape in which cam driven contact breaker points lived in easy reach behind a circular cap.

As for the sidevalve C10, well, there was rather more to it than alternator electrics. In taking every available step to keep the price down to rock bottom, the C10 was rationalized into the Bantam range and the new generator engine sat in what was basically a plunger-sprung D3 Bantam Major frame, including its heavier type Bantam forks and running gear. Re-labelled as the C10L (L stood for Lightened) it retained a three-speed gearbox, and some also managed on

A cheapy with a sparkling finish. For its final production year, the two-tone green C10L enjoyed a chrome plated tank, four-speed gearbox, alloy cylinder head and a welcome return of stouter C group front forks applied a measure of sophistication. Price was a mere £145 including purchase tax. (OW)

AC direct lighting — it was simply a case of value for money and for £95 the C10L also came in a duo-tone green finish, so who could possibly complain? The C10L had a three year production run and spared thousands the drudgery of pedalling to work or queueing for the bus. When the last batch left the works in 1957 a four-speed gearbox and C group forks were being fitted, it also marked the end of the trusty, 250cc side-valve BSA.

If the C10L looked like a compromise between several committees (and looks were never high on the list of consumer needs), the C11G appeared more balanced and cleaner in profile. A deep maroon finish was more commonly found than the rudimentary black and the tank carried one of the new acrylic badges bearing the BSA 'Piled Arms' motif. They even took the trouble to fit a thin steel cowl to avoid that awkward mess between engine and gearbox.

The pre-unit C range had one last final fling when the C11G inherited a swing-arm frame for the 1956 catalogue, creating the C12. Other than an oil feed pipe plumbed into the

Model	C12 (1956–58)
Engine type	Single Cylinder OHV
Bore × stroke	63mm × 80mm
Capacity	249cc
Comp ratio	6.5:1
Claimed power	11bhp at 5,200rpm
Carburation	375
Gearbox	Four-speed
Ratios	6.2; 11.1; 7.6; & 6.3:1
Tyres, front	19in dia × 3in
rear	19in dia × 3in
Brakes, front	7in dia × 1⅛in
rear	5½in dia × 1in
Suspension front	Telescopic
rear	Swing-arm
Wheelbase	54in
Weight	312lb
Fuel capacity	2¾ gall.
Top speed	62mph

rocker box cover, the engine was exactly the same as the C11G. The advantages of a better handling frame were penalized by an increase in weight, now loaded up to 312lb (141.5kg) as against 248lb (112kg) for the original 1939 C11. Top speed was trimmed back at about 65mph (105kph) but that was hardly a consideration to those who flocked to buy one 'on the knock'. The 7in front and 5in rear brakes were always on the short side of being comfortable but the C12 had good mudguarding, as indeed all the C range models had. In short, Val Page's 250cc 'utilities' were a safe bet in anyone's hands.

6

Brummagem's Best

The B Group Singles (1937–62)

Mention of BSA's medium range B group usually dismisses Val Page's family of seven models that were built from 1937 until the outbreak of war. These immensely popular models came in 250 or 350cc engine sizes, in either sidevalve or overhead valve, with either handchange or footchange controlled four-speed gearboxes and they were all based on a standard chassis.

From a modest £38, 250cc sidevalver B20 to a 350cc Sports B26, they each shared a common dry-sump lubricated crankcase that nurtured a double stage gear type oil pump

---

B Group

250cc Pre-war models

Model	B20 (1937–38)	B21 (1937–39)	B22 Empire Star (1937–39)
Engine type	Single Cylinder SV	Single Cylinder OHV	Single Cylinder OHV
Bore × stroke	63mm × 80mm	63mm × 80mm	63mm × 80mm
Capacity	249cc	249cc	249cc
Comp ratio	5.0:1	6.7:1	7.5:1
Claimed power	–	–	–
Carburation	Amal type 74	Amal type 74 type 75 (1939)	Amal type 75
Gearbox	Four-speed hand-change	Four-speed hand-change	Four-speed foot-change
Ratios	19.4; 13.2; 8.6; & 6.6:1	18.2; 12.4; 8.1; & 6.2:1	19.4; 13.2; 8.6; & 6.6:1
Tyres, front	19in dia × 3in	19in dia × 3in	20in dia × 3in
rear	19in dia × 3in	19in dia × 3in	19in dia × 3in
Brakes, front	5½in dia	5½in dia	5½in dia
rear	5½in dia	5½in dia	5½in dia
Suspension front	Girder	Girder	Girder
rear	Rigid	Rigid	Rigid
Wheelbase	52in	52in	52in
Fuel capacity	2¾ gall.	2¾ gall.	2¾ gall.
Top speed	45mph	60mph	65mph

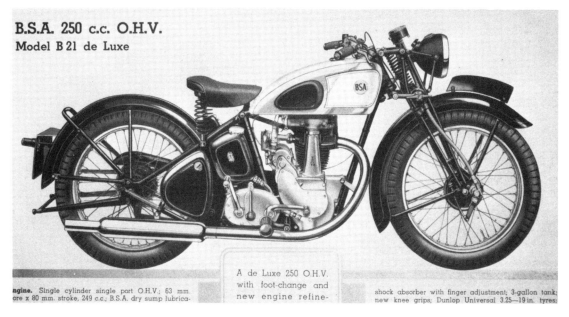

B.S.A. 250 c.c. O.H.V.
Model B 21 de Luxe

A de Luxe 250 O.H.V.
with foot-change and
new engine refine-

ngine. Single cylinder single port O.H.V.; 63 mm.
ore x 80 mm. stroke, 249 c.c.; B.S.A. dry sump lubrica-

shock absorber with finger adjustment; 3-gallon tank;
new knee grips; Dunlop Universal 3.25—19 in. tyres;

*Not quite up to Silver Star status but this de-luxe 250cc B21 still had many
refinements to commend it in 1939. (BSA Archive)*

situated at the base of the timing side crank-case. The main distinguishing feature of the type was a curved, boot-shaped timing cover, otherwise the 'B' engine was a lighter version of the heavyweight 'M' series right down to a similarly styled alloy pushrod tower and fully enclosed rocker gear for the OHV models.

Both OHV engine sizes were represented with an Empire Star while keen types could choose either the 350cc OHV B26 Sports or a high ground clearance B25 Competition, 'specially built and equipped for strenuous trials conditions'. For an extra thirty shillings any of the OHVs could be fitted with a two-port cylinder head.

For 1939, some attention to the valve gear had given an improved sealing gland between the rockerbox and pushrod tower, probably as a result of force feeding newly introduced hollow rocker spindles. The fuel tanks were reshaped and painted with matt-silver panels

to emphasise the new 'Silver Star' format.

Development of the alternative and attractively priced C10 and C11 had started to make an impression. For 1939, the basement bargain B20 had already been dropped and when an optimistic 1940 catalogue was handed out the B range had been virtually wiped out save just one interesting brew that combined the strength of the M type engine with the sprightly proportioned 'B' chassis. As we will see later, this unique replacement for the B26 Sports gave the B group BSA a new lease of life once the blackout was lifted.

In 1946, the popular motorcycling journals were at last being released from paper rationing and started to run regular roadtest features again. The first new model that *Motor Cycling* found to examine was a BSA 350cc OHV single B31. They took to it instantly during a test carried out in severe wintry conditions. A delighted rider-cum-scribe eagerly quoted

350cc Pre-war models

Model	B23 (1937–39)	B24 Empire Star & Silver Star (1937–39)	B25 Competition (1937–39)
Engine type	Single Cylinder SV	Single Cylinder OHV	Single Cylinder OHV
Bore × stroke	71mm × 88mm	71mm × 88mm	71mm × 88mm
Capacity	348cc	348cc	348cc
Comp ratio	5.0:1	6.7:1	7.5:1
Claimed power	–	–	–
Carburation	Amal type 74 type 75 (1938)	Amal type 76	Amal type 76
Gearbox	Four-speed hand-change	Four-speed foot-change	Four-speed foot-change
Overall ratios	18.2; 12.4; 8.1; & 6.2:1	15.5; 10.9; 7.1; & 5.5:1	17.0; 12.0; 7.8; & 6.0:1
Tyres, front	19in dia × 3¼in	20in dia × 3in	21in dia × 2¾in
rear	19in dia × 3¼in	19in dia × 3¼in	18in dia × 4in
Brakes, front	5½in dia	5½in dia	5½in dia
rear	5½in dia	7in dia	7in dia
Suspension front	Girder	Girder	Girder
rear	Rigid	Rigid	Rigid
Wheelbase	52in	52in	52in
Fuel capacity	2¾ gall.	2¾ gall.	2¾ gall.
Top speed	62mph	70mph	65mph

350cc Sports Pre-war models

Model	B26 Sports (1937–39)	B29 Silver Sports (1940)
Engine type	Single Cylinder OHV	Single Cylinder OHV
Bore × stroke	71mm × 88mm	71mm × 88mm
Capacity	348cc	348cc
Comp ratio	6.7:1	7.2:1
Claimed power	–	–
Carburation	Amal type 76	Amal type 76
Gearbox	Four-speed	Four-speed
Overall ratios	16.2; 11.4; 7.3; & 5.7.1	16.2; 11.4; 7.3; & 5.7.1
Tyres, front	19in dia × 3¼in	19in dia × 3¼in
rear	19in dia × 3¼in	19in dia × 3¼in
Brakes, front	5½in dia	7in dia
rear	7in dia	7in dia
Suspension front	Girder	Girder
rear	Rigid	Rigid
Wheelbase	52in	52in
Fuel capacity	2¾ gall.	3 gall.
Top speed	65mph	65mph

the B31 as 'rapid and economical transport with keen performance'. It was also the first from BSA to have the recently-patented, hydraulically-damped telescopic forks.

By the mid 1950s, the B31 was a well established favourite, and was available in rigid or plunger frame. Some estimates of B31 sales have been placed at 8,000 per year, which represents quite an achievement in production terms, but not altogether surprising since the resolute and highly reliable post-war B group singles were then typical of BSA's engineering excellence.

The B31 was really something of a hybrid that underwent development during the war years. By marrying the beefy M type bottom end into Val Page's 1937 medium weight, overhead valve 350cc model, it issued the promising model B29, intended mainly for off-road sports. This was a unique BSA in that it had hairpin valve springs contained inside a cylinder barrel moulded with integral rocker boxes. When some war contracts were being tendered it was softened up a little and the normal coil springs were restored to control valve motion. This was offered to the

Post-war models

Model	B31 (1945–59) B32 (1946–57)	B33 (1947–60) B34 (1947–57)
Engine type	Single Cylinder OHV	Single Cylinder OHV
Bore × stroke	71mm × 88mm	85mm × 88mm
Capacity	348cc	499cc
Comp ratio	6.5:1	6.8:1
Claimed power	17bhp at 5,500rpm	23bhp at 5,500rpm
Carburation	Amal 276 (pre-1955) 376 monobloc	Amal 289 (pre-1955) 376 monobloc (B33) 389 monobloc (B34)
Gearbox	Four-speed	Four-speed
Overall ratios	15.9; 11.1; 7.3; & 5.6:1 (B31) 20.1; 14.2; 9.2; & 7.1:1 (B32)	14.2; 10.0; 6.3; & 5.0:1 (B33) 15.9; 11.1; 7.3; & 5.6:1 (B31)
Tyres, front	19in dia × 3¼in	19in dia × 3¼in (B33) 21in dia × 2¾in (B34)
rear	19in dia × 3¼in (B31) 19in dia × 4in (B32)	19in dia × 3½in (B33) 19in dia × 4in (B34)
Brakes, front	7in dia × 1⅛in 7in dia × 1½in (1956–57)	7in dia × 1⅛in 7in dia × 1½in (1956–57)
rear	7in dia × 1⅛in 7in dia × 1½in (1956–57)	7in dia × 1⅛in 7in dia × 1½in (1956–57)
Suspension front	Telescopic	Telescopic
rear	Rigid, plunger option 1949–60 Swing-arm 1954–60 (B33)	Rigid, plunger option 1949–60 Swing arm 1954–60 (B33)
Wheelbase	52½in 56in	52½in 56in
Weight	324lb (B31 rigid) 410lb (B31 S/A)	340lb (B33 rigid) 421lb (B33 S/A)
Fuel capacity	3 gall., 4 gall. (1956–59)	3 gall., 4 gall. (1956–60)
Top speed	72mph (1954 B31)	78mph (1958 B33)

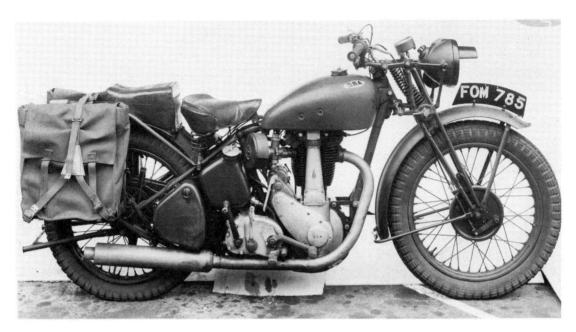

A rare photograph of the war-time 350cc OHV B30, the result of a marriage between the pre-war B series top end and the stout M series crankcase. Orders for 8,000 B30s were tendered by the War Office but this was later amended to sidevalve M20s. Apart from the girder front forks, the WDB30 was essentially the post war B31. (Courtesy The Imperial War Museum)

war department as a B30. A contract for 10,000 was received but before the tooling sections could get to work the contract was amended to that of the sidevalve M20, otherwise, the British Army would have been using mass quantities of what eventually became, with telescopic fork equipment, the post war B31.

Using established engine dimensions of 2.7in × 3.4in (71mm × 88mm), the B31 ran on a compression ratio of 6.8:1, enough to give a top speed of 75mph (120kph) and still cope with mouthfuls of the low octane fuel bought with precious ration coupons. The engine had effectively proportioned cooling fins and many of the 1939 improvements such as flat mushroom-shaped tappets helped to quell any mechanical clatter.

The first B31 was good looking, well balanced and performed with spirit. It could hold 58–60mph (95–100kph) for long periods on the open road and in town, it was sweet to handle with a light clutch operation and the engine never complained at being accelerated in top gear from low engine speeds. It had a tunefully mature exhaust note and on tick-over it was possible to stand and count each beat. At £124 the B31 was a superb all-rounder that few could ignore.

A sports version arrived at the beginning of 1946 in the form of the B32. Mainly available in off-road style, this machine had increased ground clearance, high level exhaust and chrome mudguards. This was soon followed up with a 500cc big brother for the B31, the 3.3in × 3.4in (85mm × 88mm)

B33, available from January 1947. Apart from a wider rear tyre, heavier flywheels and a slightly larger inlet valve everything else was common to the B31. The B33 was itself complemented by a sportster carrying on the numbering sequence as the B34, a big capacity competition machine with high ratio gears and available, on request, with a magneto and bulb horn instead of the complete Lucas magdyno ignition and lighting set.

Initially, the B32 and B34 Competition models had iron cylinder head and barrels, complete with a separate cast alloy push rod tunnel. During 1949, these iron components were changed to alloy replacements fashioned to the same shape. It was not until 1952 that the pushrod tunnel was eventually cast into the barrel.

The B32 and B34 Competition models held the middle ground between the road-going B31 and B33 tourers and the revered Gold Star BSAs. Even though they did not have some of the specialized parts and attentive tuning of the latter, they were an attractive proposition for anyone seeking to indulge in a spot of weekend activity in the hills.

A series of significant changes came about before the 1940s passed on. The speedometer, previously mounted in the fuel tank, was repositioned onto a bracket held from the steering upper yolk, and 1949 also marked the introduction of plunger rear suspension, BSA's cheap but effective way of providing some degree of cushioned wheel movement – provided a generous helping from the grease gun was applied!

The B33 came in for some special attention in 1953. To reduce piston rattle, noticeable on a cold engine, the con-rod was shortened by ½in (12mm) and the gudgeon pin moved down the piston skirt by a corresponding amount – all very useful for the home mechanic as it was now easy to con-

A king and his queen enjoy the freedom of the highways thanks to an ever reliable swing-arm B31. Circa 1955. (BSA publicity photo)

vert a B31 up to 500cc whilst retaining the original engine cases.

Tank colours had moved from silver-matt and chrome with small winged BSA motifs to green for the 350s and Devon red for the 500s. From 1954, Small Heath took a tip from Henry Ford and allowed the B31 and B33 to be 'any colour as long as it's maroon', but conceding chrome panels emblazoned with round 'Piled Arms' plastic badges. By then an all-welded, duplex cradle, swing-arm frame had arrived complete with plenty of extra tinware in the shape of headlamp cowlings.

In common with the A group twins, Ariel pattern full-width alloy hubs were fitted for 1956/57. This was all part of a rationalization policy that sacrificed the earlier half-width rear crinkle hub that had surely been one of the best quickly detachable wheels in the business and one of the great selling features of the entire A, B and M group BSAs since they were first issued in 1947!

The man from *Motor Cycling* was back

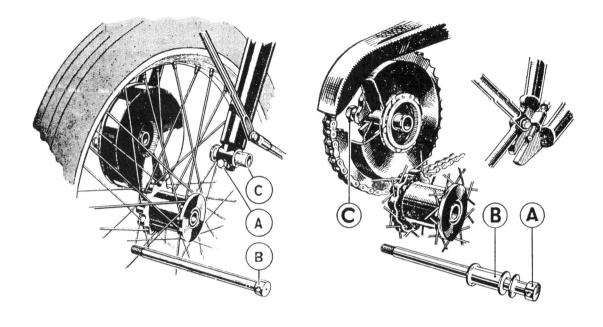

The best QD hub in the business, BSA's famous crinkle hub rear wheel began to appear on A, B and M group models from 1948 and was still specified on some models in the mid-1960s. (BSA Archive)

again in the summer of 1957 to see how the latest swing-arm alloy hub B31 had come on. At 410lb (186kg) it was only 20lb (9kg) lighter than a 650cc A10 Twin and all that extra weight had toned down some of the performance of the bike throughout the test. But for all that, it was, quoted as 'a solid and sturdy touring mount with no pretentions to sporting characteristics'. A top speed of 68mph (109kph) had been recorded and its acceleration had been stifled a little when it managed only a modest 62mph (103kph) from a standing quarter mile (0.4km) sprint that took 22 seconds. Fuel consumption however, averaged somewhere in the high 60mpg (4.7l/100km) region. The same magazine had seen 75mph (120kph) on the speedo when they rode a 1952 plunger version and the quarter mile took only 19 seconds for an impressive

69mph (111kph). But as they said, 'should the prospective customer feel he needs a 100mph "350", then a Gold Star caters for his needs'.

Arch rival publication, *The Motor Cycle* grabbed hold of one of the first 500cc B33s, with iron full width hubs and combined nacelle fork shrouds, in December 1957.

There had also been another head office decree that happily announced that all frames, forks and associated parts must be black. This set the final style for the pre-unit singles, now nearing the end of their useful production life. These latter versions had graduated to coil ignition with a very clever gear-driven contact-breaker unit occupying the spot where the magneto had been. A crankshaft mounted alternator demanded a special alloy chaincase with a large circular projection.

The final pre-unit B series singles had alternator electrical supply for lighting. Ignition was by coil using a gear-driven contact breaker with auto advance-retard. (OW)

Against a stiff breeze the test pilot for *The Motor Cycle* squeezed 81mph (130kph) before valve float had started to set in. In his final summing up he reckoned that the B33 roadster offered, 'first class steering and outstanding pulling power'.

The B33 was never made in anything like the huge quantities of its 350cc counterpart. This was perhaps due to more serious competition from, say, the Norton ES2. It did live a year longer than the B31, the last 'cooking' pre-unit single was eventually despatched in 1962. What followed the B pre-unit singles was something entirely different in many ways.

Glorious Gold – The Gold Star Singles (1938–62)

The Gold Star story was the most glittering chapter in BSA's history. When the majority of the company's output leaned towards 'bread and butter' ride-to-work bikes, the factory proved themselves just as capable of building an all-time classic that conquered so many trophies in trials, scrambles, grass track, short circuit and the Isle of Man Clubmans TT races. Sold either straight from the showroom or built to personal specification, the hand-built Gold Stars were not only super-versatile but also returned a profit when it was normally assumed that any involvement with racing machinery would be a certain loss-leader.

Although they were not to realize it at the time, BSA's blanket policy ban on racing induced by the disastrous events of 1921 did BSA Cycles Ltd a great service. Turning stubbornly away from the race-track they concentrated solely on 'useful motorcycles' building up a huge turn-over and a healthy income. Competition was strictly orientated towards reliability trials and any specially developed machines were a refined adaption of the current range. They captured silverware with monotonous ease in trials using a succession of Blue Stars and Empire Stars but within the sporting world, the company was still saddled with an image for making stodgy, unexciting, sidecar-pulling motorcycles.

A change in attitude began to come about in the late 1930s when an improved economic climate meant that high performance models were viable for manufacture, and the Val Page-designed M23 Empire star of 1937 presented a solid basis for going racing – so avoiding the costly venture of designing from scratch.

Bert Perrigo's clever scheme to win a Brooklands medal and use its title for a projected top flight model payed off handsomely. Walter Handley's gold brooch was converted by Val Page into a spectacular M24 Gold Star, shown for the first time in September 1937 and christened by BSA as 'The world's finest standard sports 500'. It was a reasoned extension to the M23 and its alloy cylinder head and barrel was considered to be a technical marvel at the time. The barrel carried an austenitic iron liner, the cylinder head having steel valve inserts, and both had an integral pushrod tunnel joined together by a bolted up flange.

During its first year in production, the

Valentine Page's masterpiece. The M24 Gold Star as it appeared in 1939. (BSA Archive)

gearbox casings were made in an Elektron alloy and the frame was constructed from Reynolds 531 tubing devoid of any sidecar lugs. Every engine was bench tested until it reached its minimum target performance of 28bhp when fuelled by petrol or 33bhp if tuned for alcohol. Buyers received a certified performance curve, a custom that continued with all Gold Stars until the end.

For the 1938 production models, an instrument panel was fitted into a silver-matt-panelled fuel tank and the cylinder head gained some extra bolts to improve cylinder head sealing. By 1939, each cam lobe had been re-profiled to remove any indiscreet tappet noise, and the M24 had become more of a high performance tourer than a potential race winner. The only notable success recorded by the M24 came when the Royal Tank Corps lifted a trophy for competing army teams in the 1938 ISDT. The same army troop together with a BSA works team were on course for a repeat performance in the following year but found that post-*Anschluss* Austria in August 1939 was not the most congenial place to forge any sporting links!

The M24 Gold Star was not altogether successful, because too many compromises in using common M type parts had been made. The gearbox was not fast through the changes and the frame and other cycle parts were essentially those of the heavyweight tourers. Less than 500 M24 Gold Star BSAs were built, including a fighting batch of thirteen that went to France with the ill-fated British Expeditionary Force.

The hybrid model B30, an experimental war-time model already mentioned in the B Group section, provided a whole new basis for a correctly balanced combination of engine and frame. When it was later mated with telescopic forks it produced the popular 1945

Selected Gold Stars	
Model	**ZB32 Gold Star 'Tourer' (1949)**
Engine type	Single Cylinder OHV
Bore × stroke	71mm × 88mm
Capacity	348cc
Comp ratio	6.5:1
Claimed power	25bhp at 6,000rpm
Carburation	Amal 10 TT9
Gearbox	Four-speed
Overall ratios	16.7; 11.5; 7.4; & 5.6.1
Tyres, front	21in dia × 2¾in
rear	19in dia × 4in
Brakes, front	7in dia × 1⅛in or 8in dia × 1⅜in
rear	7in dia × 1⅛in
Suspension front	Telescopic
rear	Plunger
Wheelbase	54¾in
Weight	374lb
Fuel capacity	3 gall.
Top speed	82mph

350cc B31, from which BSA's first post-war competition machine was developed, the 2.7in × 3.4in (71mm × 88mm) (348cc) model B32.

In 1947 some riders took up the option of an alloy head and barrel and the competition department began to handle enquiries as to whether an all-alloy trials B32 could be adapted for Clubman road racing. Bert Perrigo gained the necessary top approval from his Managing Director, Jimmy Leek, to proceed and at the 1948 show, the ZB32 Gold Star appeared on the stand. It was available in a wide range of compression ratios and cam forms, and had a Lucas racing magneto. Rather like the pre-war M24, its alloy construction also featured an integral pushrod tunnel. Normal fare included a straight-through exhaust, close ratio gears with reverse gear lever, folding kickstarter and a

The Gold Star name re-emerged in 1948 with the ZB series. Its specially bench tuned and tested engine was fitted to virtually standard 'B' type running gear. (OW)

7.5:1 piston able to live on low octane 'pool' petrol when fed from a TT10 carburettor. In standard 'Sports-Tourer' form, the ZB32 Gold Star would easily achieve the better side of 80mph (128kph) – once Len Crisp, Jack Amott (the camshaft wizard) and the rest of the competition squad had prepared it, 90mph (145kph) at 6,400rpm engine speeds were guaranteed!

Priced at only £211 9s 1d, many more than the necessary 100 models had been built for it to qualify as a production racer in time for the Isle of Man Junior Clubmans TT races. To the ardent enthusiasts who trekked over to the island, the sight of a BSA on the start-ing grid ranged from candid pessimism to pure curiosity. But the sceptics were soon sent scurrying to get their names put down for one after Harold Clark had won the Junior Clubmans Tourist Trophy at an average speed of 75.18mph (120.96kph), almost 5mph (8kph) faster than the previous year's winner. From that point on, the Gold Star never looked back and cleaned up all the Junior and Senior Clubmans titles every year until the Clubmans TT event was regrettably terminated after 1956.

A 500cc ZB34 Gold Star reappeared for the 1950 season, identical to the 350cc ZB32, it used a bore and stroke of 3.3in × 3.4in

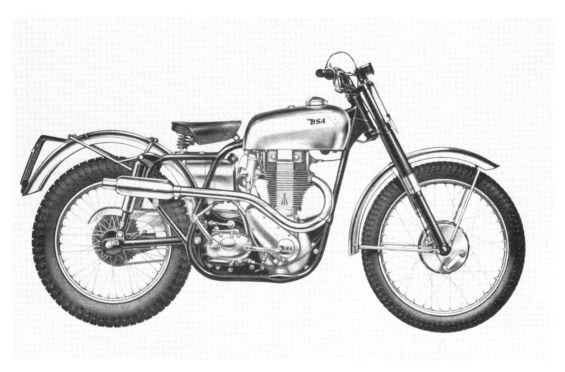

The swing-arm frame was pioneered at the 1952 International Six Days' Trial run-about in Wales. In its further developed form, it became the BB Series Gold Star as shown by this Scrambler version still with a small fin barrel engine and high-level exhaust. (BSA Archive)

(85mm × 88mm) instead of the pre-war M24 3.2in × 3.8in (82mm × 98mm). The wider bore and shorter stroke of the newcomer gave a substantial degree of improved performance due to full cylinder filling and it responded well to a wide scope of cam profiles.

By 1949, Bert Perrigo had built up a talented team of competition riders which included Fred Rist, David Tye, John Draper, John Avery and the most talented find of all, Bill Nicholson. All rode mostly Gold Stars in scrambles and trials with the freedom to carry out a wide range of modifications, breaking free of the restraints of production. Many of these race-proven alterations were applied not only to further the range of

victories won by the Gold Star but to the general model range as well. The most significant was Bill Nicholson's adaption of a McCandless type swing-arm rear suspension assisted by an 8in diameter front brake which became a Gold Star feature from 1952 and reached all the other production models in similar form in 1954.

In the design office, chief designer Bert Hopwood had been taking a close look at the Gold Star and instigated some changes that, coupled with some useful advice flowing back from the works riders further improved the Gold Star with devastating effect. From late 1951, there was a new die-cast cylinder head and barrels, the former had a 15-degree,

Model	CB34 Gold Star Scrambles (1955)
Engine type	Single Cylinder
Bore × stroke	85mm × 88mm
Capacity	499cc
Comp ratio	8.0:1
Claimed power	37.8bhp at 7,000rpm
Carburation	Amal monobloc
Gearbox	Four-speed
Overall ratios	17.0; 12.7; 9.6; & 7.3.1
Tyres, front	21in dia × 3in
rear	19in dia × 4in
Brakes, front	7in dia × 1⅛in
rear	7in dia × 1⅛in
Suspension front	Telescopic
rear	Swing-arm
Wheelbase	54in
Weight	340lb
Fuel capacity	2 gall.
Top speed	75mph

Model	CB32 Gold Star Clubman (1954)
Engine type	Single Cylinder OHV
Bore × stroke	71mm × 88mm
Capacity	348cc
Comp ratio	8.75:1
Claimed power	32bhp at 7,000rpm
Carburation	Amal GP
Gearbox	Four-speed
Overall ratios	10.2; 7.0; 5.8; & 5.3.1
Tyres, front	21in dia × 3in
rear	19in dia × 3¼in
Brakes, front	8in dia × 1⅜in
rear	7in dia × 1⅛in
Suspension front	Telescopic
rear	Swing-arm
Wheelbase	54¾in
Weight	380lb
Fuel capacity	4 gall.
Top speed	102mph

down-draught intake tract, a pair of larger valves and separate bolt-on rocker boxes. The ZB32 con-rod was reduced by ⅜in (9mm) to reduce the overall height of the engine. Hopwood's progressive changes to engine and frame resulted in an ISDT gold medal winning machine in 1952. In production form it was displayed during the following autumn as the BB series Gold Star. By then the old gearbox, which could trace its origins back to the Blue Star of 1932, was replaced by a smarter, more efficient unit derived from the A7 and A10 twins.

The quest for speed and competition success continued unabated. Bert Hopwood, in association with development engineer, Roland Pike, redesigned the engine top halves once more, primarily to meet the demands of road racing. Re-designated as the CB series and easily distinguished by their large finned cylinders, they were sent over to the TT circuit to once more snatch up both the 1954 Junior and Senior Clubmans titles.

Model	DBD34 Gold Star Clubman (1956)
Engine type	Single Cylinder OHV
Bore × stroke	85mm × 88mm
Capacity	499cc
Comp ratio	9.0:1
Claimed power	42bhp at 7,000rpm (with megaphone silencer)
Carburation	Amal GP1
Gearbox	Four-speed
Overall ratios	7.9; 6.0; 4.9; & 4.5:1 (close ratio)
Tyres, front	21in dia × 3in
rear	19in dia × 3½in
Brakes, front	7.4in dia × 2in
rear	7in dia × 1⅛in
Suspension front	Telescopic
rear	Swing-arm
Wheelbase	56in
Weight	350lb
Fuel capacity	5 gall.
Top speed	110mph plus

By 1953, the BSA Gold Star had begun to dominate totally the Isle of Man Clubman
TT races. Here another 'privateer' gets down to work. (T. Bailey)

Of the 41 finishers, 34 were BSA Gold Stars – the annual Clubmans TT had seemingly become a race for BSAs. Not surprisingly, power for the 350cc CB32 Gold Star was up to 30bhp and the 500cc CB34 pushed out 37bhp in full race trim. The CB34 type engine was remembered for having oval flywheels in order to give enough working clearance between the piston skirt and the flywheel – it took a lot of persuasion to win the confidence of the un-technically minded enthusiast!

Someone had discovered that a shorter skirted piston worked without any trouble and the 1955 DB series Gold Stars were fitted with full circular flywheels. An optional front brake with further gas-flowing improvements and Nimonic 80 valves for the cylinder head (500cc version only) in 1956 brought about the DBD series Gold Star, the final embodiment of the model after years of continuous development. To a whole generation, the DBD34 Gold Star was an icon styled on clip-on handlebars, sweptback exhaust

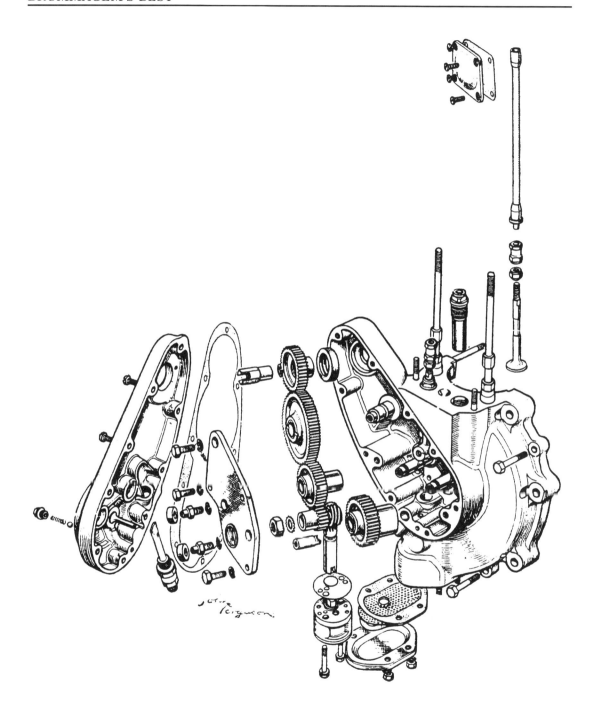

The post-war ZB series Gold Star engine with internal pushrod tunnel cast into the alloy cylinder barrel. (Courtesy The Classic Motorcycle)

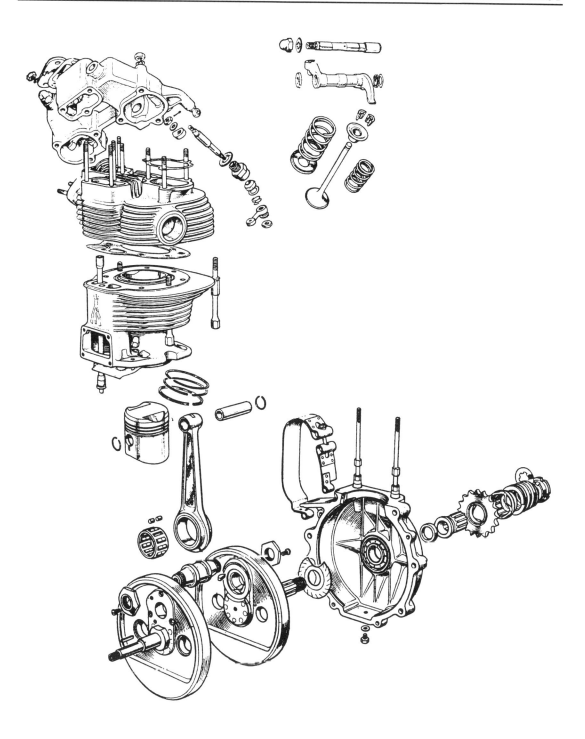

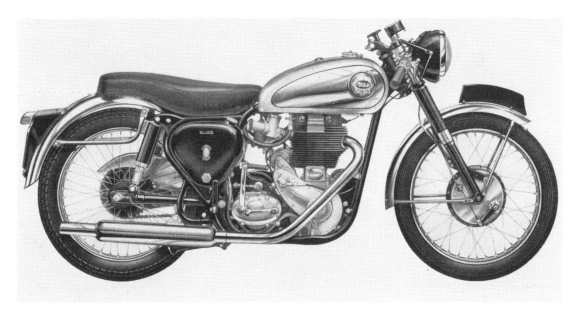

A large finned cylinder, swept back exhaust, and clip-on handle bars were featured on the final development of the DBD series Gold Star. (BSA Archive)

The sleek lines of a DBD34 Gold Star. To a generation of motorcyclists the 'Goldie' was an icon. (OW)

and acres of gleaming chrome. Thousands have marvelled at the harmony of sound and shape of a 'Goldie' ever since the last batch of DB32 versions were despatched from Small Heath in 1963. The end came about when Lucas declined to make any more magnetos, or so read the official version of events. The real reason was two-fold, one was a guarded jealousy by Edward Turner who disliked anything that threw a shadow over his own Triumph based ambitions. Secondly, although the DBD34 Gold Star was a specialized hand-built machine, it was still riding on the back of B31/B33 production and as these two old family favourites were becoming of pensionable age, BSA simply could not afford to continue to tie up valuable skilled resources when the accountants were bawling for higher production targets.

Falling interest in the Clubmans TT terminated the event after Gold Stars had totally dominated the 1956 series. BSA have been blamed ever since for allowing the Gold Star to stay streets ahead and not giving an inch of a sporting chance to any other make. Triumph had an excellent engine and, given a decent frame, they could have put up a solid fight. Norton had a pukka TT racing machine, short of a kickstarter and a batch build, they too could have gone to the Clubmans races just as BSA had always strongly expected they would. But no, no one would play, at least not in an ACU-approved capacity. In every provincial town that had the public amenity of dual carriage race track, competition was especially intense. From coffee bar to fish shop and back again before the juke box went onto the flip side, the Goldie, with a race-ready leopard-skin seat cover won a thousand uncharted victories and has become indelibly engraved into motorcycling folklore for ever more.

7

Touring Twin to Superbike

Stars, Flashes and Rockets –
The A7 and A10 Twins
(1946–63)

BSA's entry into the realms of vertical twin motorcycles was in addition to the main area of development that occupied the immediate post-war era. Anything powered by a vertical twin motor soon joined the most lucrative section of the market at a time when there was a sharp need for motor transport in any form.

After Edward Turner's Triumph Speed Twin had sent shudders throughout the industry in 1938, BSA, having selected a Val Page design from a number of prototypes built during the war years launched their own version in September 1946. Although the original idea was accredited to Page, the project was largely knocked into shape by Herbert Perkins and the early A7 Twins were referred to at BSA as 'Mr Perkins' baby'.

For varying reasons of technical development, patent or production costs, each manufacturer of a parallel two cylinder engine, be it Triumph, Matchless, or Norton, had one basic feature in its make up that would set it apart from the rest. This feature was usually the camshaft, its position in the engine and how it was driven. Page had chosen a single camshaft for his BSA scheme. It was gear driven and was located at the rear of the crankcases, with a pushrod tunnel cast into the cylinder block. It was to give the BSA twin its own definitive characteristic that lasted up until the final days of Small Heath. A BSA may not have been the most sprightly or best looking of all the parallel twins but it was certainly the most durable, oil-tight and quietest, running with the minimum of whine or clatter.

BSA's technical team were quick to acknowledge the virtues of having a pair of pistons rising and falling together, since it gave a firing stroke for every turn of the crankshaft and a multi-cylinder bike that looked no larger than a single of similar capacity. The standard A7 pitched into the fray with a 2.4in × 3.2in (62mm × 82mm) (495cc) bore and stroke motor giving a claimed 26bhp at 6,000rpm output. The crank sat on a drive side ball bearing and an Indium flash-coated bronze bush on the right-hand timing side, another endearing feature that lasted the full course. The power unit was in semi-unit construction with a four speed gearbox bolted up to the back of the engine cases. A gear-driven magneto sat at the back and a chain-driven dynamo lay across the front concealed behind a three-lobed outer cover which made the BSA twin instantly recognizable.

In October 1949, a sports version was put on the stand at the Earls Court show and was listed as the A7 Star twin. It had a pair of 7:1 compression pistons and a twin cylinder head to take a pair of Amal ⅞in (22mm) choke carburettors mounted onto an alloy manifold,

A7 & A10 Twins

Early Longstroke A7 Models

Model	A7 (1946–50)	A7 Star Twin (1949–50)
Engine type	Twin Cylinder OHV	Twin Cylinder OHV
Bore × stroke	62mm × 82mm	62mm × 82mm
Capacity	495cc	495cc
Comp ratio	6.6:1	7.0:1
	7.0:1 (1946–47)	7.5 & 8.6:1 options
Claimed power	26bhp at 6,000rpm	31bhp at 6,000rpm
Carburation	Amal 276	Amal 275 (twin carb)
Gearbox	Four-speed	Four-speed
Overall ratios	13.2; 9.0; 6.2; & 5.1:1	13.2; 9.0; 6.2; & 5.1:1
Tyres, front	19in dia × 3¼in	19in dia × 3¼in
rear	19in dia × 3½in	19in dia × 3½in
Brakes, front	7in dia × 1⅛in	7in dia × 1⅛in
rear	7in dia × 1⅛in	7in dia × 1⅛in
Suspension front	Telescopic	Telescopic
rear	Rigid	Plunger
	Plunger option (1949–50)	
Wheelbase	55in	55in
Weight (dry)	365lb	382lb
Fuel capacity	3.5 gall.	3.5 gall
Top speed	Not known	Not known

raising the A7's power output to 31bhp at 6,000rpm. There was a matt silver and chrome plated fuel tank to give it some star appeal (the standard A7s were mostly being turned out in either black or Devon red). The show visitors would also have noticed that the A7 Star Twin had a plunger sprung rear wheel as standard equipment.

Contemporary roadtests and comments relating to the initial A7s are hard to come by, because in the days of bread queues and ration books, much of Small Heath's output was labelled for export and relatively few A7s were sampled by opinionated enthusiasts. Nevertheless, consensus amongst former owners indicates that the early A7 offered a smooth ride matched with rapid acceleration and good control. The second carburettor fitted to the Star Twin made little

impact and one comment that was unanimous amongst A7 owners of old concerned its niggling habit of 'running on' long after the ignition had been killed. Its small cylinder bore and deep combustion chamber afforded by raw 'pool' petrol did not equip the A7 with the best thermodynamics, and this was one of the reasons why the BSA's technical men went back to the drawing-board for another try.

No sooner had the 500cc twin established itself in the late 1940s when it became apparent that there was a need for a larger, more powerful version with the stamina for touring or pulling a family sized sidecar. Herbert Hopwood had joined BSA in early 1949 and was soon handed a brief to re-hash the existing 500cc A7 up to a larger capacity in order to satisfy the sidecar brigade and overseas

A7 Plunger models

Model	A7 (1951–54)	A7 Star Twin (1951–54)
Engine type	Twin Cylinder OHV	Twin Cylinder OHV
Bore × stroke	66mm × 72.6mm	66mm × 72.6mm
Capacity	497cc	497cc
Comp ratio	6.6:1	7.25:1
Claimed power	27bhp at 5,800rpm	31bhp at 6,000rpm
Carburation	Amal 276	Amal 276 or TT9
Gearbox	Four-speed	Four-speed
Overall ratios	13.2; 9.0; 6.2; & 5.0:1	12.9; 8.8; 6.0; & 5.0:1
Tyres, front	19in dia × 3¼in	19in dia × 3¼in
rear	19in dia × 3½in	19in dia × 3½in
Brakes, front	7in dia × 1⅛in	7in dia × 1⅛in
		8in dia × 1⅜in (1953–54)
rear	7in dia × 1⅛in	7in dia × 1⅛in
Suspension front	Telescopic	Telescopic
rear	Rigid or plunger	Plunger
Wheelbase	55in	55in
Weight (dry)	400lb	382lb
Fuel capacity	3.5 gall.	3.5 gall.
Top speed	88mph	92mph

Sold in every corner of the world, the BSA A7 and A10 Twins had international appeal as indicated by this publicity feature. (BSA Archive)

dealers. The USA agencies thought that a 500 twin was not up to meeting the enormous pulling capabilities of a large Vee-Twin, native to that side of the Atlantic.

Strange as it may seem now, no one was quite sure if a parallel twin engine of over 600cc could attain an acceptable amount of balance. Hopwood had at least gained some experience on the matter when, as a Design Draughtsman working with Val Page at Triumph back in 1933, he had been involved with a 600cc twin cylinder project that worked smoothly and with a good enough performance at low engine speeds. Some doubts still lingered as to whether an additional 50cc was beyond the absolute limit for such an engine configuration.

To prove the point, a standard A7 was further bored out to give a near 650cc swept volume and put through an extensive test with and without a sidecar in tow. The ex-

A7 Swing-arm models

Model	A7 (1954–62)	A7 Shooting Star (1954–62)
Engine type	Twin Cylinder OHV	Twin Cylinder OHV
Bore × stroke	66mm × 72.6mm	66mm × 72.6mm
Capacity	497cc	497cc
Comp ratio	6.6:1 7.0:1 (1959–62)	7.25:1 8.0:1 (1957–62)
Claimed power	28bhp at 5,800rpm	32bhp at 6,250rpm
Carburation	Amal 376 monobloc	Amal 376 monobloc Amal 276 (1954)
Gearbox	Four-speed	Four-speed
Overall ratios	13.6; 9.3; 6.4; & 5.3:1	13.6; 6.9; 6.4; & 5.3:1
Tyres, front	19in dia × 3¼in	19in dia × 3¼in
rear	19in dia × 3½in	19in dia × 3½in
Brakes, front	7in dia × 1⅛in 8in dia × 1⅜in (1954–55)	8in dia × 1⅜in 7in dia × 1⅛in (1956–57)
rear	7in dia × 1⅛in	7in dia × 1⅛in
Suspension front	Telescopic	Telescopic
rear	Swing-arm	Swing-arm
Wheelbase	56in	56in
Weight	425lb	416lb
Fuel capacity	4 gall.	4 gall.
Top speed	88mph	93mph

periment proved that there was no reasonable cause for concern, in fact the test riders were all impressed by its lack of vibration and ability to pull hard over a wide range of engine speeds.

Using as many of the existing A7 components as possible, a decision was made to press ahead with the 650 'A10' design. It took Bert Hopwood a matter of ten days to lay down the A10 scheme. The principal variation from the older design was born of the need to obtain a more efficiently cooled cylinder head. Hopwood achieved this by splaying out the exhaust ports and allowing air to flow between and around separate exhaust valve wells. The crankshaft was increased in size and the driveside bearing was changed from a ball type to a roller type. Light alloy conrods were called for to keep reciprocating masses to a minimum. The tappet arrangement and timing gear geometry was revised too, but one of the finest Hopwood touches was to create an oil-trough in the crankcase castings for the camshaft.

The A10 was one of the great all time feats of design and manufacture, carried out at a hectic pace. Seldom did any other machine go together so easily and pass through the test and development section with so few snags. By August, the prototype engines had been on the dynamometer and had shown 35bhp on the scale against a crankshaft speed of 5,700rpm. A team of three riders working in interminable shifts ran up 12,800 miles (20,600km) in just over three weeks.

All was well! The testing was completed and the new BSA A10 Golden Flash took its place on the showstand, shimmering under

All gold. A shortage of chromium plating in 1952 meant an all-painted tank for the A10 Golden Flash. Capable of 100mph (161kph), the A10 was BSA's proud flagship throughout the 1950s. (OW)

the spotlights in an all-over livery of golden-beige. Its reassuring stance and functional curves truly represented the very best of BSA when the company was at its greatest. On the move, the A10 was capable of roaring past that tantalizing 'ton', and production versions started to appear in January 1950 with a price tag of £193 for a rigid frame model and £205 for the plunger sprung tail model.

The power plant was based upon a bore and stroke of 2.7in × 3.3in (70mm × 84mm) with a compression ratio of 6.5:1 and a cast-iron cylinder head fed by a single $1\frac{1}{16}$in (27mm) Amal 276 carburettor. Weighing in at 408lb (185kg) dry, the first A10 Golden

Flashes had to contend with a diet of 73 octane Pool petrol but could still graciously return a fuel consumption in the high sixties.

In view of the enormous risks that BSA took to produce the A10, the hasty testing sessions had uncovered only a handful of minor problems and the A10 turned out to be a roaring success, loved and respected by thousands and a big money spinner for BSA. If conclusive evidence was needed to substantiate that fact, one only needed to see how many A10s were parked in the bike sheds at Small Heath.

A year after the launch of the A10, Hopwood's methods were applied to the 500cc

A10 Golden Flash models

Model	A10 Golden Flash Plunger (1950–54)	A10 Golden Flash Swing-arm (1954–63)
Engine type	Twin Cylinder OHV	Twin Cylinder OHV
Bore × stroke	70mm × 84mm	70mm × 84mm
Capacity	646cc	646cc
Comp ratio	6.5:1	6.5:1 (7.0:1 1958–63)
Claimed power	35bhp at 5,500rpm	34bhp at 5,750rpm
Carburation	Amal 276	Amal 376 monobloc
		Amal 389 monobloc (1960–63)
Gearbox	Four-speed	Four-speed
Overall ratios	11.4; 7.7; 5.3; & 4.4:1	11.7; 8.0; 5.5; & 4.5:1
Tyres, front	19in dia × 3¼in	19in dia × 3¼in
rear	19in dia × 3½in	19in dia × 3½in
Brakes, front	8in dia × 1⅜in	8in dia × 1⅜in
rear	7in dia × 1⅛in	7in dia × 1⅛in
Suspension front	Telescopic	Telescopic
rear	Rigid or plunger	Swing-arm
Wheelbase	55in	55in
Weight	408lb	430lb
Fuel capacity	4¼ gall.	4 gall.
	3½ gall. option (1950–51)	
Top speed	96mph	96mph

A7. On a revised bore and stroke of 2.5in × 2.8in (66mm × 72.6mm), the A7 stood as the smaller capacity version of the A10. Its flexible, sweetly running engine was preferred by many. It also appeared in sporty Star Twin form but fitted out with just a single carb. With a 90mph (145kph) top speed, matched with good brakes, it was superbly balanced. It was just the sort of thing that BSA had in mind when a trio of these models captured their third and final Maudes Trophy win in 1952.

Slowly, the 1950s were turned upside-down, from ration coupons to the 'never had it so good' era. Docile sidecar-hauling sloggers gave ground to a new generation based on speed and excitement. Higher compression ratios had been available, and in 1953 a new alloy cylinder head was developed for racing and export only. But it was not until

1954, along with the general introduction of the swinging-arm frame, that the alloy head sports engines at last became available to home buyers, who could lash out on an A7 Shooting Star or an A10 Road Rocket. Chrome mudguards and a lusciously finished red fuel tank provided the necessary sparkle for the Road Rocket man to take on the Norton Dominators and Triumph Tigers out on the Saturday night circuit. The A7 Shooting Star had one of the best colour schemes ever presented by BSA, a deep bottle green frame with contrasting light polychromatic green tank, mudguards and panels.

The swing-arm frame created a true pre-unit build, utilizing a separate gearbox fixed between plates with drawbolt primary chain adjustment. Demand for the plunger sprung models still remained high from die-hard sidecar users and they plodded on cour-

The A7 Star Twin of 1952 was chosen for BSA's memorable Maudes Trophy victory.
The post 1951 500cc A7 set a new standard for flexibility and reliability and its sweetly
running engine was favoured by many. (OW)

ageously until production ended in 1958. Although the plunger type engine did inherit the wider finned barrel and head that came along with the swing-arm models, BSA's quickly detachable wheels and efficient half-width hub brakes were retained.

It took some time for the new frame to be accepted, and riders found that the rear brake lacked response due to a less efficient cross-over shaft and cable link. Full-width alloy hub brakes did little to restore faith in its stopping ability. But that apart, the welded duplex downtube rear swing-arm frame handled as well as anything on offer at the time and would take any amount of punishment in its stride.

Another round of changes for 1958 gave the A10 an improved crankshaft forging with a radially bolted flywheel and larger big-end journals. Cast-iron full-width hubs and a nacelle type headlamp with combined fork-shroud completed the new look. The A10 Sports twin was re-christened the Super Rocket to carry on the tradition of the top performance 650. A Super Rocket roadtest written over thirty years ago makes for some hair-raising reading. The tester, whose protective headgear consisted of a woollen bobble hat, wrote 'Sizzling up to Scotch Corner gave me my first taste of Super Rocketing at over the ton. One hundred and four miles

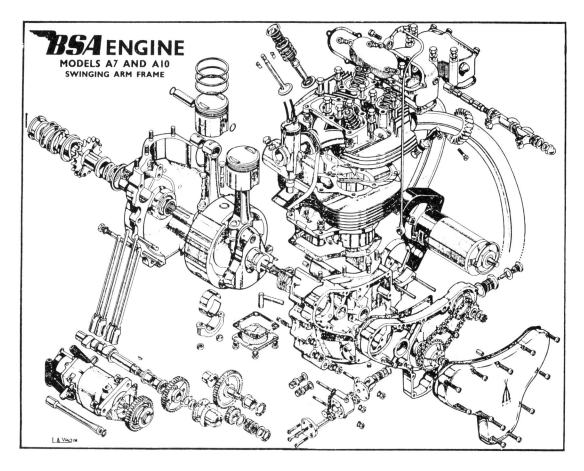

Exploded drawing of the A7/A10 power unit. Camshaft and magneto were driven by gears. The dynamo, lying across the front of the engine was powered by a light chain. The drawing also shows a post-1958 unit with radially bolted flywheel. (Courtesy The Classic Motorcycle)

[167km] per hour without really trying and rock steady on course. It inspires the confidence necessary for fast travel in safety.'

But there were different people in charge at BSA in the late 1950s and the basic A7 and A10 Golden Flash went through all sorts of cosmetic changes. Golden-beige was now a scarce colour option as frames for all models were churned out in a take-it-or-leave-it gloss black. One livery inflicted upon the once proud A10 was Peacock blue! Slowly

and sadly, the glory was surely fading away.

The end finally came in 1963 when Lucas stopped making dynamos and K2F magnetos, and the basic layout of the power plant was grafted into unit form. Fortunes now turned to the A50 and A65 story. . .

But there was one last, enthralling chapter to play out.

Aided and abetted by Gold Star racing specialist, Eddie Dow, BSA built a hybrid by combining a 45bhp Super Rocket motor with

A10 Sports models

Model	A10 Road Rocket (1955–57)	A10 Super Rocket (1958–63)	A10 Rocket Gold Star (1962–63)
Engine type	Twin Cylinder OHV	Twin Cylinder OHV	Twin Cylinder OHV
Bore × stroke	70mm × 84mm	70mm × 84mm	70mm × 84mm
Capacity	646cc	646cc	646cc
Comp ratio	8.0:1	8.3:1 9.0:1 (1962–63)	9.0:1
Claimed power	40bhp at 6,000rpm	42bhp at 6,000rpm	46bhp at 6,250rpm
Carburation	Amal TT9 or 389	Amal 376 Amal 389 or TT9 (1960–63)	Amal 389
Gearbox	Four-speed	Four-speed	Four-speed
Overall ratios	11.7; 8.0; 5.5; & 4.5:1	11.7; 10.0; 5.5; & 4.5:1	7.9; 6.0; 5.5; & 4.5:1
Tyres, front	19in dia × 3¼in	19in dia × 3¼in	19in dia × 3¼in
rear	19in dia × 3½in	19in dia × 3½in	19in dia × 3½in
Brakes, front	7in dia × 1½in	8in dia × 1⅜in	8in dia × 1⅜in or 190mm option
rear	7in dia × 1½in	7in dia × 1⅛in	7in dia × 1⅛in
Suspension front	Telescopic	Telescopic	Telescopic
rear	Swing-arm	Swing-arm	Swing-arm
Wheelbase	56in	56in	56in
Weight	418lb	418lb	395lb
Fuel capacity	4 gall.	4 gall.	4 gall. 2 or 5 gall. option
Top speed	109mph	106mph	115mph

Another variant of the A7/A10 series was the USA specified Road Rocket Gold Star of 1958. (BSA Archive)

116

Probably the most sought-after BSA by collectors was the 1962–63 A10 Rocket Gold Star, a superb blend of tuned Super Rocket engine and Gold Star chassis and fittings. It was capable of over 115mph (185kph). (OW)

Thunderbolt and Lightning – The A Group Unit-Twins (1962–73)

Looking back some thirty odd years, it is still hard to believe that BSA's unit twins were viewed with so much scepticism and mistrust. Just imagine – BSA took a blisteringly successful design such as the A10, completely updated the electrics with an alternator and gave it coil ignition, removed all the clutter of a separate gearbox, lost 2in (5cm) in the wheelbase and reduced its operating weight by 30lb (13.6kg), only to find that Mr Public treated it with contempt! Still, motorcyclists always were a stubborn lot, and the old A7 and A10 twins had been a hard act to follow. After all, there had always been a separate gearbox since Grandad's day, so why change now?

Anything wrong, even the slightest misdemeanour or malfunction, soon spread through the coffee bar grapevine and once a bad name... Well, maybe it was fashionable to write off the BSA A50 and A65 twins. Sure, some of the highly tuned versions of the mid-1960s were perhaps a little too overdone for their own good and BSA were going through traumatic times and having plenty of trouble with a decaying quality control system. But amidst a mish-mash of various model types there were some excellent motorcycles, vindicated after three decades by enthusiasts who have kept them in constant use.

Triggered off by Joseph Lucas's reluctance to carry on winding magnetos and dynamos, plans were put into operation to simplify things by planting all the prime movers and transmission gear into one set of die-cast alloy cases, taking the parallel twin motorcycle into the unit-construction age. With just two years of design and development behind it, the new 500cc A50 and 650cc A65

Gold Star cycle parts. For the trunk-road racer it was offered with a full range of accessories and options including a five gallon alloy fuel tank, Siamese exhaust, 7in diameter front brakes and a bench test certificate to guarantee a show of blistering acceleration up to a 115mph (185kph) top speed. Built only during 1962 and 1963, the A10 Rocket Gold Star was a final and fitting tribute as one of the best designs to proudly carry the 'Piled Arms' trademark.

A50 & A65 Twins

A50 Models

Model	A50 Star (1962–65)	A50 Cyclone (1964–65) A50 Cyclone Clubman (1964–65)	A50 Wasp (1965–66) A50 Royal Star (1965–70)
Engine type	Twin Cylinder OHV	Twin Cylinder OHV	Twin Cylinder OHV
Bore × stroke	65.5mm × 74mm	65.5mm × 74mm	65.5mm × 74mm
Capacity	499cc	499cc	499cc
Comp ratio	7.5:1 8.0:1 (1964–65)	9:1	10.5:1 (A50W) 9.0:1 (A50RS)
Claimed power	28.5bhp at 6,000rpm	38.5bhp at 6,750rpm	35bhp at 6,750rpm (A50RS 1969)
Carburation	Amal 389 monobloc	2 × Amal 389 monobloc	Amal 389 monobloc Amal 626 concentric (1967–70) (two carbs A50W)
Gearbox	Four-speed	Four-speed	Four-speed
Overall ratios	13.1; 8.4; 6.0; & 5.1:1	10.4; 7.5; 5.9; & 5.1:1	10.5; 7.6; 5.7; & 5.2:1 (A50W) 13.6; 8.6; 6.2; & 5.4 (A50RS)
Tyres, front	18in dia × 3¼in	19in dia × 3¼in	19in dia 3½in (A50W) 19in dia × 3¼in (A50RS)
rear	18in dia × 3½in	19in dia × 3½in	18in dia × 4in
Brakes, front	7in dia × 1⅛in	8in dia × 1⅛in	8in dia × 1⅝in
rear	7in dia × 1⅛in	7in dia × 1⅛in	7in dia × 1⅛in
Suspension front	Telescopic	Telescopic	Telescopic
rear	Swing-arm	Swing-arm	Swing-arm
Wheelbase	55in	55in	55in
Weight	385lb	390lb	390lb
Fuel capacity	4 gall.	4 gall. 2 gall. (option)	1⅔ gall. (A50W) 3½ gall. or 4 gall. option (A50RS)
Top speed	95mph	105mph	98mph (A50RS)

Stars made their tentative debut in January, 1962. Both were built around a stroke of 2.9in (74mm), with the A50 cylinders 2.5in (65.5mm) in diameter and the A65 further bored out to a slightly over-square 2.9in (75mm). The resulting large combustion area gave enough space for a pair of big valves with unrestricted gas flow and an ability to take a second carburettor, something that had never produced any worthwhile effects on the A10 types. The rest of the engine section was still based on the earlier pre-unit A10 with a single camshaft lying behind the cylinders. The tappets had rectangular feet to prevent them from rotating against each other and above, the rocker gear was supported on trunnion brackets cast onto the upper surface of the alloy cylinder head, so

118

that the rockerbox was merely a cover, and was under no stress and therefore easy to seal.

At the bottom end, a ball race bearing held up the drive-side of the crank and the timing-side main bearing still used a plain bush slightly larger than that of the A10 at 1¼in (31mm) in diameter. Driven by a triplex chain, the gearbox cluster sat on a large circular plate and was accessible from either the timing side or from the primary drive by removing an aperture plate, after pulling off a four spring clutch. The initial 1962 models were fairly soft at 38bhp for the A65 and 28.5bhp for the A50. Compression ratios were a modest 7.5:1, capable of spinning the motors up to 6,000rpm.

In appearance the new Star twins resembled chunkier versions of their predecessors – 'cobby' was one term commonly used. The frame, mudguards, tank and wheel hubs were more or less as before except for smaller 18in tyres and a pair of large side panels covering the battery and toolbox compartments picked out with a large circular winged BSA motif. In all, it was a tidy, clean and compact layout with no gaping spaces or fresh air surrounding a big egg-shaped engine.

Motorcycling ran an A50 around the MIRA test track at Nuneaton in July 1962, and had the speedometer needle nudging very close to the 100mph (160kph) mark. It started easily whether hot or cold, and apart from some cold start piston slap, it was also very quiet. But reading between the lines, they were not very keen on its tingling vibration and could not understand why the A50 with only a 7in front brake was expected to dissipate the same energy output as its near

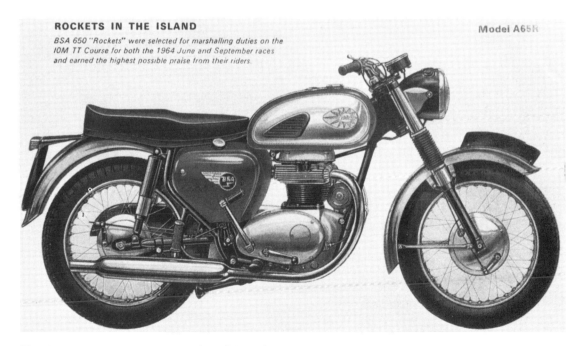

ROCKETS IN THE ISLAND

BSA 650 "Rockets" were selected for marshalling duties on the IOM TT Course for both the 1964 June and September races and earned the highest possible praise from their riders.

Model A65R

The A65 Rocket was an outstanding high performance motorcycle. Tank and centre compartment were deep red – guaranteed to make the blood race. (BSA Archive)

119

A65 Models

Model	A65 Star (1962–65)	A65 Rocket (1963–65) A65 Lightning Rocket (1964–65) A65 Lightning Clubmans (1964–65)	A65 Thunderbolt (1965–70) A65 Lightning (1964–70)
Engine type	Twin Cylinder OHV	Twin Cylinder OHV	Twin Cylinder OHV
Bore × stroke	75mm × 74mm	75mm × 74mm	75mm × 74mm
Capacity	654cc	654cc	654cc
Comp ratio	7.5:1	9.0:1	9.0:1
Claimed power	38bhp at 5,800rpm	38bhp at 6,250rpm (A65R)	40bhp at 6,250rpm (A65T) 53bhp at 7,000rpm (A65T)
Carburation	Amal 389 monobloc	2 × Amal 389 monobloc (A65R)	Amal 928 concentric (A65T 1968–73) 2 × Amal 930 concentric (A65 1968–73)
Gearbox	Four-speed	Four-speed	Four-speed
Overall ratios	11.1; 7.2; 5.1; & 4.3:1	10.9; 6.9; 4.9; & 4.3:1 (A65R) 9.3; 6.7; 5.2; & 4.6:1 (A65LR & A65LC)	12.3; 7.8; 5.6; & 4.9:1
Tyres, front	18in dia × 3¼in	18in dia × 3¼in (A65R) 19in dia × 3¼in	19in dia × 3¼in
rear	18in dia × 3½in	18in dia × 3½in	18in dia × 4in
Brakes, front	8in dia × 1⅛in	8in dia × 1⅛in	8in dia × 1⅝in
rear	7in dia × 1⅛in	7in dia × 1⅛in	7in dia × 1⅛in
Suspension front	Telescopic	Telescopic	Telescopic
rear	Swing-arm	Swing-arm	Swing-arm
Wheelbase	55in	55in	55in
Weight (dry)	390lb	390lb	420lb
Fuel capacity	4 gall.	4 gall.	4 gall.
Top speed	100mph	105mph	101mph (A65T) 108mph (A65L)

identical A65 big brother fitted out with a stouter, 8in 'stopper'.

The A65 story really started to gather pace when the first of many sports models came about in October 1963. To replace the highly glamorized A10 Rocket Gold Star, the A65 Rocket stepped in to fill the void. 'A BSA to make the blood race,' said *Motor Cycle Weekly*, and they simply raved about its 105mph (170kph) performance and surging acceleration. It would also potter through the town without any fuss, and the engine sat down to 800rpm despite a row of aggressive cams and a 9:1 piston. Slim valanced, chrome plated mudguards and a Siamese exhaust system completed the sporty looks.

'A policeman's lot' . . . BSA supplied A65s in various specifications to the Constabulary. This example has a twin leading shoe front brake, QD wheels and a small seat presumably to make room for a radio intercom. (BSA Archive)

By the end of 1964, the programme had exploded to ten models. Twin carburettors were all the rage as the A50C Cyclone and Cyclone Clubman gave the 500s something to shout about, with the Clubman racer also getting a close ratio gearbox and a full complement of competition accessories. The A65 versions were called the Lightning and Lightning Clubman, and both had bench tested engines, capable of a thoroughly good 110mph (180kph).

The greater part of BSA's sales drive was dedicated to the American market, and A50/A65 progress was overwhelmingly influenced by such grandiosely-named machines as the A65 Spitfire-Hornet or A50 Wasp, a pair of the rorty monsters that contributed to Small Heath's 85 per cent export drive. No lights,

energy transfer ignition, skimpy valanced chrome 'fenders' and a pair of high level straight-through exhausts (sans muffler) were all essential ingredients for a long track racer with 'mule kick' acceleration.

Back home, things were kept in more sober proportions, with twelve volt electrics, flamboyant paint finishes and plenty of chrome setting the style for the new A50 Royal Star and A65 Thunderbolt, 1966 replacements for the Star models. A Thunderbolt came through a *Motor Cycle* roadtest with flying colours in October that year. Now with a 9:1 compression ratio and high-lift cams taken from the twin carburettor 'Lightning', it still proved to be a useful tourer, never getting hot and bothered either in town or out on the open road. The test singled out the brakes

Model	A65 Spitfire Mk II (1966) A65 Spitfire Mk III (1967) A65 Spitfire Mk IV (1968)	A65 Thunderbolt (1970–73) A65 Lightning (1970–73) A65 Firebird (1970–71)
Engine type	Twin Cylinder OHV	Twin Cylinder OHV
Bore × stroke	75mm × 74mm	75mm × 74mm
Capacity	654cc	654cc
Comp ratio	10.5:1 (Mk II) 10.0:1	9.1:1 7.5:1 option
Claimed power	55bhp at 7,000rpm (Mk III)	46bhp at 7,000rpm (A65T) 52bhp at 7,000rpm (A65L)
Carburation	2 × Amal GP2 (Mk III) 2 × Amal 932 concentric	Amal 928 concentric (A65T) 2 × Amal 930 concentric (A65L & A65F)
Gearbox	Four-speed	Four-speed
Overall ratios	12.3; 7.8; 5.6; & 4.9:1	12.2; 7.8; 5.6; & 4.9:1
Tyres, front	19in dia × 3¼in	19in dia × 3¼in
rear	18in dia × 4in	18in dia × 4in
Brakes, front	7½in dia × 2in 8in dia × 1⅝in (Mk IV)	8in dia × 1½in
rear	7in dia × 1⅛in	7in dia × 1⅛in
Suspension front	Telescopic	Telescopic
rear	Swing-arm	Swing-arm
Wheelbase	55in	57in
Weight	382lb (Mk III)	420lb
Fuel capacity	4 gall.	2.5 gall. 4 gall. option
Top speed	110mph	105mph

for particular praise – they were old half-width hub patterns dating back to the early 1950s, but were still the best QD design in the business!

Some of the excesses of the American models began to rub off when the mean, lean and occasionally fragile A65 Spitfire with its blood red fibre-glass fuel tank began to make an impact. Starting out as a Mk II in 1966, the Spitfire was the hottest thing on the roads. 'Style and speed as never before,' said a promotional hand-out. 'Here is a model that looks like 120mph [193kph] and actually does it: and the Spitfire can annihilate a standing quarter mile [0.4km] in 13.6 seconds.' Spitfire pilots also had to withstand plenty of knuckle-shattering vibration and run the risk

of pulverizing a set of expensive mainshaft bearings if that kind of treatment was kept up for too long. . .

The Spitfire Mk III for 1967 came out with a finned rocker box, a slightly lowered compression and a pair of Amal Concentrics which at least enabled the engine to tick over at a regular tempo instead of the over-exuberance of the GP types. In its last year, now up to a Mk IV, the Spitfire finished off with a twin leading shoe front brake and a steel fuel tank.

The endless quest for more power and speed was taking place at a time when BSA was bedevilled by severe defects in the basic design. The main bearings, still based on the modest sidecar hauling models of the 1950s,

The twin carburettor A65 Lightning entered a new phase when the 1971 models had a 'tall' oil carrying frame and conical pattern hubs. Often criticized, the oil-in-frame A65s have since attracted a devoted following. (BSA Archive)

were simply not up to matching any further seasonal increases in performance, and rogue sparking caused by a deficient ignition system and the frailty of an alloy-bodied oil pump all contributed to the widespread derision. But it was a revolutionary frame that was to cause greater controversy when the 'new era' models were shown in November 1970 at a lavish press and trade beanfeast.

The new oil-carrying frame was a classic example of work being carried out by people who had little or no experience of actually riding a motorcycle. Well constructed, strong and with good handling it may have been, but the brilliantly-schooled minds that conceived the oil-in-frame overlooked the fact that it

needed a full six-footer in stockinged feet to be able to sit astride the thing. BSA's team of testers had warned every level of management that the frame was a good 2in (5cm) too high. So did the journalists in their polite, and tactful way, but it was no good, and their sound advice fell on deaf ears.

The big spiny frame also came with new conically-shaped hubs carrying a twin leading shoe front brake, and a pair of forks showing exposed stanchions on each side of the wheel spindle, and secured by a cluster of four stout bolts.

'Is the touring five-hundred a dodo?' asked one eminent journalist. 'Definitely not,' said BSA, but by August 1971 the last oil-in-frame Royal Star was wheeled away for despatch. By then the twin cylinder range had been clipped down to just three models as the company began to sink almost without trace into financial ruin. Home buyers could either take a Thunderbolt or a twin Carb Lightning although they were denied an export only, Firebird Street Scrambler, a virile creation if ever there was one, with its twin pipes high up on the nearside and covered by a mesh grille. The front and rear fenders were the skimpiest ever seen, still, who ever went street scrambling in places like Slough or Market Harborough?

It was a little ironic that the final, last ditch 1972 A65 Thunderbolt and Lightning twins were amongst the best of the breed when restored to flat touring bars and a more European influenced tank with real knee-grips. It is these latter models and the very early, soft-tuned 'Stars' that have always been the pick of the bunch.

In Triplicate – The Rocket Three (1968–73)

As the covers came off the BSA Rocket Three and T150 Triumph Trident in September 1968, years of rumour and speculation about a mysterious development going on within the group ended. First reports heralded the triple cylinder models as 'a most significant innovation by the British motorcycle industry'. But it did not take people long to realize that this 'new innovation' was in fact strongly based on an existing Triumph twin power unit whose lineage dated back to 1936! The pundits called it 'a tiger and a half', pointing out that as a design it was a Triumph to the core. Separate gear-driven exhaust and inlet cams ran across the crankcase in front of and behind the cylinder block respectively, with the pushrods concealed within chrome plated

Rocket Three	
Model	**A75 Rocket 3 (1968–73)**
Engine type	Three Cylinder OHV Transverse
Bore × stroke	67mm × 70mm
Capacity	740cc
Comp ratio	9.5:1 (9:1 1970–72)
Claimed power	58bhp at 7,250rpm
Carburation	3 × Amal 626 concentric
Gearbox	Four-speed
Overall ratios	11.95; 8.3; 5.83; & 4.89:1
Tyres, front	19in dia × 3¼in
	19in dia × 4⅛in (1970–72)
rear	19in dia × 4⅛in
Brakes, front	8in dia × 1⅝in
rear	7in dia × 1⅛in
Suspension front	Telescopic, Hydraulic two-way damping
rear	Swing-arm
Wheelbase	58in
Weight	468lb
Fuel capacity	4¼ gall. (2.5 gall. export/option)
Top speed	120mph

tubes nestling between the cylinders. But as a sop to avoid any accusations of 'badge engineering', a few features were applied to distinguish the BSA Rocket Three from the Triumph Trident. The BSA's cylinder block was raked forward by 15 degrees and was held in a duplex cradle frame, while its timing cover gave the impression that the engine section was in-unit with the transmission. On the other hand, the Triumph had an upright block and a crankcase that retained the traditional Triumph heart-shaped outer cover, and its frame was a single down-tube type with a separate rear section.

The original idea was conceived one evening in 1963 by Bert Hopwood and Doug Hele. Hopwood considered the idea of extending a twin cylinder engine as an interim project to

Drive side view of the Three. The superbike era got underway when this high speed, high mileage machine arrived in 1968. (R. Shufflebottom)

meet an urgent demand for larger and more powerful machinery. A few hasty calculations appeared to show that it had all the potential for a compact unit with low vibration and excellent power delivery prospects. There was an acute problem of overall width to overcome but this was more than satisfied by dispensing with the central flywheel and substituting a car type crankshaft with integral bobweights. Relocating the alternator to the timing side and specifying a single friction plate diaphragm clutch made the task all the more attainable.

At first, BSA-Triumph group management was unreceptive and dismissed the proposal. 'Three is potty' formed the basis of one analysis. It was only when some news of a Japanese 'Superbike' came filtering back that the go-ahead was given and by 1965, the first complete 750cc engine had been fired up on the test bench and all the anxieties about good balance factors and power delivery were dispelled.

The 750cc engine had a bore and stroke of 2.6×2.75in (67mm $\times 70$mm) and a crankshaft that was a masterpiece of the forge. The blank was given a couple of twists after each heating process to throw the big-end journals around at 120 degree intervals for a one-three-two firing sequence. The crank sat on four main bearings: a pair of split-shell plain bearings in the centre, a ball type outer drive-side bearing and a roller bearing forming the outrigger support on the timing side. As an expedient measure to get the machine into production many Triumph components were retained and the crankcase construction retained the time-honoured vertical joints (and the accompanying oil spills). The cylinder block was a beautifully crafted, light alloy casting, square finned with spigotted liners and flange mounted onto the crankcase assembly. A one-piece alloy cylinder head with hemispherical combustion chambers and well proportioned valve ports was fed by a bank of three 1in (26mm) Amal Concentric carburettors topped off with a finned rocker box. Long tappet covers and tappet caps completed the job. Keeping to BSA practice, a high capacity dual stage oil pump formed the heart of a dry sump lubrication system which, on the production models, was assisted by an oil cooler hung beneath the fuel tank.

According to its creator, there were only a few minor development problems and the bike could have been launched in its Triumph format straight away. Instead the project was dragged through the bureaucracy of consultants and marketing analysts and was 'tossed like a ball' from one committee to another.

The finished product was 'different' to say the least, with a quirky mixture of new ideas, such as a long, slab-sided 4¼ gallon (19.3 litre) tank, side panels as big as dinnerplates and bags of fittings such as high rise handlebars and skimpy 'fenders' to keep the American lobby happy. Most noticeable were the ray-gun silencers: long, flared and flat-sided and with three stumpy little tubes poking out at the tail end. The standard issue colour scheme was deep red for the tank and side panels, while the optional version in lime green with red striping took some getting used to.

Public reaction to the Rocket Three ranged from lukewarm to ecstatic. The engine, pumping out 58bhp at peak revs of 7,250rpm gave a genuine 120 +mph (195+ kph) top speed. With the motor kept above 4,500rpm the Three had vivid acceleration and plenty of pace. Many enthusiasts became addicted to seeking out empty stretches of trunk road, and listening to those ray-guns blasting away!

Handling was solid and reliable except when the silencers touched down early and cornering was assured by Dunlops K81 TT100 tyres specially developed for the purpose. 'The motor's unburstable,' said chief tester, Percy Tait. 'You can take it flat out all the way down the motorway and it'll still be running as sweetly at the other end.' The pay off was that the Rocket Three only returned 30mpg (9.4l/100km) of high octane poured into the intake tubes. But who cared when there was no 70mph (110kph) speed limit and there was a Jaguar up ahead. . .

On the race track, the BSA showed the way with a speed demonstration at Daytona in 1969. Records were shattered as an unfaired Rocket Three flashed past the 5, 15, 20, and 50 mile markers at an average speed of just over 130mph (210kph). 'Beat that', ran the BSA slogan as the rest looked on in disbelief. In those heady days before BSA-Triumph had to call in its racing team, the Triples dominated the short circuit racing scene.

Each production year brought a few changes. The most significant came in 1971 when a complete re-hash of the cycle parts rendered the beast virtually unridable. The fuel tank became a ridiculously pear-shaped effort just short of three gallons (13.6 litres) capacity, and the idea of painting the frame in light dove grey did not go down well with owners battling to keep their machines looking smart. This was also the year of the conical hub wheels and cast alloy fork legs, both products of the ill-founded and ill-fated Umberslade Hall establishment. The new brakes were little better than the original 8in twin leading front shoes, a dubious set-up for a machine that registered 490lb (222kg) on the scales. The ray-gun silencers were exchanged for a more conventional, slow, reverse-cone shape but other changes to the carburation, gearing and compression ratio made the 1971 models that little bit more responsive to the throttle.

The long delays in launching the Triple cost the company dearly for no sooner had the fanfare of publicity faded away when Honda unveiled their 67bhp 750cc Four with disc brakes and electric starter. Then came the Kawasaki Mach III two-stroke . . . and potential Rocket Three sales evaporated overnight.

But before the BSA name was bulldozed into oblivion, the Rocket Three had reverted back to most of its 1970 specification. The bigger tank was back, finished in deep burgundy, and with a black frame. Without doubt the later versions had all the right equipment and better visual appeal.

8

Forever Single

The Clockwork Cockerel – The Bantam Two-Stroke (1948–71)

After the Second World War, one particular motorcycle rose above all others as the first name in basic, dependable two-wheeled transport. It became a household word. If anyone had been stopped in the street and asked to name any popular motorcycle, they would most likely have said 'Bantam'.

The Bantam story began in 1948 when BSA announced that they were supplying some two-stroke engines to fulfil a Swedish contract. The unit had a capacity of 123cc and it incorporated all the very latest in two-stroke know-how, with twin, 180 degree, Schnurle-loop transfer ports cast into an iron cylinder barrel and capped with an alloy cylinder head. Both parts were held down to the crankcases by four long studs. Breaking a traditional but unwritten law, the primary

Bantam Models			
Model	D1 (1948–63)	D3 (1954–57)	D5 (1958)
Engine type	Single Cylinder, two-stroke	Single Cylinder, two-stroke	Single Cylinder, two-stroke
Bore × stroke	52mm × 58mm	57mm × 58mm	61.5mm × 58mm
Capacity	123cc	148cc	174cc
Comp ratio	6.5:1	6.4:1	7.4:1
Claimed power	4bhp at 5,000rpm	5.3bhp at 5,000rpm	7bhp at 4,750rpm
Carburation	Amal 361/8	Amal 523/1	Amal 375 monobloc
Gearbox	Three-speed	Three-speed	Three-speed
Ratios	22.1; 11.7; & 7:1	22.0; 11.7; & 7:1	20.2; 10.7; & 6.5:1
Tyres, front	19in dia × 2¾in	19in dia × 2¾in	18in dia × 3in
rear	19in dia × 2¾in	19in dia × 2¾in	18in dia × 3in
Brakes, front	5in dia × ⅝in	5in dia × ⅝in	5in dia × ⅞in
rear	5in dia × ⅝in	5in dia × ⅝in	5in dia × ⅞in
Suspension front	Telescopic	Telescopic	Telescopic
rear	Rigid 1948–54 Plunger 1950–63	Plunger 1954–56 Swing-arm 1956–57	Swing-arm
Wheelbase	50½in	51¼in	52in
Weight	153lb	183lb	216lb
Fuel capacity	1¾ gall.	1¾ gall.	2 gall.
Top speed	46mph	50mph	56mph

drive was taken on the right-hand side, using a non-adjustable chain to transmit power from the crankshaft to a multi-plate, six spring clutch.

The overall appearance of the engine was very neat and clean, gone were the external flywheel and supplementary oiling devices usually associated with two-strokes. Inside BSA's tidy and compact unit with its egg-shaped casings and forwardly raked cylinder was a positive stop, three speed gear cluster and a roller big-end bearing assembly. The crankshaft was supported on three ball bearings, two main bearings held up drive side and one supported the opposite side main-shaft jutting out from a pair of full circular flywheels.

On the nearside, a Wico-Pacy magneto generator combined with a heavy permanent magnet flywheel was locked to the crank-shaft. The clutch was disengaged by a simple cable operated mechanism situated beside the generator set, which worked through a helix and pushrod running inside a hollow

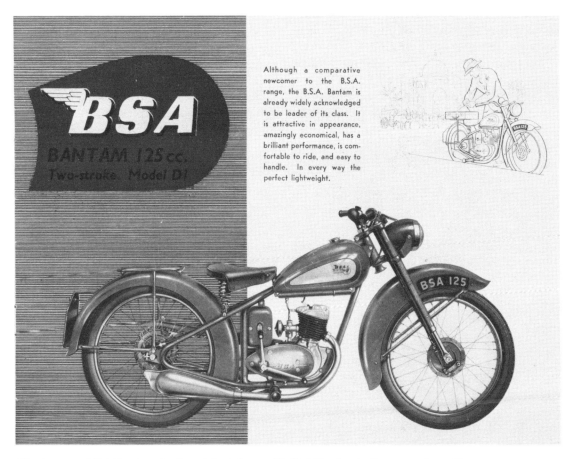

Although a comparative newcomer to the B.S.A. range, the B.S.A. Bantam is already widely acknowledged to be leader of its class. It is attractive in appearance, amazingly economical, has a brilliant performance, is comfortable to ride, and easy to handle. In every way the perfect lightweight.

The immortal D1 Bantam in its original form with 'flat Bantam' silencer and small finned barrel. Setting new production records, the 150,000th Bantam came off the production line in February 1957. (BSA Archive)

gearbox mainshaft. Over on the drive side, a kick start lever and foot operated gearchange worked on the same shaft axis. The engine was fed by an Amal 261 carburettor with a built-in air filter and strangler. Power output for the 'petroil' lubricated unit was put at a modest 4bhp, rated at 5,000rpm.

In June that same year, a further press release stated that a complete machine was undergoing final preparation. The engine was now slung into an all welded frame holding together an unsprung rear wheel and a pair of telescopic front forks. Front wheel movement was controlled by a long spring and grease packed bushes offered the only chance at damping any recoil.

The first road test for the new model D1 Bantam appeared in October 1948. The *Motor Cycle* gave a bright account of the young fledgling. They thought it was a cinch to ride and its performance about-town was brisk, with safe brakes and handling. More than that, it was said to be impossible to overdrive the motor and a fuel consumption return worked out at 128mpg (2.21l/100km).

The early bird could scuttle along at 21, 41 and 47mph (33, 66 and 75kph) in each gear; it also managed to reach the 30mph (50kph) barrier in 6.6 seconds. The Bantam's clean lines and easy maintenance made for an ideal economy motorcycle and with a price tag of only £60, plus purchase tax, BSA were quite right to consider themselves on to a winner, and so indeed they were.

By 1953, after barely five years in production, the 100,000th Bantam had been wheeled from the production line. Along all the trunk roads and lanes throughout both town and country, BSA's little gem, painted in an all-over coat of mist green with cream tank side panels ran about in droves. Bantam clubs sprouted up all over the place – it was a classic example of automania delivered by a harmless looking creation which had cast a spell upon every member of society.

It proved to be a gutsy little fowl too, as demonstrated by the number of folk prepared to load it with bundles of clothing, camping equipment and even the dog for trans-continental expeditions. BSA responded to the call of serious tourists by offering, from 1949, a plunger sprung rear wheel.

Demand was so high that Wipac could not cope, so a consignment of 5,000 machines were built with Lucas generator sets. These were known as de-luxe Bantams. There was also a competition model on offer, which had an upswept exhaust and a cylinder head decompressor to attract off-road trialists.

It was not until many years after the introduction of the Bantam that its true origins began to be questioned. Out of the bag came an admission that the 123cc engine design was in fact some war booty brought home in a bundle of blueprints from the bomb-ravaged remains of the German Zschopauer Motorradwerk, the original makers of the DKW RT125 'power egg'. BSA had merely converted the drawings to inch dimensions and good old Whitworth threads. To arrange the gearshift onto the conventional right foot position, the original format was relayed into its mirror image.

It came as no surprise when in October 1953, BSA announced an uprated Bantam. This turned out to be the 150cc D3 Bantam Major that was bored out to 2.26in (57mm) in order to create a virtually 'square' volume whilst retaining the original stroke of 2.28in (58mm). Claimed power output for the pepped-up Major was 5.2bhp at 5,000rpm and yet it still qualified for the same taxation class as the D1.

The D3's running gear had heavier front forks, taken from the Competition D1 model.

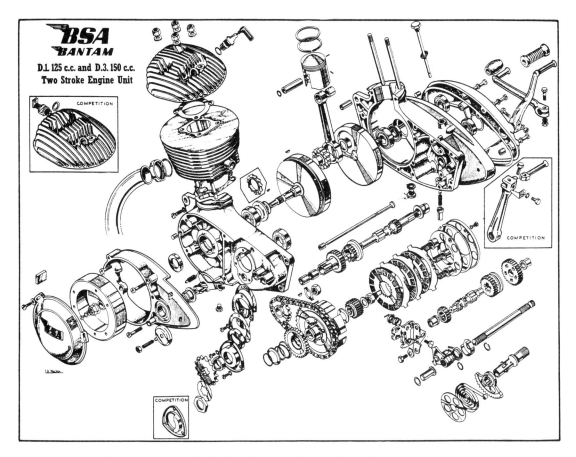

From 1954, the Bantam engine had wider finning, though the basic layout remained virtually unchanged throughout its life span. (BSA Archive)

Apart from that and its pastel grey finish the frame assembly was generally shared with the D1. The Major engine had a new style cylinder barrel and head with larger finning. Inside the crankcases, heavier flywheels and an uprated big-end bearing using ¼in × ⅜in (6mm × 9.5mm) long rollers required the flywheels to be recessed at the crankpin eye. The humble D1 received the same treatment, and gone too was the old 'flat Bantam' silencer which was now replaced by a long cigar-shaped version with removable baffles to allow easy de-coking (a regular chore for

keeping a two-stroke in tune when using 1950s oils). To ring the changes, the front mudguard arrangement was also altered to a smoother looking shallow valanced style supported from the lower fork stanchions and matched above by a more appealing headlamp cowl.

In 1956, the D3 Major acquired a spanking new swing-arm rear chassis using Girling telescopic dampers. The bigger Bantam now boasted excellent road-hugging prospects but at the cost of being fattened up to tip the scales at 226lb (102.5kg). Once again, *The*

131

Model	D7 (1958–66)	D10 (1966–67)	D14/4 (1968–69) D175 (1969–71)
Engine type	Single Cylinder, two-stroke	Single Cylinder, two-stroke	Single Cylinder, two-stroke
Bore × stroke	61.5mm × 58mm	61.5mm × 58mm	61.5mm × 58mm
Capacity	174cc	174cc	174cc
Comp ratio	7.4:1	8.6:1	10:1
Claimed power	7.4bhp at 4,750rpm	10bhp at 6,000rpm	12.6bhp at 5,750rpm
Carburation	Amal 375 monobloc	Amal 375 monobloc	Amal 626 concentric
Gearbox	Three-speed	Three-speed (Four-speed D10 Sports)	Four-speed
Ratios	17.4; 9.3; & 6.6:1	17.4; 9.3; & 6.6:1	18.68; 12.04; 8.55; 6.58:1
Tyres, front	18in dia × 3in	18in dia × 3in	18in dia × 3in
rear	18in dia × 3in	18in dia × 3in	18in dia × 3in
Brakes, front	5½in dia × 1in	5½in dia × 1in	5½in dia × 1in
rear	5½in dia × 1in	5½in dia × 1in	5½in dia × 1in
Suspension front	Telescopic	Telescopic	Telescopic
rear	Swing-arm	Swing-arm	Swing-arm
Wheelbase	52in	50in	50in
Weight	220lb	215lb	215lb
Fuel capacity	2 gall. (1.9 gall. D7 de-luxe)	1.9 gall.	1.9 gall.
Top speed	56mph	65mph	65mph

MotorCycle took one out for a spin. 'Ample power for touring, fuel economy and docility in traffic are among the attributes of a striking two-stroke lightweight' ran the headline. It was that 'docility in traffic' that the author can vividly remember. Well, so speaks the voice of experience? I'm afraid so, for a 1956 D3 was my first BSA, a ratty old Rooster with good scrap-yard potential, but for £7 10 shillings who was I to complain. My beloved Bantam may have been beyond the 'clapped-out' stage but it took all the punishment an ill-informed novice could mete out, and still remained faithful to the bitter end. What about spares? No problem. All one had to do was to insult a BSA dealer and he would virtually throw a spare engine at you!

The D3 Major's production run came to an end in late 1957, when it was replaced by the first 175cc, the Bantam D5 Super. A 2.4in (61.5mm) bore helped to restore an acceptable ratio of power to weight which had been sapped by the swing-arm frame. Colours were now either maroon or black and the D5 could be identified by its more bulbous two gallon fuel tank.

The D1 carried on with little change other than some of the crank assembly features now found on its big brother. The D5 had only one year in production when Edward Turner's influence began to tell. It took the shape of a completely re-styled D7 Super Bantam which was introduced in time for the 1958 season. Turner's obsession for clean

132

Smooth lines and a neat headlamp nacelle identify a 1959 Bantam Super. Hampered by having only three gears, the D7 still enjoyed excellent sales. (OW)

lines gave the 175cc Bantam rounded covers and a combined fork shroud and headlamp nacelle, and even fitted an extra engine case to cover up the clutch mechanism. It was finished off with a 'Super' inscription scrawled across its surface.

The D7 ran on until 1966, outliving the hugely popular D1 that had finally departed in 1963. D7 Bantams were available in two forms during 1965. One was a cheap 'silver' Bantam with all-painted fuel tank, the other a 'Super de-luxe', the first to have a re-styled, 'jelly mould' fuel tank lavishly painted in a variety of red, blue or black finishes matched against chrome plated side panels.

Eager to make the Bantam a little more 'with it', BSA took a step forward by re-developing the engine to produce a new sporty image. Out went legshields, bulb-horns, drab paint finishes and the famous Bantam cock motif. In came flamboyant polychromatic paint finishes, 'racing' handle-bars and moulded acrylic silver star tank badges. Wipac had given up making their range of series 55 Mk 8 ignition generators, and so modern A/C rectified, coil ignition alternators took over the electrical work. The contact-breaker points now lived in a circular chamber on the right hand side of the motor behind a round cover featuring a flashy finned profile.

A claimed output of 10bhp (hence the new

133

The D7 Bantam de-luxe of 1965 was the first to have a new style 'jelly mould' fuel tank. Now up to 175cc the Bantam had outgrown its three-speed gearbox. (BSA Archive)

D10 designation) had been achieved with re-shaped transfer ports and riveted flywheel compression plates. The clutch also took on an extra friction plate to cope with the 40 per cent increase in output power.

So in July 1966, the range of four 175cc D10 Bantams was released to the motor-cycle press. A cheap and cheerful Bantam Silver was still among the list although the former de-luxe model was now retitled the Bantam Supreme. The third in the line-up was the D10 Sports, fitted with a tiny nacelle-mounted flyscreen, upswept ex-haust, humped seat and full-width hub brakes. 'Go-faster' decor amounted to a strip of black and white chequered tape running along the upper flank of the fuel tank. More significantly, a four-speed gear cluster had been installed for the first time. 'About time too!' everyone said. That extra prod on the gearshift gave the D10 Sports another punch, while the

other models remained hampered by a dis-mally antiquated selection of three wildly spaced gears.

MotorCycle Mechanics, a magazine never shy of a few home truths when they pre-sented a road test, took a Bantam Sports for a few laps of Snetterton. They were mildly impressed by the four-speed gearbox and the vastly improved performance of the 8.65:1 compression ratio engine that set a top speed of 62mph (99.75kph) and jumped from a standing start to 50mph (80kph) in 15.9 seconds. The quarter mile (0.4km) took 25.3 seconds with a terminal speed of 57.6mph (92.6kph) shown on the clockface. Fuel con-sumption for a hard day's work still came out at a penny pinching 90 mpg (3.14l/100km).

The fourth member of the D10 Bantam family was certainly an attractive proposi-tion, with its special frame giving two inches of additional ground clearance and its trials

*'One meets the nicest people on a Bantam.'
Bantamite meets swinging sixties socialite
complete with harpoon and goosepimples. The
Bantam is a 1967 D10, note the circular
points cover and suede desert boots! (BSA
publicity photo)*

specification, Intended primarily for the rough
ground of the Australian outback, the D10
Bushman remained a rarity on our home
shores.

But the D10 story was not all extra gears
and progress. It developed an infamous
service record, linked with a crankshaft
assembly that was hard pressed to live with
the dramatic increases in power taken from
an engine that was still betraying its 1948
vintage. By the end of 1967, the BSA Bantam was starting to lose its dominance of

the lightweight market, giving up precious
ground to a vast invasion of mainly Japanese
products. To keep the enemy from the door,
BSA's development men further raised the
compression rate to 10:1 and fitted a larger
bore exhaust system which raised the Bantam's power rating to 13bhp. A batch of 600
D13 Bantams had been shipped off before
someone thought of the superstitious impli-
cations and renamed the latest brood the
D14/4, emphasising that all models now had
the four-speed gearbox. The D14 motor settled down nicely at a cruising speed of 55mph
(88kph) with a wide power band and no low
speed snatch when pulling away in top gear.
At full throttle, 60mph (100kph) action was
pretty lively work, and noisy with it too, as
the bigger pipe yelled out a fairly harsh rasp.

At £130, a D14/4 Supreme still offered
good value and when it came to totting up bills
for fuel, oil, spares, and general wear and
tear there was still none better. The trouble
with the later Bantam was that it was trying to
suit two opposite camps and failed to satisfy
either. No longer was it a true unisex utility
appreciated by both young and old, yet as an
attempt at the youthful 'tearaway' market, it
fell short on zip and looked like an antique.

After the initial appearance of the D175
Bantam in 1969, the final version, *Meccano
Magazine* printed an honest and commonly-
held opinion of the Bantam. 'As a means of
transport, the Bantam has much to commend
it. Comfort, good roadholding and sound construction give the impression that it will provide many years service.' But the same
report also lambasted its old-fashioned looks
and lack of useful extras such as a steering
lock and a reserve fuel tap.

From any standpoint, the D175 looked
identical to the D14/4 apart from having a
centrally located sparkplug and a pair of
stronger, rubber-gaitered front forks pre-

The Bushman was an exciting new concept for a lightweight, off-road sports machine. It had a 2in increase in ground clearance and an energy transfer ignition system. The Bushman was a relatively scarce bird on home ground, since most were sent to Australia. (BSA Archive)

viously only found on the D14/4 Sports. The engine, however, had been extensively changed. BSA had taken the trouble to make completely new crankcase and cylinder patterns. The crankshaft was also unique to the D175, having increased bearing journals.

The end came in late 1970 when the D175 joined an unfortunate line-up of models being hyped-up to try to rekindle the flagging fortunes of a once mighty empire. Instead, by

Final inspection for a D10 Bantam Supreme. The side panel transfers have yet to be applied. (BSA Archive)

the following March, Bantam production was terminated as the 'leaders of the industry' had all the jigs and tooling fixtures unforgiveably, unceremoniously and most cynically smashed to pieces, purely to thwart a reasonable offer made by a well-known Bantam specialist. For twenty-three years, it had provided cheap, safe and sensible transport for many thousands of people, not to mention generations of learners. Although the service provided by half a million Bantams was cruelly terminated, the author was, and still is, proud to have been a 'Bantamite'.

Still Single – The Unit Singles (1958–73)

BSA's tidy, one-piece construction singles will always be remembered with a mixture of love and loathing. As a replacement for the old separate gearbox C12, the uncomplicated C15, first introduced in September 1958 was, for many motorcyclists, their first taste of a 'real' bike. For others, the 250 Star and its derivatives earned themselves infamy for eating big-end bearings and leaking oil like a sieve.

137

Model	C15 Star (1961)	B40 Star (1960)
	Selected Unit Singles	
Engine type	Single Cylinder OHV	Single Cylinder OHV
Bore × stroke	67mm × 70mm	79mm × 70mm
Capacity	247cc	343cc
Comp ratio	7.25:1	7.0:1
Claimed power	15bhp at 7,000rpm	21bhp at 7,000rpm
Carburation	Amal 375 monobloc	Amal 376 monobloc
Gearbox	Four-speed	Four-speed
Overall ratios	15.9; 10.5; 7.6; & 6.0:1	14.6; 9.6; 7.0; & 5.4:1
Tyres, front	17in dia × 3¼in	18in dia × 3¼in
rear	17in dia × 3¼in	18in dia × 3½in
Brakes, front	6in dia × ⅞in	7in dia × 1⅛in
rear	6in dia × ⅞in	6in dia × ⅞in
Suspension front	Telescopic	Telescopic
rear	Swing-arm	Swing-arm
Wheelbase	51¼in	52½in
Weight	280lb	307lb
Fuel capacity	2½ gall.	3 gall.
Top speed	72mph	75mph

Tipping the scales at only 280lb (127kg), the 'Ceefer' showed an amazing power to weight ratio; its punchy 249cc, 2.6in × 2.7in (67mm × 70mm) OHV engine handed out 15bhp, revved freely up to its maximum 7,000 rpm and yet behaved calmly at low speeds with an easy tick-over. The early unit single BSA reflected the two sides of Edward Turner. On the exterior, the C15 showed his uncanny brilliance at reading the market and supplying just what everyone wanted – something light, sleek and easy on the eye. It was a salesman's dream, a bike that people would buy as soon as they had seen one, and at £179 19s it was not only a good looker but also a good buy. On the other hand, it was as they say, 'value engineered'; certain features, such as the thickness of the crankcase sealing faces had been skimped and as a basis for further development, it should have had a limited shelf life. Instead, for a thirteen year span, twenty-two basic model versions were built to fulfil almost every aspect of motorcycling, and the number of modifications and seasonal changes to extract more power and come to terms with the deficiencies of the basic design were countless.

There was nothing all that unusual with the C15. Its vertically split engine had a cast-iron cylinder barrel and alloy head all held down tight on four long studs. The tappets could be easily adjusted after unscrewing a pair of circular caps; the oil sump plate was simple to get at and the pre-1965 models had the contact-breakers housed in a 'lollipop' distributor, poking upwards just behind the barrel. This latter feature was one of the culprits responsible for some of the nastier incidents experienced by owners.

The power unit betrayed some earlier work by Turner and it did not take much intelligence to see that it was based on his Triumph Terrier, dating back to 1953. The C15 was more or less an enlarged edition

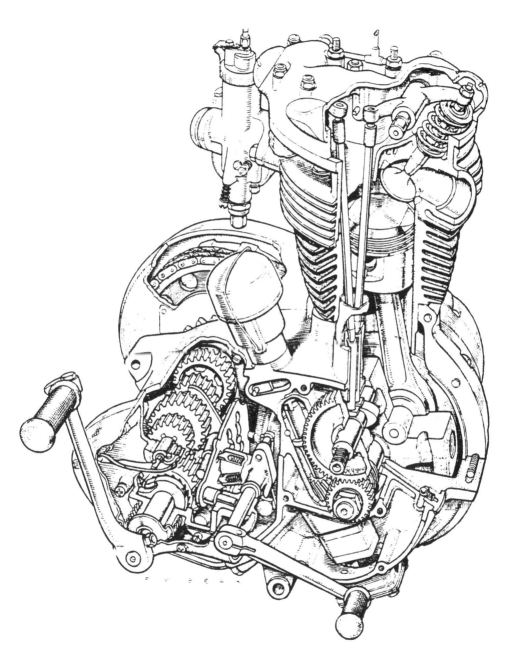

Introduced in September 1958, the 250cc C15 engine formed the basis of a whole new generation of BSA power plants. The drawing shows a pre-1965 version with the dreaded 'lollipop' distributor. (Courtesy The Classic Motorcycle)

with an upright cylinder and a pair of dural pushrods jigging about inside a chrome plated tube, and operated from a single camshaft. The crank drove a double stage gear pump connected to the distributor drive, whilst the opposite end of the crankshaft spun an alternator rotor and a four-spring oil bath clutch, all covered with a stylish alloy chain case. A separate compartment for the four-speed gear-cluster was built into the oval-shaped engine cases and the kickstarter movement was transmitted through a ratchet and pawl mechanism housed inside an outer layshaft gear. This was another ill-considered device that taught many an L-plate novice to master the art of a TT bump start!

The factory's development section played a major part in making something out of Turner's 'commercial' specifications. The single downtube frame opened out at the forward engine mounting lug to form a duplex cradle,

the engine in fact, being offset slightly towards the offside to correct the centre of gravity.

First impressions given by journalists and owners alike ranged from moderately favourable to greatly excited. The new 250's smoothly valanced mudguards stood up well to the first winter, a set of 17in wheels kept the saddle height down to just 30in (76cm), and both brakes and handling earned a big tick. A blast around the MIRA proving ground registered 78mph (125kph) on the Smiths speedo, with a remarkable and miserly consumption figure of only 90mpg (3.14l/100km) at a steady all day cruising speed of 50mph (80kph). Some owners found it difficult to come to terms with BSA's habit-breaking, up-for-up gearchange and worried about the apparently high running temperature of the gearbox living next door to the engine department.

A dependable motorcycle with a clean appearance and a reasonable price ensured a good order book for the C15 250 Star, first introduced in 1958. (BSA Archive)

Model	C15 Sports Star 80 (1961)	B40 Sports Star 90 (1962)
Engine type	Single Cylinder OHV	Single Cylinder OHV
Bore × stroke	67mm × 70mm	79mm × 70mm
Capacity	247cc	343cc
Comp ratio	8.75:1	8.75:1
Claimed power	20bhp at 7,250rpm	24bhp at 7,000rpm
Carburation	Amal 376 monobloc	Amal 389 monobloc
Gearbox	Four-speed	Four-speed
Ratios	12.6; 9.9; 7.2; & 6.0:1	12.2; 5.6; 6.9; & 5.8:1
Tyres, front	17in dia × 3¼in	18in dia × 3¼in
rear	17in dia × 3¼in	18in dia × 3½in
Brakes, front	6in dia × ⅞in	7in dia × 1⅛in
rear	6in dia × ⅞in	6in dia × ⅞in
Suspension front	Telescopic	Telescopic
rear	Swing-arm	Swing-arm
Wheelbase	51¼in	52½in
Weight	288lb	316lb
Fuel capacity	3 gall.	3 gall.
Top speed	83mph	85mph

A couple of off-road versions of the C15 were proclaimed to the sporting enthusiasts in February 1959. A 20in front tyre with an 18in rear created the necessary ground clearance, while careful selection of gear ratios, high level exhaust and a host of other requirements for the rough and tumble were specified for both the C15S Scrambler and the C15T Trials. Prototype models entered by works riders had already begun to show that the days of the big banger were doomed as the lightweight C15-derived models skipped over any obstacle and were certainly easier to control. Both sportsters had a shortened seat and a sump guard. Lacking lighting gear and battery, the alternator worked on an energy transfer system that fell well short of expectations and few could fathom it out.

It was two and a half years before a road-going sports model appeared. The 1961 C15 Sports Star 80 cashed in on new legislation that restricted learners to 250cc. Boasting a caged roller big-end instead of the original, fragile plain shell type bearing, the C15 SS80 also had a larger inlet valve, a little more cam lift and a high 8.75:1 compression ratio to match. Classed as a genuine 80mph (130kph) plus, 250cc sportster, it certainly looked the part with lashings of chrome plate contrasted against a royal blue finish; the magazines queued up to try one out.

Motor Cycling found that the 20bhp motor delivered a maximum speed as high as its name implied with plenty of 'hang on hard acceleration'. In common with its standard version, its light clutch and snappy gear-changes meant that it could get about very quickly, and all this for less than £190.

Resembling an overgrown 'Ceefer', the long-awaited replacement to the 350cc B31 was presented at the annual show at Earls Court in October 1960. Intended as a general purpose, 'everyman's' model at a rock-bottom price of £205 all-in, the B40 350 Star took on the role of the middle-weight challenger. Standing on 18in wheels, the B40 was slightly taller than the C15, and its distin-

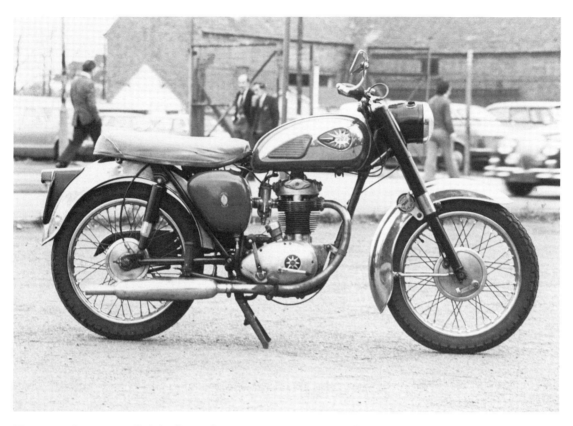

The tuned B40 was called the Sports Star 90 on account of a claimed top speed of 90mph (145kph). Certainly one of the fastest 350s to be built by BSA, its larger inlet valve and cam profiles were handed down from the company's victorious scrambling machines. (OW)

guishing feature was a cast-in pushrod tunnel and a 7in diameter front brake. In a fairly gentle state of engine tune, its over-square 3.1in × 2.7in (79mm × 70mm) motor thrived on revs, pulled like a 500cc and yet handled as well as a 250cc lightweight. *Motor Cycle Mechanics* had one for the weekend and kept it cruising easily between 65 and 70mph (105 and 112kph) on half throttle. From a standing start it raced up to 50mph (80kph) in just 7.5 seconds flat.

If that was not enough, a B40 Sports Star 90 came about for 1962. Rated as one of the

fastest 350ccs ever to carry BSA badges it conformed to the usual tuning tricks of high compression piston, aggressive cam profiles and a large inlet valve. And could it do 90mph (145kph)? Well, the author had a 1965 'lolli-pop' distributor SS90 and still occasionally wakes up in the middle of the night in a cold sweat after re-living those experiences in the nether regions of peak revs in top gear – pity that the erratic movement of a poor magnetic speedometer never told the truth. . .

The C15 eventually finished up as the Sportsman in 1966, its last year, by which

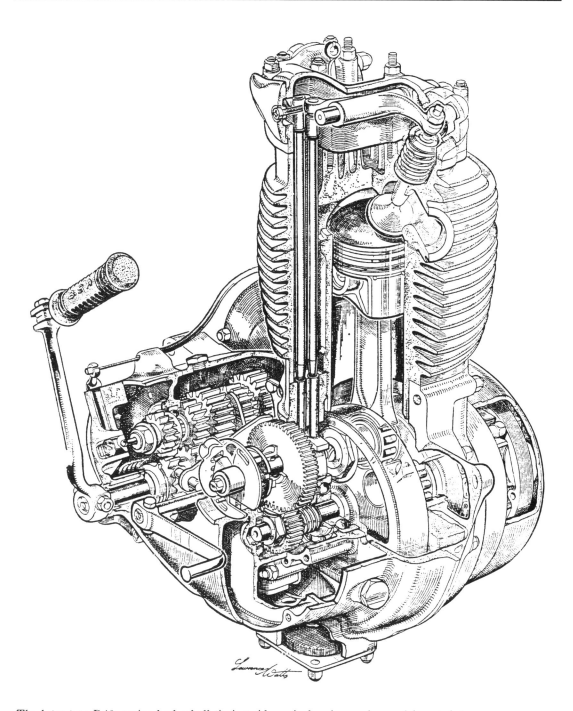

The later type B40 engine had a ball timing side main bearing and cam driven points developed from BSA's competition successes. (Courtesy The Classic Motorcycle*)*

143

In 1967, after a lengthy 10,000 mile (16,100km) reliability test programme, the army placed a large order for B40s. An all-enclosed rear chain case and in-line oil filter went a long way towards making the B40WD a very tough and tractable motorcycle. (BSA Archive)

time it had gone through many changes. For 1965, the contact-breaker points were mounted on the side of the engine, taking the drive from the cam pinion. Double row roller big-end bearings were fitted to both the 250cc and 350cc models, while the C15 Sportsman even had a roller timing-side main bearing instead of the dubious bronze bush, which bore an extra burden of responsibility by acting also as an oil distributor.

Sales of the C15 had been very high and had provided BSA with at least one outstanding financial success during the 1960s. The B40, however, was not quite so lucky, and the days of the all-encompassing 350 were over. It did have a brief new lease of life in 1967, when the British Army placed an order for 2,000 B40s built to a special WD specification which included an in-line oil filter, fully enclosed chain case and the welcome return of the old and faithful QD crinkle hub rear wheel. But for a dismally restricted butterfly valve carburettor, the gently tuned B40WD has since been regarded within BSA Owners Club circles as one of the most reliable and tractable singles produced in the 1960s.

The B40 also formed the basis of Jeff Smith's world beating Grand Prix scrambling machines. In return, many of the improvements that stood up to the test of moto-cross were paid back into the development of the unit single BSA. A special BSA group supplement was issued in November 1966 which outlined the new replacement for the C15. 'Britain's fastest production two-fifty' it said, 'into which BSA boffins have ploughed all the know-how which gained them two World Moto-cross Championships.' Called the C25 Barracuda, it featured 12 volt electrics, two-way damped forks and a glass-fibre tank. Inside the engine there was a one-piece forged steel crank with radially bolted flywheels running on roller drive-side and ball timing-side main bearings. The boffins, so it transpired, must have got their sums wrong, since the C25 plain shell type big-end bearing did not take many miles of punishment before it extruded itself from its original shape.

The next year the C25 became B25 Starfire, taking the name from a USA export single. Legislation forced the tank to be re-made from steel, while the square-finned all-alloy engine eventually reverted back to a roller big-end. Some enthusiasts may have

scoffed, but the B25 Starfire was rated as the fastest 250cc roadster of its era, with all the feel and sound of a 'big single'. If riders did not like starting that high 10:1 compression engine they could opt for the milder B25 Fleetstar – as its name suggested, this was a latter day attempt at catching bulk order contracts for government and private despatch duties. Usually it came complete with BSA-Motoplas windscreen, panniers and even a pair of legshields!

The 1965 B44 GP carried many of the features of the 'Victor Scrambler'. It had a hard-chrome plated alloy barrel with the piston stroke extended to 3.5in (90mm) giving a swept volume of 441cc. For 1966, it was available as the Victor Roadster, a semi-road-trail machine with an odd mix of humped seat, polished chrome colour with a bright yellow Victor Scrambler tank and an exhaust that wormed its way over the engine cases to a small cigar-shaped silencer hovering just above the rear swing-arm pivot. The square-

Model	B25 Starfire (1968)	B44 Shooting Star (1968)
Engine type	Single Cylinder OHV	Single Cylinder OHV
Bore × stroke	67mm × 70mm	79mm × 80mm
Capacity	247cc	441cc
Comp ratio	9.5:1	9.4:1
Claimed power	25bhp at 8,000rpm	29bhp at 5,750rpm
Carburation	Amal 928 concentric	Amal 930 concentric
Gearbox	Four-speed	Four-speed
Ratios	18.3; 11.4; 8.6; & 6.9:1	14.2; 8.8; 6.6; & 5.3:1
Tyres, front	18in dia × 3¼in	18in dia × 3¼in
rear	18in dia × 3½in	18in dia × 3½in
Brakes, front	7in dia × 1⅛in	8in dia × 1⅝in
rear	7in dia × 1⅛in	7in dia × 1⅛in
Suspension front	Telescopic	Telescopic
rear	Swing-arm	Swing-arm
Wheelbase	52in	53in
Weight	306lb	342lb
Fuel capacity	2 gall.	3¼ gall.
Top speed	82mph	88mph

The 250cc B25 Starfire typified the later unit-constructed singles. It was a keen performer with lively handling but a little noisy and too highly tuned for everyday practical use. (BSA Archive)

finned cylinder carried a liner and was fed by one of the newly introduced Amal Concentric carburettors. For the following season, a more homely exhaust set was fitted and one of the new style shaped fuel tanks similar to that of the C25 Barracuda.

For some strange reason, known only to a growing army of marketing consultants, the revered Victor name was then changed to Shooting Star, a name previously given to the 1950s A7 alloy head sportster. The 441 single was simply not in the same class as BSA's products of the previous decade. *Motor Cycle Mechanics* magazine was one of the more influential journals of the era and a 1968 article entitled 'Still Single' questioned BSA's motives for holding fast to the high compression single cylinder. In terms of handling, braking and overall quality, the 441 Shooting Star came out well, but its performance against its sister 250 Starfire model was a big disappointment, for those extra 200 cubic centimetres provided little more low-down torque and precious little else. It had a top speed of 80mph (128kph) and took 18.4 seconds for the standing start quarter mile (0.4km) with plenty of 'chunky vibration'. Moreover, the test bike was never in the mood for easy starting.

The final clutch of BSA singles appeared amidst a brave but ill-fated 1971 line-up. They bore some of the long-awaited fruits of the Umberslade Hall 'aero-engineered' concepts. Oil-carrying frames inconveniently

Photographed in the grounds of Umberslade Hall, the 1971 B50 SS 'Gold Star' gave the unit single BSA a last – if short lived – lease of life. (BSA Archive)

painted in dove-grey, conical pattern hubs and a high level exhaust with a stainless-steel perforated guard set the tone of a virile 'Street Scrambler'. Hard for any enthusiast to stomach, was BSA's ill-considered idea to call them 'Gold Stars'. Their main feature was a large spined frame that could carry four pints of oil. The rear swing-arm used needle roller bearings and could be adjusted by a pegged snail cam. The fork legs had light-alloy bottom sliders with two-way damping, controlled by a clack valve, and were pivoted on taper roller bearings instead of grit-grinding ball bearings.

Whereas the 250cc B25 SS Gold Star was virtually a Starfire in new clothing, its 500cc B50 counterpart was more definitely an exciting proposition. Again based on moto-cross developments, it appeared in three forms as the B50 SS Gold Star, B50 T Trail and the B50 MX Scrambler. Bored out to 3.5in (89mm) using the Victor 3.54in (90mm) stroke it was the last of the strong and able big bangers, capable of singeing performance as demonstrated by the Mead and Tomkinson B50 Endurance racer that was stunningly victorious at Barcelona and Holland. With corrected gearing and a larger fuel tank, it

Model	B50 SS (1971)
Engine type	Single Cylinder OHV
Bore × stroke	84mm × 90mm
Capacity	499cc
Comp ratio	10:1
Claimed power	34bhp at 6,200rpm
Carburation	Amal 930 concentric
Gearbox	Four-speed
Ratios	16.0; 10.0; 7.5; & 6.1:1
Tyres, front	18in dia × 3¼in
rear	18in dia × 3½in
Brakes, front	8in dia × 1¼in
rear	7in dia × 1⅛in
Suspension front	Telescopic
rear	Swing-arm
Wheelbase	54in
Weight	308lb
Fuel capacity	2 gall.
Top speed	95mph

could be a very useful tourer capable of high cruising speeds and acceptable vibration levels. From the ashes of the fallen BSA empire, Alan Clews bought up a stock of B50 components and launched the CCM Scramblers that extended the life of the BSA-based unit single until the end of the 1970s. It had come a long way indeed from the peppy little 250cc 'Ceefer'.

9

All Things to All Men

Miscellaneous Machinery

BSA's sixty year history of motorcycle manufacture was littered with countless prototypes and hybrids that ranged from the sensible to the pure bizarre, many of which failed to reach the production stage. Over the years the author has, in his capacity as a sort of BSA 'agony uncle', pulled many strange and wonderful, non-standard items from his regular postbag. Even some of the production models were not immune to the quirks of research and development launched onto an unsuspecting public. I can recall the case of a rare 750cc A10 Golden Flash given a tryout during the mid-1950s, and it is always a delight when a limited production, alternator-powered A10 comes to the surface. Then there is the case of the scarce, long-stroke A65 which was originally sent to the USA, and otherwise known as the 751cc A70, or an extremely rare 350cc version of the C group singles called the C12 that was built for the 1940 civilian catalogue, but actually went across to France with the BEF and became posted as 'missing, presumed dead'.

Against a long list of successes, the company were also quite capable of pulling off the odd spectacular disaster. This chapter will look at a few of these oddities that added a variety of flavours to the BSA story.

By all accounts the BSA-Triumph Scooter was well up to standard. Available with 175cc two-stroke single cylinder or 250cc OHV twin cylinder engine. It was an Edward Turner design sold either as a BSA Sunbeam or a Triumph Tigress. Built in the years 1958–64, it struggled to emulate the more successful and well-entrenched Italian designs. (Loaned by A. G. Cave)

The Terrible Two-stroke

To follow up their resounding success with the immortal 250cc sidevalve, model B Round Tank, BSA tried to go one better and made a tentative stab at building a new ultra-lightweight two-stroke, which appeared as

149

B.S.A. 1.74 h.p. model A29

the model A28 at the 1927 Olympia show. The engine was all of 174cc using a bore and stroke of 2.36in × 2.42in (60mm × 61.5mm) and had a two-ring deflector piston running in a one-piece cylinder head and barrel. A roller big-end bearing sat on a cantilevered pin, while the main shaft carried a pair of gears that ran in constant mesh with a two-speed output shaft, which meant that the flywheels ran backwards! The motor was started by a folding handlever tucked behind an exposed flywheel and connected straight to the main-shaft. The frame was made up of pin-jointed straight tubes, reminiscent of an early Francis Barnet, to tie the price down to just £28 10s. For a few extra shillings the A28 could be ready fitted with maglita lighting set.

The showstand billboard heralded the little stroker with 'Here is a BSA Motorcycle for all the family. From fourteen years of age, including the ladies, it is everyone's motor-cycle.' But no one wanted it. The engine was so puny and utterly gutless that the poor wretched thing could hardly propel itself along. Probably because of the high tooling up costs already committed, BSA stubbornly refused to give in, and instead fitted a tear-drop tank and a few other de-luxe extras and dropped £2 from the price but even so, the huddled masses still would not buy it, so by mid-1930 the model A two-stroke was dead and buried.

In 1939, Small Heath produced a prototype 98cc autocycle codenamed the F10. In many ways this wee little 'putt-putt' carried on a few ideas from the model A but the war killed it off. Eventually the Second World War brought BSA's only resoundingly successful two-stroke – the ex-Wehrmacht, DKW-inspired Bantam.

The Fluid Flywheel Folly

The BSA stand at the Olympia show in November 1933 produced something of a

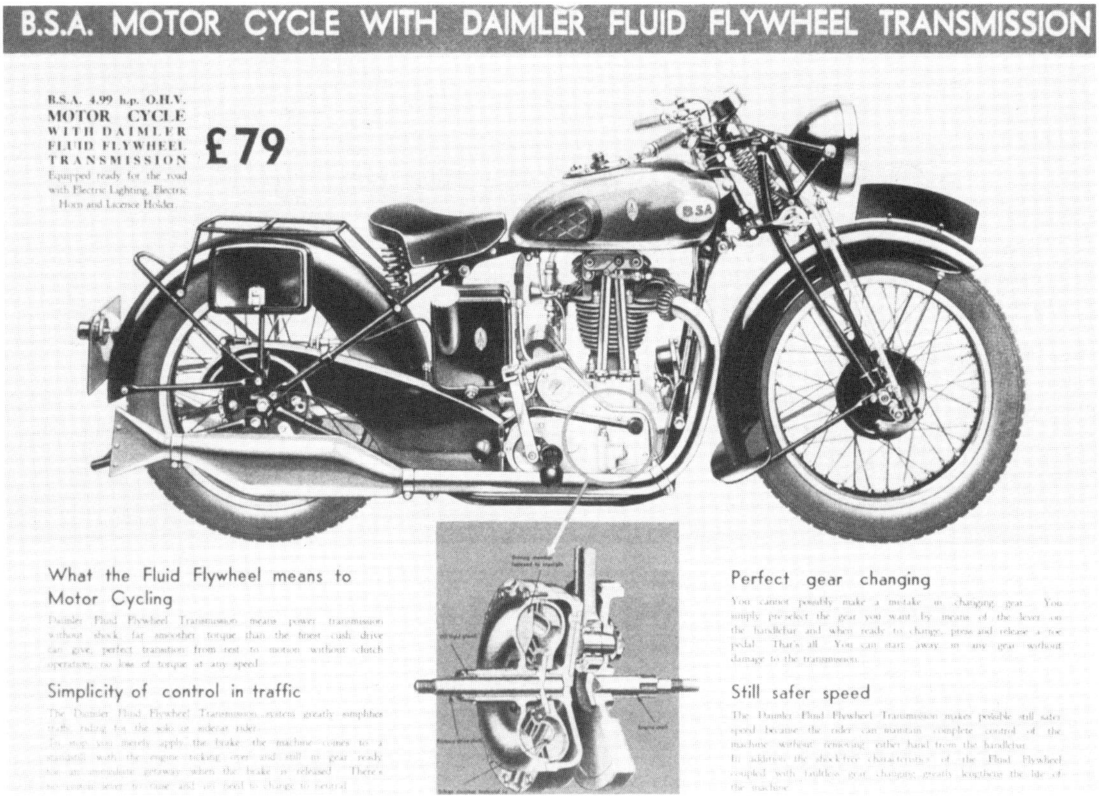

B.S.A. MOTOR CYCLE WITH DAIMLER FLUID FLYWHEEL TRANSMISSION

B.S.A. 4.99 h.p. O.H.V.
MOTOR CYCLE
WITH DAIMLER
FLUID FLYWHEEL
TRANSMISSION
Equipped ready for the road
with Electric Lighting, Electric
Horn and Licence Holder.

£79

What the Fluid Flywheel means to Motor Cycling

Simplicity of control in traffic

Perfect gear changing

Still safer speed

*BSA's 1934 catalogue included a fluid flywheel 500. An ambitious project that failed to
live up to expectations and consequently never reached production. (BSA publicity
photo)*

sensation when a unique twin-port 500cc single with clutchless fluid flywheel transmission and pre-selector three-speed gearbox was put on display. It was the result of a joint venture with BSA's Daimler and Lanchester car-making division who were the acknowledged experts in this ultra-smooth method of power control. At the time, any royal pageant would have been accompanied by an endless column of majestic Daimler motor-cars silently drifting past with only a faint whine coming from the fluid flywheel.

The fluid flywheel used a system of vanes to throw oil by centrifugal force onto an im-

peller, to which the take-off sprocket was attached. A handlebar-mounted lever selected the appropriate gear inside a Wilson epicyclic gearbox, after which a foot pedal engaged the gear to take up the motion. To by-pass the fluid drive, the kickstart drove the crankshaft through a separate gear train.

Only a handful of privileged riders took up the opportunity to ride the show-prepared model FF BSA. All were totally enchanted by the machine but just how many fluid flywheel equipped BSA motorcycles were actually built remains a mystery. Some reports indicated that the show model was one of a batch

151

of eight – after all, it was featured in a full colour catalogue for 1934 and a considerable amount of tooling up had been prepared. At £70, the FF was very expensive – £52 10s bought a 500cc Blue Star – and the Daimler-Lanchester drive absorbed too much power, making the machine hopelessly slow. It was a brave attempt by BSA to show some innovation but it unfortunately came at a time when the market was severely depressed.

For Gentlemen Only

The Sunbeam S7 and later S8 were pure BSA engineering from tip to tail and yet they are seldom found at any gathering of BSAs. And all because of that badge on the fuel tank.

As early as 1943, Jimmy Leek wanted to produce an up-market model in readiness for a return to post-war production. Leek had paid good money for the posh Sunbeam name during the war and set a car and bus designer, Erling Poppe, onto the task of building a 'gentleman's motorcycle' in order to capture the luxury end of the two-wheeler market.

Poppe's design for BSA's new Sunbeam division was based on a pre-prepared brief that included an old experimental two cylinder, overhead-cam engine that had been lying about at Small Heath since 1932. The main criteria included such needs as rider comfort, big 'wallowy' tyres, soft suspension and a clean appearance with no external clutter – supposedly all the things that motorcyclists had been carping about for years.

The production prototype, completed dur-

The first all-black Sunbeam S7 with rigid engine mountings prior to despatch to South Africa. Later rubber mounted S7s were painted mist-green with orange badges. (BSA Archive)

Miscellaneous Models

Model	Sunbeam S7 (1945–57)
Engine type	Twin Cylinder In-line OHC
Bore × stroke	70mm × 63.5mm
Capacity	487cc
Comp ratio	6.5:1
Claimed power	25bhp at 5,800rpm
Carburation	Amal 376
Gearbox	Four-speed
Overall ratios	14.5; 9.0; 6.5; & 5.3:1
Tyres, front	16in dia × 4¾in
rear	16in dia × 4¾in
Brakes, front	8in dia
rear	8in dia
Suspension front	Telescopic
rear	Swing-arm
Wheelbase	57in
Weight	434lb
Fuel capacity	3½ gall.
Top speed	70mph

ing the last days of the war, was built around a hefty looking all-alloy engine with its cambox, cylinder head, block and sump all piled up one on top of the other. The twin-in-line OHC unit was over-square at 2.7in × 2.49in (70mm × 63.5mm) (478cc). A neat looking shaft drive on the off-side drove the rear hub through an underslung worm and wheel. Even Lucas had contributed a special pancake dynamo that protruded from the front of the cylinder block. In all, the Sunbeam 'car on two wheels' had some thirty patents lodged against it. Surprisingly it had no electric start, instead a kick-start lever had to transmit through bevel gears to retain a conventional backward swing.

The first Sunbeam S7s came off the Redditch factory production line finished in gloss black, and were hurriedly shipped off to South Africa to act as escorts for a visit by King George VI. They were soon back! The first in a series of disasters had struck as chronic vibration rendered the machines virtually unridable. With everyone in a mad panic, the problem was eventually solved by using rubber bushes to act as anti-vibration engine mountings. This worked well enough, but then they realized that the exhaust pipe needed a flexible joint at the silencer box.

On paper at least, a claimed output of 25bhp at 5,800rpm was considered quite good, almost up to the power of an OHV twin A7, but the hopelessly inefficient rear hub sapped and stifled any life trying to get to the tyre. Top speed was a mere 80mph (130kph), with sluggish acceleration to match. On the credit side, the air-cooled engine was exceptionally quiet, the pair of Y-alloy pistons could only be heard when the engine was cold and the valve gear was commendably noiseless.

With a monstrous £175 price tag slapped on the S7, sales were doomed to be no more than a trickle. The Sunbeam division instigated an unfruitful salvage operation by giving the S7 a new, all-over lick of mist-green paint (the same as the D1 Bantam built on the adjoining track) and an orange badge. In 1949, a lightened S8 version appeared with standard tyres and a front fork assembly arrangement taken straight from the A7. S8 colours were either silver-grey or black. Both models dawdled on to a silent and ignominious withdrawal in late 1957.

The OHC in-line twin layout could have opened up countless opportunities. Plans had been drawn up to shift the carburettor to the near side, and cross-flow the cylinder head, but that final drive clamped a limit on input power. Although a higher compression model was offered, the Sunbeam luxury twin remained a docile softie and it never achieved the popularity it may have deserved.

Had the MC1 racer gone to plan, it could have formed the basis of a whole new generation of low-slung single cylinder models. In the event, this futuristic design was relegated to the back-burner. (OW)

The MC1 Racer

This is a sad and unfortunate story of an inspired, purpose-built racing machine that failed because of politics. Bert Hopwood answered his managing director's call for a new breed of racing machine and during his initial (and brief) period as a forward product designer, he laid down a scheme for a 250cc four-valve, overhead-cam, single cylinder performance engine. The cylinder lay in a virtually horizontal position to keep the centre of gravity close to the ground.

Work on the A10 Golden Flash and all the general hurly-burly of the drawing office relegated the 250cc racer drawings to the shelf until Hopwood's assistant, Doug Hele, picked up the drawings once more in 1951.

Two carburettors, each having their own inlet tract, fed an over-square cylinder measuring 2.7in × 2.5in (70mm × 64.5mm). The frame was revolutionary for the time, using Reynolds famous 531 tubing built to a triangulated rear arm pattern and damped by a single shock absorber mounted underneath the seat. The steering headstock had cross-over bracing, while the forks had leading link geometry modelled on an Earles type principle.

On a test track, the secret racer code-named MC1, pushed out 32bhp at 10,250rpm. Charlie Salt ran it around the MIRA test track at 100mph (160kph) to prove its durability. Geoff Duke later put in thirty laps at Oulton park and even without a fairing, the MC1 showed an impressive and competitive edge. Then everything started to go horribly wrong. . .

Duke was so thrilled with the MC1 that he entered it for a forthcoming race as a GDS (Geoff Duke Special). The press and television people got to hear about the origins of the GDS and spurious claims began to appear in the papers. Back at BSA, James Leek, not wishing to plunge BSA into another repeat of the 1921 'terrible TT' realized that failure on the race track would ruin all prospects for future models based on the MC1 idea. He personally hauled Hopwood and Hele over the coals about the press leaks and demanded a promise that should the bike race, it must be *guaranteed* to win. Faced with such an impossible task, especially as the MC1 had not even completed its development programme, Doug Hele reluctantly withdrew the machine from the starting list, effectively writing out the death warrant for one of BSA's most astonishing post-war racing projects.

Winged Wheels

Whereas the mainstream rash of post-war clip-on bicycle motors powered a tyre-shredding friction roller, BSA's beautifully designed and made Winged Wheel unit was a complete add-on assembly consisting of a double reduction drive and multi-plate clutch contained within the rear hub. For £25, it came complete with a fuel tank, control cables and fixing kit. Later, it could also be bought ready installed in a BSA-built, sprung fork ladies' or gents' style cycle, and included a lighting set powered by a coil from a Wipac flywheel-magneto. BSA published some performance figures that rated the 1.41in × 1.37in (36mm × 35mm) (35cc) two-stroke at 1bhp at 6,000rpm, good enough for a cruising speed of 25mph (40kph) . . . on the flat! The slightest up-gradient called for generous helpings of LPA (light pedal assistance). The

Model	W1 Winged Wheel (1953–57)
Engine type	Single Cylinder two-stroke
Bore × stroke	36mm × 34mm
Capacity	35cc
Comp ratio	6.5:1
Claimed power	1bhp at 6,000rpm
Carburation	Amal type 335/1
Gearbox	Single-speed
Ratio	18.7:1
Tyres, front	26in dia × 1¼in
rear	26in dia × 1¾in preferred
Brakes, front	3in dia × ½in
rear	9½in dia × ⅝in
Suspension front	Webb, parallel link
rear	Rigid
Wheelbase	44in
Weight	27lb (Engine unit only)
Fuel capacity	½ gall.
Top speed	25mph (flat surface!)

Winged wheeler. The engine unit was designed to fit any cycle frame but BSA soon supplied a complete machine with webb sprung forks, while a ladies' frame could also be specified. (OW)

half-gallon (2.27 litre) petrol tank lasted for 100 miles (161km) and the silencer had to be stripped down every 1,000 miles to scrape out the carbon-coated barnacles. But did 'Mr and Mrs Winged Wheel user' ever get used to the lawnmower type controls and a front brake swopped over onto the left hand handlebar?

The W1 Winged Wheel was made at BSA's subsidiary 'New Hudson' factory in Coventry Road, Birmingham. Unfortunately, the clip-on engine mania was almost over by the time it came about in May, 1953 and when BSA's cycle interests were sold to Raleigh in 1957, this simple, charming device, unkindly nick-named 'the Stink-Wheel' faded away.

Dandy Days

Another two-stroke utility that failed badly was Bert Hopwood's idea for a light-weight scooter using a pressed steel open chassis and an ingenious two-speed pre-selector gear mechanism. Its low-slung engine had ball and roller bearings throughout and its pressed-steel banana-shaped spine included a weather shield. With soft rear damping, 15in diameter wheels, effective leading link forks and safe brakes this fuel-miserly run-about should have had a rosy future. Instead, the BSA Dandy 70 Scooterette has long been misunderstood on two accounts. Firstly, when Hopwood departed BSA in 1955, he left behind a design scheme calling for a high, heat-dissipating, alloy barrel with a chrome plated bore. His terms were based on the belief that such a technological advance was well within the realms of the BSA industrial empire, since BSA Monochrome Ltd were then the leaders in the field of metal coatings. However, persons unknown decided to take a cheap view of the matter and fashioned the cylinder out of good old cast-iron at once

Standard Dandy riding gear was a bobble hat and Mum's leatherette gloves. Even with an ingenious two-speed pre-selector gearbox, few novices chose a Dandy 70 for their first bike. (BSA Archive)

condemning the poor Dandy to suffer piston seizures. Secondly, when launched for the 1956 programme, the trade and press castigated the flimsily-constructed Dandy for having its ignition contact-breaker points inconspicuously hidden inside the engine. This was a harsh treatment for Hopwood's judgement that most Dandy owners would have had their machines serviced by a BSA-approved agent and that it was also reasonable to assume that the points would not require any attention between 10,000-mile (16,100km) services. As it happened, few Dandys ever went past that milestone before needing a premature and unwelcome over-haul to replace a seized piston!

Had BSA's technicians engineered it correctly the Dandy could have pre-empted the Japanese step-thru of later years. Instead,

Model	Dandy Scooterette (1956–62)	K1 Beagle (1963–65)
Engine type	Single Cylinder two-stroke	Single Cylinder OHV
Bore × stroke	45mm × 44mm	47.6mm × 42mm
Capacity	70cc	75cc
Comp ratio	7.25:1	9.0:1
Claimed power	–	–
Carburation	Amal 365/1	Amal type 19
Gearbox	Two-speed pre-selector	Four-speed
Overall ratios	21.2; & 9.7:1	34.4; 23.8; 15.1; & 11.5:1
Tyres, front	15in dia × 2½in	19in dia × 2¼in
rear	15in dia × 2½in	19in dia × 2¼in
Brakes, front	4in dia × ⅞in	4½in dia × ⅞in
rear	4in dia × ⅞in	5in dia × ⅝in
Suspension front	Leading link	Leading link
rear	Swing-arm	Swing-arm
Wheelbase	40in	46in
Weight	115lb	140lb
Fuel capacity	¾ gall.	2 gall.
Top speed	40mph	48mph

Dandy production staggered on in small doses until 1962.

Ladybird, Ladybird, Fly Away Home. . .

There was the Messerschmitt, the Heinkel, the BMW-built Isetta and even the Goggomobile, those dinky little bubble cars that spluttered about the place in the 1950s. But what about the one that BSA built? This was a quaint little run-about that came of age far too late to be of any interest.

It was really a desperate attempt by Edward Turner to find another use for his 249cc OHV twin, Sunbeam scooter engine. A milk-float was the first idea but eventually they opted for the bubble-car theme. Starting as a Triumph project, BSA's Carbodies plant got involved in the development work when the job got underway in 1960. This blimpish little object that could only ever have been an

The only known BSA Ladybird to survive has recently turned up in the USA. It was powered by a 250cc OHV twin cylinder engine originally intended for the BSA-Sunbeam Scooter. (Anon.)

157

Lady and the tramp. The Beagle had a 75cc OHV engine and plenty of pressed-steel construction. It was a dismal failure and BSA finally lost the art of making small capacity motorcycles. (BSA Archive)

interim stepping stone between motorcycle combination and a 'nice little car' was to be sold as a BSA Ladybird carrying a price tag of £285. Someone even suggested a paint finish of red with a few black spots! Its lack of a reverse gear meant that sixteen year olds could drive it with L-plates, but by 1962 when a second prototype was under review the bubble had really burst as the Issigonis BMC Mini put paid to any further work. The first prototype was last heard of in the USA – but we'll never know if it could have knocked the spots off a Messerschmitt!

Every Dog Has Its Day

How could anyone take a motorcycle seriously if it was adorned with a name like 'Beagle'? Edward Turner's whimsical 75cc four-stroke was brought out for 1964 in answer to the demands of a marketing survey. As he had done with the 250cc C15, he had gone back to his old Triumph Terrier drawings, sketched out a pressed steel frame to carry the motor and then left designer, Ernie Webster to hold the pup.

Turner's specification, in fact, called for

two models, a 50cc Ariel Pixie and the 75cc BSA Beagle (surely 'Whippet' would have been a better choice?). Both engines used the same 1.6in (42mm) stroke but the Beagle's cylinder was bored out to 1.8in (47.6mm).

In theory, the Pixie/Beagle design had some very interesting features. Both used the same cylinder head with an elliptoidal combustion chamber – well, that's what they called it! The rocker gear was said to have 'stalactitic' lubrication, which was purported to be a projection cast into the underside of the rocker inspection cap so that oil mist would collect on the end and form a drip feed onto the rocker. And that was not all – its incredibly complicated wet-sump oiling system employed a rotary breather, oil pockets, ante-chambers and a labyrinth of internal oilways. The crankshaft was a two-piece forging with integral bobweights, pushed around by an H section con-rod and located with a burnished surface big-end bush. A four-speed gearbox rather like a scaled down C15 cluster was driven by a pair of gears inside the primary drive case and to reduce weight, a clutch drum was omitted by using the clutch plates as the driven gear.

When it was launched in 1963, the press actually said some very kind things about how it would hold 40mph (65kph) and make a top speed jutting past the 50mph (80kph) mark whilst its fuel consumption was a remarkable 155mpg (1.8l/100km). With a two gallon fuel tank it had a very long range between fuel stops and a Wipac lighting set provided primitive but effective electrics. Although it was a get-to-work bike, it had some sporty looks with a readily accessible over-hung engine, 19in wheels and a leading link front fork.

At £92, in the days when roadtax was just £1, it was expected to be a winner. It was not. The K1 Beagle flopped badly, getting a sound thrashing in the market place from the functional and attractively priced Honda step-thru. Mickey Mouse engineering was one of the common terms used by long-suffering BSA agents.

It was never likely to be a worthy replacement to the Bantam. A change of colour scheme in 1965, from green to royal red and ivory did not make a scrap of difference. In America it was sold as an ultra-light sports 'Starlite'. Grave doubts remain as to whether there were any takers and in the following year the Beagle was finally put to sleep.

In its short and unhappy life it had suffered many weaning troubles. Jack Harper, for many years the life and soul of BSA's service department, was once given a Beagle to try out and had nothing but trouble with its big-end bearing, until someone who happened to be a Rolls-Royce bearing expert, paid a visit by chance to the service shop and spent most of his lunch hour chalking out a suggested re-design!

Raging Fury

Edward Turner bounced back out of retirement with a burning desire to build a 'hot 350' for the price of a cheap 250. Working in a freelance capacity, he was given some space in the corner of the Redditch works and by 1968 he had come up with a twin cylinder, double-overhead-cam unit slung into what was virtually a lightweight Triumph Tiger Cub frame. In prototype form, it circulated the MIRA test track at well over 100mph (160kph) from 27bhp at 8,000rpm. It also looked sensational, as so many ET productions did, a tribute to his amazing talent for putting the right shapes and proportions together. Something very special was clearly in the air – it was after all, the first completely

One of only a handful of BSA Fury 350cc OHC twins. In truth it was badly engineered and would have needed an extensive re-design if it was to save BSA-Triumph. (OW)

new British design since the 1958 Ariel Leader. Yet Turner still went back to his old Triumph Speed Twin sketches for inspiration for camshaft profiles.

The engine unit was raked forwards and a one-piece 180 degree crankshaft sat on ball and roller main bearings powering a pair of chain and gear-driven camshafts. Further work raised its power output up to 34bhp at 9,000rpm driving through a five-speed gearbox. Turner wanted it to be a Triumph and came up with the name Toledo, but the car people pinched the name before it could be safely registered. By then BSA's ruling class

were getting excited about the bike and started to move into the operation.

The money-spending Umberslade Hall Research Establishment started to play about with it, made a few changes to the engine and planted it into a new duplex cradle frame, but other than that the precious time was being wasted on deciding names and colour schemes. They finally opted for a garish metallic purple aptly named 'Plum Crazy' and badge-engineered the names as Triumph Bandit and BSA Fury. As if oblivious to the machines' somewhat flimsy proportions and skimped design the Bandit and Fury

160

Model	Fury 350 (1971)
Engine type	Twin Cylinder OHC
Bore × stroke	63mm × 56mm
Capacity	349cc
Comp ratio	9.5:1
Claimed power	35bhp at 9,000rpm
Carburation	2 × Amal 926 concentric
Gearbox	Five-speed
Overall ratios	17.2; 12.0; 9.0; 7.4; & 6.4:1
Tyres, front	18in dia × 3¼in
rear	18in dia × 3½in
Brakes, front	8in dia × 1½in
rear	7in dia × 1⅛in
Suspension front	Telescopic
rear	Swing-arm
Wheelbase	58½in
Weight	340lb
Fuel capacity	2½ gall.
Top speed	95mph

appeared for the first time at a big posh London dinner in November 1970 and dealers started to take bookfuls of orders.

Bert Hopwood remained sceptical about it, and insisted on a test and development programme. The ruling regime scoffed at his suggestion and started to tool up for it. On the test bench, the prototype smashed its way through two crankshafts and gulped down four pints (2.2 litres) of oil during the equivalent of 100 miles (161km). It was noisy, it rattled and was self-destructive – within 4,000 miles (6,440km) the whole power unit had to be re-built four times. After a lot of persuasion, heart-searching and intense argument, the panic button was thumped, killing off the BSA Fury once and for all. It might well have been the bike which could have saved BSA/Triumph; instead it cost them a fortune and actually contributed to the company's ultimate demise. It remains nothing more than a memory of an empty promise.

10

Competition Glory

Star Riders

Mention of BSA's competition history always throws up talk about the Gold Star and its total domination of 1950s production racing through to its total steal of the Isle of Man Clubmans TT races from 1948 onwards. The story reached its ultimate conclusion in the 1956 races when Bernard Codd won both the Junior 350cc and Senior 500cc titles – no one

Phil Palmer is congratulated by BSA Managing Director James Leek after winning the 1954 Junior Clubmans TT at a new record speed of 81.83mph (131.66kph). Of the forty-nine starters, forty two were BSAs. Eight machines retired. (Loaned by A. G. Cave)

else, it seemed, would come out to play so an avenue of great pleasure for BSA was effectively closed off.

But there was more to BSA's racing past than the Gold Star. Taking full stock of Small Heath's sixty year involvement in motorcycle sport, BSA won more trophies than any other British factory in every section of competition. Long before the calamitous and embarrassing TT saga in 1921 there had been some notable successes. In 1913, Kenneth Holden, acting chief machine tester entered a standard 3½hp '500' at Brooklands and came out a clear winner, knocking aside some of the big names, notably the Collier brothers and their much fancied Matchless.

Gold Stars aside, race track antics were for the best part spasmodic and when the initials BSA appeared in print it was either due to a speed test session or to the noble efforts of a privateer. And the Isle of Man was not the only happy hunting ground. In

the early 1950s, factory-tuned racers were shipped over the Atlantic to take part in the Daytona races and the honours did not all go to the Gold Star singles. In the 1954 races, the first two positions were claimed by 500cc A7 Star Twins, with Gold Stars in the next three places.

There was yet another sport where BSA twins totally dominated. . . In 1962, a quite amazing thing happened. BSA won a full TT title! Chris Vincent's astounding sidecar victory came completely out of the blue; certainly, his A7-powered kneeler outfit was competitive but it wasn't expected to trouble the highly laudable BMW outfits piloted by Florian Camathias and Max Deubel. But when the former crashed into an embankment and the latter's engine seized into a solid mass, the road to a memorable victory lay open. The last time a British sidecar outfit had won the TT was way back in 1924! Chris Vincent's series of BSA twin cylinder-

Chris Vincent and passenger Eric Bliss get up a head of steam at Mallory Park. (BSA Archive)

Eddie Dow The Gold Star King (1924–)

Captain W. E. Dow RASC, riding a BSA Gold Star, led a volunteer Army 'A' team in the 1951 International Six Days' Trial held at Trieste, and collected a matching Gold medal in the process. Thus began a long and glorious association with the Gold Star.

Applying a meticulous approach to preparation of both men and machines in true military style, Captain Dow's action was decorated with a full set of gold medals for all the team in the 1952 event. Already mentioned in despatches, Dow, albeit in an amateur role, was 'recruited' by BSA when he bought his own BB series Gold Star and made the rapid transition to Clubman racing.

In his first Isle of Man TT he topped the practice leader-board but after carving out an insurmountable lead he crashed badly and spent three months in a traction ward nursing multiple fractures and a punctured lung.

1955 brought a hard fought and thoroughly deserved Senior Clubmans TT victory when the race was held on the Clypse course. Piloting a DB34 Gold Star he won at an average speed of 70.73mph (113.8kph), the bike had been timed at 110mph (177kph) with revs running to an astonishing 7,000rpm. Even then Dow was holding back the throttle, taking care not to spoil an otherwise superb day out.

The oil had hardly been given a chance to cool down before he was at it again! Sharing a ride with team mate Eddie Crooks in a Thruxton nine-hour thriller, they took turns to rattle through 221 laps at a winning average speed of 67.86mph (109.1kph), keeping more than one lap ahead of their nearest rivals.

Eddie Dow left the army in 1957 and set up his own business in Banbury, specializing in Gold Stars, selling both new or rebuilt machines along with a range of top quality racing equipment. His most famous after-sales accessory was a specially developed silencer ideally suited to the large amount of valve overlap found in the Gold Star. As the engine drew breath, the silencer gave out a characteristic twittering song.

In the early 1960s he took an order for a gentleman who wanted a carefully prepared 650cc A10 Super Rocket engine mounted in a Gold Star rolling chassis. This provoked a glut of enquiries at which BSA, keen to shift a stock of sports A10 motors, produced the legendary, road-roasting A10 Rocket Gold Star – a lasting tribute to Eddie Dow, the man who put the gleam, and twitter into the fabulous BSA Goldie.

---

powered combinations spearheaded a generation of famous three-wheeler 'barrowboys' throughout the 1960s and early 1970s. Vincent himself won seven British championship titles in the ten years from 1961.

In solo form, BSA twins were less spectacular but were still capable of pulling off the odd special extra. In 1965, Mike Hailwood flew to victory in the Hutchinson 100 at Silverstone on an A65 Lightning; a year later, the same title was claimed by the people's favourite, John Cooper on an A65 Spitfire. This time

the race was held on the Brands Hatch circuit and the winning speed was an impressive 80.12mph (128.91kph).

The last great vestige of BSA's tarmac adventures came soon after the launch of the 750cc Rocket Three triples in 1969. The first year of racing was spoilt by a combination of teething troubles, pure bad luck and a certain Honda Four. But 1971 proved to be the big year for the bright-scarlet coated Rocket Threes and the long awaited Daytona victory came when Dick Mann found an average

Eddie Dow at work during the 1953 Senior Clubmans TT. After lapping in 26 minutes 51 seconds he was forced to retire on lap three. (Anon.)

speed of 104.73mph (168.5kph) enough to get over the finishing line first. Mike Hailwood had led the first part of the race until his Three dropped a valve, precisely the way it had deprived him of victory in the previous event.

Before the final curtain came down on BSA's competition shop in 1971, there was an exciting series of match races between Great Britain and the USA. All the riders in the Transatlantic races rode either Rocket Threes or similar specification Triumph Tridents, and with all the big names equally 'tooled up' the action gave the full capacity crowds at three meetings some of the tightest racing ever seen. Ray Pickrell riding a

BSA won three of the legs. Yet it was not only an international competition, for there was also tribal contention between the two factions that made up Britain's last great motorcycling empire. The British may have won the series as a whole, but to most, a blue fairing represented a Triumph, while red stood for BSA, and that mattered most of all!

Rough and Tumble

From the earliest times, manufacturers of the new fangled motor-bicycle were ever keen to pit their produce against each other

Three of a kind. Victor Scramblers piloted by (left to right) Brian Povey, Jeff Smith and John Banks, going in leaps and bounds at Hawkestone Park in 1965. (Loaned by A. G. Cave)

and let chance, rider ability and weather elements decide the outcome if machine design and durability failed to provide a clear result.

Before the First World War, the long distance reliability trial presented a test by which a machine could be measured against another. The first trials were a 'point-to-point' affair to assess good time-keeping, and it soon became obligatory practice to place one or two listed hills *en route* in order to weed out any no-hopers. Then came improvements to transmission, stronger frames,

better valve materials and more efficient engines and the trials started to take on awesome ravines, mountainous tracks and water-logged moorland. The observed section was introduced to invoke penalty marks if a rider had to place a foot on the ground to retain balance. In 1924, on Camberley Heath, another type of trial was organized. Instead of a timed and observed section, all the riders set off together in a 'free-for-all' race to the finishing line. 'It'll be a right scramble,' someone remarked, and thus the term 'Scramble'

Winners all. At the 1950 British Experts Trial, Bill Nicholson and ace sidecar man
Harold Tozer share the spoils. Tozer's 'chairman', Jack Wilks also collects some silver and
some hearty congratulations from senior BSA management. (Loaned by Bill Nicholson)

was coined, although 'Moto-cross' was later introduced as a more up-market title for racing over rough ground.

Trials and Scrambles were to be the main theatre of BSA's competition operations after they had discovered from the hard lessons of 1921 that circuit racing held little return. Tourist Trophy racing on the Isle of Man was left to firms such as Velocette and Norton who could spend hard cash on developing race winners. The shrewd businessmen at Small Heath recognized that the time trial and mad scramble presented the true proving ground for machines that had a

more faithful resemblance to the one ordered from the showroom.

Whilst BSA were never an autonomously organized company, their astonishing achievements in the rough and tumble sporting world could be attributed largely to one man, Albert E. Perrigo, the great competition mastermind whose career spanned from 1926 until his retirement in 1968. After just one year with BSA, Perrigo had won a vast array of trophies including the first ever British Experts Trial in 1929 and he continued to win silverware for the next decade until war clouds started to gather again. In his best

John Cooper Rocket Man (1938–)

John Cooper's exploits on BSA machinery lasted for only a relatively short time, but in the two years 1971/72 he gave BSA fans plenty to cheer about when everything else was rapidly going to rack and ruin.

Born in Derby, John began riding in the early 1960s, winning his first international race at Scarborough in 1961 riding a Ray Petty-prepared single cylinder Norton (using outdated machinery to outsmart top class opposition on home circuits was typical of his early successes). Though never a supporter of the Isle of Man Tourist Trophies, his strength lay in short lap racing particularly over the 1.35m (2.17km) Mallory Park Circuit in Leicestershire, where he picked up the nickname 'Mooneyes' on account of his steel-rimmed spectacles. In 1964, having already won a 350cc ACU Star, he won the Mallory staged Race of the Year. From 1966 he enjoyed a useful spell riding Colin Seeley-developed Yamaha twins and picked up his second Race of the Year title in 1970.

In 1971, he managed to loan a works-prepared BSA Rocket Three for the Great Britain versus USA Transatlantic series, and eventually worked his way into the factory team. In the following Mallory Park Race of the Year, he took on Giacomo Agostini and his supposedly invincible MV Augusta and in a long duel, Cooper and Ago slugged it out, constantly exchanging the lead. A large crowd held its breath as they went into the final lap neck and neck, but coming down from Devil's Elbow it was the man with the 'Mooneyes' helmet leading – the red and white BSA stormed over the line first with only inches to spare. A week later, as if to hammer home the point, he beat the legendary Italian again at Brands Hatch. Later in the season, he flew out to California and won the classic 250 miler at Ontario. Then, after a brilliant year, he was voted *Motor Cycle News* Man of the Year.

In 1972, he had another good series of outings on the 750cc triple cylinder BSA, with a worthy win in the MCN sponsored Superbike Championship. But by then the BSA Competition shop had closed down and Cooper transferred to Norton. He broke a leg after a bad accident at Brands Hatch and opted for early retirement. After a career spanning nearly twenty years, John Cooper was the local 'scratcher' come good and the last BSA star rider.

years, he represented Great Britain in six International Six Day Trials for both Vase and Trophy teams and came out with a gold medal on each occasion. If there was one outstanding victory, it was at Merano, Italy, in 1932. On the last day the British team stood on level points with their hosts and went into a deciding fixture based on a one hour speed test. In lashing rain, Perrigo's BSA Blue Star Special faltered as water worked into the spark-plug and snuffed out all life. Undaunted by the prospect of letting team and country down, he breathed new life into his machine and rode the race of his life,

firm footing through the corners like a modern speedway professional to snatch back the honours.

After the war, he built up an invincible trials and scrambles squad, passing on much of his know-how to a long list of star riders who were once the pride of BSA Competition teams. There was Fred Rist, a regular soldier who was given support by BSA and re-paid them with a hatful of wins in all forms of off-road sport. In sidecar events the powerful figure of Harold Tozer recorded five wins in the British Experts Trial making the sport almost his own. Then there was the small

John 'Mooneyes' Cooper rocketing his BSA Three at Mallory Park in 1972. (Loaned by John Cooper)

frame of Johnny Draper who harnessed the power of the Gold Star to win many a fine Scrambles Victory but still demonstrated enough skill and poise to carry off a series of trials wins. There were many others who were spotted and schooled by Bert Perrigo's masterclass, including one young man who passed an interview with the great man and after a modest term in trials sport went on to become the greatest TT and short circuit racer in the post war era. His name was Geoffrey Duke and his long road to fame only began when he asked Perrigo for some assistance with an WD M20 trials machine!

In 1953, Perrigo moved to the sales department and for a brief period, worked with the associate company Ariel Motors, and his place as leader of the Competition team was taken on by former journalist, Dennis Hardwicke, who carried on the Perrigo tradition by selecting the best up-and-coming riders. He was amongst the first to have the vision to see that the brutish Gold Star power plant could not go on for ever and bravely, against many odds, fomented the idea of the Bantam lightweight two-stroke. When he transferred to BSA industrial engine sales in 1957, the responsibilities of carrying on BSA's untouchable tradition were shouldered by Brian Martin, who eventually gained official recognition for the task in 1960. His reign carried on until the closure of the department in 1971. It was primarily a story of how the lowly 250cc C15 was turned into a world beater and the ascent to international championship status of Jeff Smith.

Fred Rist Soldier of Fortune (1906–1995)

Fred Rist was a serving regular in the Second Battalion, Royal Tank Corps in 1938, when he volunteered for motorcycle duties, despite virtually no previous experience on powered two-wheelers. Within the year, he had won his first International Six Days' Trial gold medal, riding a BSA M24 Gold Star for the RTC team when the event was held in Wales.

From Stokesley near Middlesbrough, Fred Rist was a tough farmer's lad turned soldier, who dominated the trials and scrambles scene just before and after the Second World War. After the 1938 ISDT, he was given the use of a BSA works model B25 and picked up a trio of top class awards at the first time of asking and the RTC squad often showed well against many of the top factory entries in team events.

In the Scottish Six Days' Trial, Fred Rist was in an army team that went into the fray riding standard army issue machines. Rist opted for a sidevalve BSA M20 fitted with a 21in front wheel to increase its ground clearance. His tank training must have come in useful for he picked up a silver medal – tank or BSA M20, was there any difference?!

During late August, 1939, Fred was having another go at the ISDT when it was being held at Salzburg, Austria. On the fifth day the Royal Tank Corps team (made up of L/Cpl A. C. 'Paddy' Doyle, Sgt F. M. Rist, and Pte S. 'Jackie' Wood, all riding works-prepared khaki drab Gold Stars) were all still on a clean sheet and heading for victory on Nazi territory when the orders came through that war was imminent and that they should beat a tactical retreat to Switzerland. (A BSA team also with no marks lost had long since scarpered!)

After five years of active overseas service with the RTC, Rist stormed back into the news with an impressive Colmore Cup Trial win in 1946 and followed it up with another clear win in the Victory Cup Trial.

In 1949 he got involved in sand racing and made his presence felt on Pendine Sands in south Wales riding a B32 Gold Star. He also ran an A10 Golden Flash that was capable of ploughing along a beach at 125mph (200kph). Winning on the sand was not only confined to Pendine – at St Andrews in Fife, he beat the Scottish lads on their own beach in every class but one, riding either the A10 or a specially built pre-war 'flying 250' B21.

During the late 1940s, Fred was a regular winner in numerous trials and scrambles events, constantly battling against his arch rival, Bill Nicholson, also riding BSAs. The ACU selected him again for ISDT duty and from 1948 to 1951 he captured a gold medal every time and never got a single penalty mark.

To be near his beloved Pendine Sands, he began to set up a business in Neath in 1952. But before the premises were opened he had one more crack at the ISDT, held in Austria, having been asked by Bert Perrigo to form a BSA trio to ride off-the-peg A7 Star Twins, in an ACU observed expedition. The result of this was the Maudes Trophy victory (the last time it was ever won by a British factory) and an ISDT team trophy brought back from Austria after one of the toughest events ever had destroyed every other British team entered. For Fred Rist, his unblemished ISDT record was still intact, and it was a fitting way to end a really great career.

But to outline all the big names who rode for BSA and to list every entry in the trophy cabinet would only become tedious and moreover trespasses outside the scope of this book. It is only in recent times that anyone has tackled the monumental task of laying out in words the full story of BSA competition success. It was quite fitting that Norman Vanhouse, a former war-time despatch rider with thirty-five years' sales experience with

Fred Rist (far left with plaster on nose!) makes up a Royal Tank Corps Team with R. Gillam (centre) and J. T. Dalby. They clinched the 'Motorcycling Trophy' at the 1938 ISDT. The threesome are mounted on factory-prepared M24 Gold Stars. (Loaned by A. G. Cave)

Ariel and BSA should write the full account (*BSA Competition History* published by Haynes). Norman Vanhouse was well placed within the post-war sporting fraternity to record in detail many of the events and characters; he himself was one of the heroic three who, with pennants flying, won what was probably the greatest all time victory by any British firm – the 1952 ISDT and Maudes Trophy double.

Speedmen and Speedway

About 100 miles (161 km) from Salt Lake City,

USA, lie the Bonneville Saltflats. They measure some fifteen miles (24 km) in length and are about eight miles (13 km) across. On a sparkling white surface, glistening like snow under a hot sun, Gene Thiessen shattered two USA speed records for BSA in 1952.

In class 'C', for standard production machines limited to a maximum allowable compression ratio of 8:1 and a diet of ordinary pump 'gas', Thiessen hurled a 500cc A7 Star Twin along at a measured 123.69mph (199.01kph). For an unlimited dope-tuned class 'A' run, he took a 650cc A10 Golden Flash up to 143.54mph (230.95kph). Both machines were stripped of their respective

Bill Nicholson Ulster's Unapproachable (1917–1994)

For eight blistering years, between 1946 and 1954, Billy Nicholson tore into the post-war trials and scrambles scene giving BSA fifty top awards. The press dubbed him 'the unapproachable Ulsterman'. He was technically and tactically way in front of his rivals and graced the sporting world with his fluent and precise style. Strong as an ox, his short and stocky build blended well with the tough and powerful four stroke singles that dominated post war rough terrain motor sport.

His interest in motorcycles began in 1939 when he was working for a BSA dealer in Belfast. He managed to get his hands on a rare 350cc B30 and managed to get it going quickly enough to scoop up a few wins in the Irish Republic during the war. He began to mix with Artie Bell, a top racer and Rex McCandless whose damped swing-arm rear wheel suspension had revolutionized motorcycle frame design. After a brief spell trying his hand at Grand Pix and grass track racing he started to take up trials and scrambles using a McCandless type framed BSA special.

In his first mainland appearance in 1946, he won the Colmore cup trial and Bert Perrigo snapped up his signature and gave him the free reign of the competition department, where he demonstrated his talent for building forward-thinking, trophy winning machines. The following year, he proved to be equally successful, winning the Cotswold, Lancashire Grand National, Sunbeam point-to-point and a whole host of other trade supported events.

During the 1949 season, he started to use an A7 twin, fitted with lightweight 'C' group forks, a 21in front wheel and a Siamese exhaust system, spurred on by arch rival, Jim Alves' successes on a Triumph twin. The Nicholson A7 was lighter than a 500cc single B34 but it needed a lot of careful development and for Nicholson, hampered by an eye injury sustained during a practice session, the year did not live up to its promise. Even so, he still won all BSA's top National awards before the year was out.

In October 1950, he constructed a trials frame that had the front down tube pulled back to clear the mudguard when the telescopic forks were fully compressed under 'trials conditions'. He also increased the trail from 2½in (63mm) to 4½in (114mm) which greatly improved the weight distribution. Three straight wins in the Southern classic, Scott Trial and British Experts were proof enough that Nicholson had found the correct geometry! It was both lighter and easier to make than the then-existing brazed forged lug design. BSA's policy makers were loath to accept the idea until Bill won Jimmy Leek's approval to have the frame put into production. It later became the chassis on which Eddie Dow's army team competed in the 1951 ISDT.

He then designed and built his own version of the swing-arm frame using a pair of modified girling damper units. It eventually became BSA's standard twin-loop chassis when it was put into production in late 1953. In its 1951 prototype form, Nicholson won the first of his two ACU stars. In passing he won the Scott Trial again with the best performance in both observation and time, probably his greatest victory. His rear-pivoting fork 'special' was seen as his own personal bike, because as a BSA works rider he was under obligation to ride the relatively-outdated plunger sprung machinery.

Increasingly discouraged by BSA's complacent attitude and lack of interest in his ideas, Bill became deeply involved with a prototype 250cc racer (the MC1 project) and when the order was issued to withdraw the machine because it could not be 'guaranteed to win', Bill Nicholson left and took up a development engineering job with Jaguar Cars.

In 1968, he was offered a top job by Herbert Hopwood and Bert Perrigo, whose primary intention was doing away with the blighted, money-guzzling, Umberslade Hall Research Establishment. After giving the offer some consideration, he declined the position, having already built up his own garage business. Who knows what may have happened if William Nicholson's outspoken and forthright methods had been returned to BSA?

fenders and other unnecessary fittings. Mr Thiessen himself wore only the flimsiest of tee-shirts, jeans and a pair of baseball boots. It was a pity that the people back home in Small Heath did not make any further mileage out of the event otherwise there could well have been a BSA A10 Bonneville!

But what about the humble M20 that managed to reach 103mph (165kph)? This occurred in Tasmania during 1960 when B. W. Chaplin fitted 'Goldie' cams and a special 6:1 compression ratio piston into a 500cc side-valve rigid frame M20. The inlet tract was blanked off to enable a 1⅛in (28mm) Amal TT carburettor, located in a position down by the tappet chest, to blast an updraught feed into the combustion chamber. Apart from that, the rest of the old stager used standard M20 components. The engine was reputed to wind up to a keen 7,000rpm. This certainly puts things into perspective considering the way an ordinary, off the-shelf M20 putted and panted with only a 5:1 compression ratio!

Kicking Up Cinders

Speedway came to us from the other side of the globe in the late 1920s. An Australian dirt-field race developed into a fully fledged sport with purpose-built cinder tracks laid down from the residue of coal fired industry. Some stadiums such as Coventry's Brandon or Manchester's Belle Vue, were built from scratch, but most were adapted greyhound tracks. Speedway, or dirt-track as it was more commonly known, became a craze and it called for a new kind of sportsman – hard gutsy riders, who could still glide a snarling motorcycle with finesse and grace around four corners. The greatest of these men was Jack Parker.

In 1928, Jack Parker was working in BSA's experimental department, test riding and fault finding anything the factory gaffers wanted checking over. While on a weekend trip to Wales with Bert Perrigo, a message from Small Heath HQ instructed them to make a diversion and head for the newly set-up Kings Oak track near Ilford and investigate the inaugural meeting of British League dirt-track racing. Jack was riding a 500cc Sloper Combination, while Bert was on a 350cc upright single. There and then, the BSA lads decided to 'have a go'. Jack unhitched the chair, took the lights off and replaced the large three-gallon (17-litre) fuel tank with something smaller found lying about in a nearby garage. Neither Jack nor Bert Perrigo knew how to 'broadside' but in the first race, a handicap, Jack took full advantage of the generous lead the organizers gave him and romped home a clear winner!

Although Jack Parker was really a trials expert (winner of the 1928 Colmore Cup) he took to oval track racing in a big way. After the Kings Oak meeting he put in a report to BSA management which convinced them that speedway could be a lucrative venture. Behind the Small Heath works a disused tip was turned into a makeshift track and Parker built a prototype BSA Dirt Track Special. He decided that a Sloper was no good for the job and set about using an upright bottom end assembly grafted with a Sloper barrel and cylinder head which gave the engine a distinct updraught carburettor intake. The frame was based on a 350cc single, with a solid rod replacing the fork spring to make the chassis totally rigid.

It was on the BSA dirt-track that Jack Parker taught himself a new trade and the unwritten art of laying a bike down into the corner. He went on to become speedway's greatest, skippering Coventry, Southampton, Clapton, Lea Bridge, Haringey and

Jack Parker demonstrates his cornering technique around BSA's Small Heath sports field in 1928. Chinese army cadets form an unusual and inscrutable audience! (BSA Archive)

finally, Belle Vue. He also represented England in numerous 'needle' matches against the Aussies over the ensuing years.

BSA announced their S29 Dirt-Track model in time for the first full league season in 1929. It was, of course, based on Jack Parker's intrepid creation and sold for £65. Bore and stroke for the machine was 3.4in × 3.8in (80mm × 98mm), the same as the 500cc Sloper. A twin-port head, open exhaust pipes and a hefty double row roller big-end bearing were specified. To prevent dust and grit being kicked into the carburettor intake, a 'Protectormotor' canister air cleaner was fitted and the magneto also had a mesh

screen. The frame was completely revised to give a shorter wheelbase, and the front forks had short links and a single heavy spring to give them just a mite of controlled movement. The engine was lubricated by a tank-mounted hand pump that fed oil straight into the crankcase. Clutch and gearbox were standard BSA components although the gearbox was a half-empty shell with a direct 8.55:1 gear driving a fifty-toothed rear sprocket.

Something in the region of 400 S29 DT's were sold, and many went overseas – notably to the land 'down under'. All the bikes were tested by Jack Parker himself around the

Jeff Smith MBE World Champion (1934–)

After a dramatic series of fourteen hard-fought battles against the cream of the world's scrambling stars, Jeff Smith and his 420cc BSA finally won the world Moto-cross championship in 1964. Man and machine had won seven of the encounters against crack Swedish riders such as Rolf Tibblin and Sten Lundin, coming second in six races and third in one. Throughout the whole series, the BSA never failed to finish, such was the stamina of BSA's works scrambler, and such was the toughness and single-minded dedication of the greatest rider who ever represented his country – and BSA.

Jeffrey Vincent Smith was originally born in Colne, Lancashire, but his family moved to Birmingham when he was only three years old. Yet he still chose the red rose emblem to decorate his helmet throughout nineteen glorious years in top class competition. Ever since he won his first trial aged only fifteen in 1949, Jeff Smith always had that supremely natural ability for riding a motorcycle over rough terrain, be it on the slippery rocks of an observed section against the clock or against his fellows in the mad dash through mud and water towards the finishing tape.

He was still only nineteen when he won his first national title riding a 500cc Norton which qualified him for a stab at the British Experts Trial. He finished a highly creditable fourth (he was only just pipped for third position by Bill Nicholson) and Norton Motors quickly snapped him up for their works team. At the time he was just starting a five year engineering apprenticeship at BSA and caused a bit of a stir every day by riding up Armoury Road on a works Norton! In 1952, when Norton closed down their off-road competition team, Jeff Smith was immediately signed up for BSA and remained in the squad until the fateful end of trophy winning at BSA in 1971. By the time he was twenty-one years old, he had won both the Scottish Six Days and the British Experts Trials and continued to do so again and again and. . .

During 1954, Jeff took up scrambling and won the Dutch Grand Prix, with a second place in the French. In the following year his biggest win among so many others, was a fine victory in the British Motor-cross Grand Prix. Victories piled up until it reached the point where he only made the headlines if he lost!

He did his two years' National Service in the REME from 1956 but was still able to collect two more wins in the British Experts, and an ISDT gold medal not to mention a host of silverware collected from international scrambling competitions.

In the early 1960s he helped Brian Martin, then Competition Department Manager, to make a world beater out of the stock 343cc B40 with the intention of attacking the world Moto-cross championships. Fitness and dedication to the tough task were one of his keys to success. He trained with Maurice Herriot, a Tokyo Olympic silver medallist who worked on BSA's assembly line in Small Heath. After a dramatic and meticulously planned win in the final round in Spain the trophy was proudly displayed at Small Heath in 1964. Using a more powerful 440cc 'Victor' Scrambler, he repeated the performance in the following year, and by an even greater points margin.

In the years when scrambling enjoyed keen patronage by television, Jeff won the 250cc BBC Grandstand Trophy in 1968, having already won just about everything in trials and scramble (several times over). To his many fans, Jeff Smith was articulate and accessible, and he was a true model for any sportsman both in victory and defeat. In 1970, he was awarded an MBE for his services to motorcycle sport, which was a fitting tribute to BSA's greatest rider.

Brian Martin Sports Supremo (1932–)

Another Bert Perrigo 'find', Brian Martin was only twenty years old when he was signed up to replace Norton-bound Johnny Draper. In his first test for BSA colours he clinched the Colmore Trial 350 Cup, and then picked up a premier trophy in the Victory cup trial. This was good enough for Perrigo to select him for the three-man squad that, under ACU scrutiny took three off-the-shelf A7 Star Twins on a 4,500 mile (7,240km) jaunt across Europe in 1952, taking in the International Six Days' Trial. Brian Martin's contribution, with a faultless gold medal, only months after joining BSA was an astonishing start to a long career with BSA that lasted until the competition shop closed down in 1971.

His Majesty's armed forces invited Brian to do his obligatory two-year stint but weekend leave, wearing either civvy or army clothing, enabled him to keep his hand in, winning many trials and scrambles awards.

In 1954, he resumed his BSA work as both rider and engineer. His enthusiasm for getting things on the move, man-managing people and resolving awkward situations eventually led him to the Competition Department Manager's job in 1960 – the third and last man to fill that position.

In the early 1960s, he championed the cause of the light-weight, low capacity, single cylinder machine. The basic tool for the job was the 250cc OHV C15 but from the start it was beset with problems caused by a flimsy distributor drive and a poor plain big-end bearing. Brian Martin's team turned it into a world beater, and Brian himself was deeply involved throughout the whole story from lowly 'Ceefer' to the 343cc B40 and on to the development of the 420cc and later 441cc Victor scramblers that proved ultra-reliable under the severest conditions and which eventually gave Jeff Smith his first World Moto-cross Championship.

For 1966, the Competition team further enlarged the Victor Scrambler engine up to 494cc but kept the weight down by using magnesium cases and a titanium conrod. To take the issue to its full extent, the frame was also made from titanium tubing. It was a revolutionary gamble that did not pay off – in fact it ran up a massive bill, but in the mid to late 1960s BSA could afford to throw money about as if it were water. Titanium welding needed a special vacuum chamber, which meant that frame breakages couldn't be repaired at the trackside unless some primitive blacksmith's bodge up was used. Going into a new Grand Prix season with an untried machine proved disastrous. Brian Martin forced a return to mild-steel tubing after a few initial races, but by then the impetus for another championship win was lost.

In the few years leading up to the close of the Competition Department, Brian Martin's players had in their ranks the best of British star riders such as Vic Eastwood, Keith Hickman, John Banks and Dave Nichol to name but a few of the Scrambler men who struggled to keep the BSA four-stroke alive against the ever-growing packs of howling two-strokes.

Small Heath track. But many of the ideas and suggestions put forward by Jack Parker had been overlooked and the BSA S29 lived in the shadow of the flat-twin Douglas and the later, four-valve Rudge. BSA declined to make a further batch for 1930.

BSA's involvement in speedway had been short and sweet but they had at least made an important contribution to the fledgling sport. That might have been a tidy end to the story but no, we must tear our way through forty-three years over the cinders to the year 1972. By then the Czechoslovak Jawa power-plant dominated the sport but these were somewhat hard to find, because Iron-curtain countries took precedence for de-

Brian Martin launches his Gold Star into action during a 1956 Scrambles meeting. There was no time to repair that broken front mudguard! (Courtesy Motor Cycle News)

liveries. This prompted a delegation of speedway promoters to approach BSA to see if they could fill the void. The company were sceptical at first but eventually set about making a complete machine based on a 500cc B50MX engine held down in a special

*Number One. The legendary Mike ('The Bike') Hailwood wins the Hutchinson 100
with a BSA A65 Lightning on the rain-drenched Silverstone circuit in 1965. (Loaned
by A. G. Cave)*

frame designed by Rob North, a leading frame builder (though they later reverted to a Jawa frame). The power-house was looked after by Cyril Haliburn, one of the great Gold Star engine specialists who worked on various developments at Small Heath.

The project had got as far as stage two when speedway stars such as Nigel Bookcock, Ray Wilson and Ivan Mauger tested it, running up 700 laps between them without any mishaps. It was found to be well up to standard and certainly a lot more durable than the Jawa. A press release quoted its performance at 45bhp at 7,100rpm (this was later shown to be pessimistic, its true output was more like 60bhp).

Sadly, just as things were getting close to the production stage with a further developed four-valve model coming off the drawing-board, history had caught up with the newly re-structured BSA Engineering Ltd and insufficient funds drowned the promising BSA B50MX Speedway for good. It was the last Small Heath designed and built BSA.

11

The Wheels Keep Turning

Before the contractors were sent in to flatten BSA's once-thriving Small Heath factory, a great funeral pyre of files, drawings and photographs was set ablaze. A number of years later, the site became a municipal training ground. The final ironic twist in the story saw scores of young motorcyclists riding small Japanese two-strokes as if in a gleeful dance on the grave of Britain's fallen industry.

The wheel makes a full turn. Eighty-five years have passed and former Small Heath Works Manager Alistair Cave tries out a 1905 Minerva built chiefly from BSA cycle parts. Looking on and offering a helping hand is the curator of the National Motorcycle Museum. (Loaned by A. G. Cave)

The Japanese Meguro-Kawasaki company copied the BSA 650cc OHV A10. One of these Japanese intruders has been surrounded by BSA Owners Club hardcore who look on with intense curiosity and scepticism. (OW)

But the sign of the 'Piled Arms' is still in existence. A walk through any street will find the badge with three rifles fixed to the headstock of a modern bicycle. Raleigh of Nottingham have always found a saleable name in the initials BSA.

In 1980, Dennis Poore, Chairman of NVT relaunched the name on a range of small two-stroke machines built predominantly from foreign bought-in parts assembled in Coventry. The 50cc Beaver, Brigand and the more ambitious 175cc Tracker never quite caught on – the tables had been turned since BSA had been out of the room and the name now had little appeal to a new generation. Of late,

the BSA Company Ltd still fight on down in Gloucestershire supplying third world demand with a cheap and simple two-wheeler. Try as they might, most BSA enthusiasts have long been resigned to the notion that BSA died for keeps back in 1973.

It was only when the smoke was clearing from the rubble that a resurgence of interest in old motorcycles suddenly found another gear. In a typically British way, the public cruelly smirked at the way the company's affairs had been handled in the last ten years of its existence but in the morning after the funeral they awoke to the stark realization that motorcycling was left with an overbearing diet of character-lacking Japanese tin-plate and plastic. So what if you, like me, could never accept anything else but a faithful old Beesa? Maybe through circumstances and not choice you are now the proud owner of an ex-farmyard D7 Bantam or have been bequeathed old Uncle Arthur's maroon C11G, still lying under an old coat in the potting shed. Perhaps you couldn't resist making a bid for that gorgeous pre-war over-head valve job, but where do you turn for help?

Back in 1958, a Sheffield pub became a regular meeting place for a group of enthu-siasts who formed 'The BSA Owners Club'. The news spread throughout the country and in 1963, a National BSA Owners Club was organized. Throughout the 1960s the high-light of the yearly BSAOC social calendar was a 'Field Day' held on the BSA Sports and Social Club grounds adjacent to the Small Heath factory. Rally visitors were treated to a round of fun and games and a tour of the works which was eagerly finished at the spares and service department. To this day, a BSAOC Field Day is still held every year bringing together owners, riders and enthu-siasts from every corner of the country and the BSAOC can proudly boast nineteen bran-ches in Britain and twenty-two associated clubs throughout the world. Through its magazine, *The Star*, machines, spares, books and paraphernalia are sold and ex-changed, while technical wizards read the mail and offer advice. BSA, once the supplier of millions of riders is now kept alive by those riders. However, if your tastes are for a fuller involvement in all old motorcycles then the Vintage Motorcycle Club is the one to try. The VMCC, founded in the late 1940s, has over 10,000 members, 'united by a common appreciation of the engineering skill and vision of those who built the pioneer machines'.

Through its aim, the VMCC sets out to en-sure that 'such machines are not preserved as lifeless exhibits in Museum. . .' Now there lies the very key to survival. Whilst both the BSAOC and VMCC do not themselves run a spares supply business, they are fully active in encouraging the everyday use of old machinery. To meet this end, a considerable cottage industry has blossomed over the last few years supplying every need from new big-end bearings, exhausts or pistons to new seat covers, cables and even those fiddly little cork inserts found in every petrol tap.

So there you go, and if I am ever asked 'where can I get a new rocker spindle for a 1948 plunger frame B31?', the answer is simple, join the club, read the monthly 'Classic' journals on sale at all High Street news-agents, or get along to the next autojumble!

In his time, this author has done his fair stint as a BSA agony uncle. The main topic has always been about colours, finishes and small fittings requested by owners intent on restoring to original condition. Colours have always been a hoary old subject, but the truth is the paint was ordered on a week-to-week basis and could (and did) vary slightly in shade and tone but even on the most cor-rupted 'basket case' there's a chance that a flake of the original paint will survive and there are numerous car body re-spray specialists who can mix up a good match. Otherwise, some of the spares dealers advertised in monthly 'Classic' journals have ready made-up tins for most of the popular models.

As for transfers, these delicate items are usually the last thing to complete a rebuild and how many get it wrong! Watch out for cheap fakes, the correct 'Piled Arms' trans-fers should state: 'BSA Cycles Ltd' for machines built before 1954; to mark the occasion of becoming a motorcycle division the transfer upper lettering should read 'BSA

The annual BSA Owners Club Field Day attracts everything from Round Tanks to Rocket Threes. (O.W.)

Motorcycles' and it is only in recent times that good quality reproductions with the correct lilac garter colouring instead of bright red have become available.

Another tiny detail often overlooked even by professional restorers concerns the polished copper fittings. BSA plated everything in the old days – all handlebar fittings and fuel pipes were nickel plated before chromium plating took over in the late 1920s.

But let us spare the trivia – a BSA motorcycle standing idle, either in a rusty derelict outhouse or restored back to full glory is just an inert mass of metal. Open the fuel tap, push the piston over compression, follow through with a sure lunge on the kickstarter and just listen and feel the sensation as the miles ahead open up, and BSA's wheels continue to turn. Anyone who has rebuilt, renovated or simply ridden a BSA motorcycle has also had a part to play in The Birmingham Small Arms story. BSAing? It's the best!

182

Appendix 1

BSA MODELS 1930–40 *(Heavy Weight Groups)*

TYPE	YEAR AND FRAME/ENGINE PREFIX LETTERS										
	1930 X	1931 Y	1932 Z	1933 A	1934 B	1935 E	1936 D	1937 H	1938 J	1939 K	1940 W
500cc SV	S30–7* S30–9DL S30–18*	S31–7*									
			W32–6	W33–6	W34–7	W35–6	W6				
								M20	M20	M20 M20DL	M20 M20DL
500cc OHV	S30–19L S30–12* S30–13*	S31–9* S31–10 DL*	S32–8*								
			W32–7 W32–7 BS	W33–7 W33–8 BS W33–9 SP	W348 W34–9 BS W34–10 SP	W35–7 W35–8 BS W35–9 SP					
							Q7 Q21 BS Q8 ES	M22 M23 ES	M22 M23 ES M24 GS	M22 M23 SS M24 GS	M23 SS
557cc CV 600cc SV	H30–8* H30–10 DL*	H31–8*	H32–9*								
				M33–10	M34–12	M35–10	M10				
								M21₊	M21●	M21●	M21●
500cc OHV Twin				J34–11	J35–12 J35–15 WO	J12					
750cc OHV Twin 770 SV Twin 1000cc SV Twin								Y13	Y13	Y13	
	E30–14 G30–15 G30–16 WT	E31–11 G31–12 WT	G32–10 WT	G33–12 G33–13 WT	G34–14 WT	G35–14	G14	G14	G14	G14	G14

				BORE & STROKE				
DL	De LUXE	GS	GOLD STAR				M● MODELS	82mm × 112mm
L	'LIGHT'	SP	'SPECIAL'	S	MODELS	80mm × 98mm	Q ,,	82mm × 94mm
BS	BLUE STAR	WO	WAR OFFICE	H	,,	85mm × 98mm	J ,,	63mm × 80mm
ES	EMPIRE STAR	WT	WORLD TOUR	W	,,	85mm × 88mm	Y ,,	71mm × 94.5mm
SS	SILVER STAR	*	'SLOPER' ENGINE	M	,,	82mm × 94mm	E ,,	76mm × 85mm
				M₊	,,	85mm × 105mm	G ,,	80mm × 98mm

BSA MODELS 1930–40 *(Light and Medium Weight Groups)*

TYPE	YEAR AND FRAME/ENGINE PREFIX LETTERS										
	1930 X	1931 Y	1932 Z	1933 A	1934 B	1935 E	1936 D	1937 H	1938 J	1939 K	1940 W
174cc 2-stroke	A30–2										
150cc OHV				X34–0	X35–0	X0					
250cc SV	B30–3	B31–1		B33–1	B34–1	B35–1	B1				
								B20	B20		
									C10	C10	C10
										C10 DL	C10 DL
250cc OHV	B30–4	B31–2 B31–3 DL	B32–1	B33–2	B34–2	B35–2	B2				
							B18				
				B33–3 BS	B34–3 BS						
						B35–3†	B3†				
								B21	B21	B21	
								B22 ES	B22 ES	B21 DL	
										C11	C11
350cc SV	L30–5 L30–6	L31–4 L31–5 DL	L32–2 L32–4 DL								
								B23	B23	B23 B23 DL	
350cc OHV	L30–11*										
		L31–6 DL	L32–3 L32–5								
				R33–4	R34–4		R17				
			L32–5 BS	R33–5 BS	R34–5 BS	R35–5 BS	R20 BS				
							R3 ES				
							R4†				
						R35–4†	R19†				
					R34–6 SP						
								B24 ES	B24 ES	B24 SS	
								B25 C	B25 C	B25 C	
								B26	B26	B26	
											B29 SS
											B30
											C12
								M19	M19		

DL De LUXE	SP 'SPECIAL'	BORE & STROKE		C12 ONLY	71mm × 88mm	
BS BLUE STAR	C COMPETITION	A MODELS	60mm × 61.5mm	L MODELS	72mm × 85.5mm	
ES EMPIRE STAR	* 'SLOPER' ENGINE	B ,,	63mm × 80mm	M ,,	68.8mm × 94mm	
SS SILVER STAR	† 'HIGH CAM' ENGINE	B ,,	71mm × 88mm	R ,,	71mm × 88mm	
		C ,,	63mm × 80mm	X ,,	52mm × 70mm	

Appendix 2

**Badges, Books,
Bits and Pieces**

'Winged BSA', used from 1945 onwards.

'BSA Motor Bicycles', used from 1914 to 1923.

'BSA The Most Popular Motorcycle in the
World', used from 1945 to 1963.

The famous 'Piled Arms' badge.

BSA Club Addresses

The BSA Owners Club
Jim Seabrooke
6 Langdown Lawn Close
Hythe
Southampton
Hampshire
SO45 5GW

The Vintage MotorCycle Club Ltd
Ann Davy
Wetmore Road
Burton-on-Trent
Staffordshire
DE14 1SN

The Gold Star Owners Club
Brian Standley
7 Austliss Close
Hunt
Redditch
Worcestershire
B97 5NZ

Bantam Owners Club
Peggy Clark
2 Willis Waye
Kingsworthy
Winchester
Hampshire
SO23 7QT

The BSA Front Wheel Drive Club
P. D. Cook
13 Rosemary Drive
Guildford
Surrey

Trident and Rocket Three Owners Club
Deena and Kieron Carvell
138 Cubbington Road
Hall Green
Coventry
Warwickshire
CV6 7BL

The British Motorcyclists Federation
129 Seaforth Avenue
Motspur Park
New Malden
Surrey
KT3 6JU

Specialist Booksellers

Bruce Main-Smith Retail Ltd
1 Featherby Drive
Glen Parva
Leicester
LE2 9NZ

Chater and Scott Ltd
8 South Street
Isleworth
Middlesex
TW7 7BG
Tel: (0181) 568 9750

Mill House Books
The Mill House
Eastville
Boston
Lincolnshire
PE22 8LS
Tel: (0120 584) 377

Motor Books
33 St Martin's Court
London
WC2N 4AL
Tel: (0171) 836 5376

Leading BSA Spares Dealers

C & D Autos
1,193–1,199 Warwick Road
Acocks Green
Birmingham
B27 6BY
Tel: (0121) 706 2902

Bri-Tie
'Cwmsannan'
Llanfynydd
Carmarthen
Dyfed
SA32 7QT
Tel: (01588) 668579

Lightning Spares
157 Cross Street
Sale
Cheshire
M33 1JW
Tel: (0161) 969 3850

Kidderminster Motorcycles
60–62 Blackwell Street
Kidderminster
Worcestershire
DY10 2EE
Tel: (01562) 66679

Anglo-Moto
Unit 9
Park Lane Industrial Estate
Kidderminster
Worcestershire
DY11 6TT
Tel: (01562) 742559

Vale-Onslow
104–115 Stratford Road
Birmingham 11
Tel: (0121) 772 5837

Russell Motors
125 Falcon Road
London
SW11
Tel: (0181) 228 1714

Appendix 3

BSA Bibliography

The Story of BSA Motor Cycles Bob Holliday (Patrick Stephens Ltd)

The Giants of Small Heath Barry Ryerson (Haynes Publishing Group)

BSA Competition History Norman Vanhouse (Haynes Publishing Group)

BSA Gold Star and Other Singles Roy Bacon (Osprey Collectors Library)

BSA Twins and Triples Roy Bacon (Osprey Collectors Library)

British Motor Cycles Since 1950 Vol 2 Steve Wilson (Patrick Stephens Ltd)

Whatever Happened to the British Motorcycle Industry? Bert Hopwood (Haynes Publishing Group)

The Gold Star Book written and published by Bruce Main-Smith Retail Ltd

BSA Gold Star Super Profile John Gardner (Haynes Publishing Group)

BSA Bantam Super Profile Jeff Clew (Haynes Publishing Group)

BSA A7 & A10 Twins Super Profile Owen Wright (Haynes Publishing Group)

BSA M20 & M21 Super Profile Owen Wright (Haynes Publishing Group)

Index

Italic numerals denote page numbers of illustrations